Early Childhood Education in Social and Political Transitions

Also Available from Bloomsbury

Education in Radical Uncertainty, Stephen Carney and Ulla Ambrosius Madsen
Anthropocene Childhoods, Emily Ashton
Children's Transitions in Everyday Life and Institutions,
edited by Mariane Hedegaard and Marilyn Fleer
A Critical Anthropology of Childhood in Haiti, Diane M. Hoffman
A History of Education for the Many, Curry Malott
Education, Individualization and Neoliberalism, Valerie Visanich
International Schooling, Lucy Bailey
Teaching in Unequal Societies, John Russon, Siby K. George, and P. G. Jung
Education in Radical Uncertainty, Stephen Carney and Ulla Ambrosius Madsen
A Cultural-Historical Approach towards Pedagogical Transitions,
Joanne Hardman

Early Childhood Education in Social and Political Transitions

The Legacy of the Open Society Foundations Step by Step Program

Sarah Klaus, Jan Peeters and Tatjana Vonta

BLOOMSBURY ACADEMIC
LONDON • NEW YORK • OXFORD • NEW DELHI • SYDNEY

BLOOMSBURY ACADEMIC
Bloomsbury Publishing Plc, 50 Bedford Square, London, WC1B 3DP, UK
Bloomsbury Publishing Inc, 1359 Broadway, New York, NY 10018, USA
Bloomsbury Publishing Ireland, 29 Earlsfort Terrace, Dublin 2, D02 AY28, Ireland

BLOOMSBURY, BLOOMSBURY ACADEMIC and the Diana logo are
trademarks of Bloomsbury Publishing Plc

First published in Great Britain 2024
This paperback edition first published in 2026

Copyright @ Open Society Foundations. Authored by Sarah Klaus,
Jan Peeters and Tatjana Vonta, 2024.

Sarah Klaus, Jan Peeters and Tatjana Vonta have asserted their right under the Copyright,
Designs and Patents Act, 1988, to be identified as Author of this work.

For legal purposes the Acknowledgments on pp. xvi–xvii constitute an
extension of this copyright page.

Cover image: Children playing in the Roma settlement of
Pušča, Slovenia (2013) @Aljoša Rudaš

This work is published open access subject to a Creative Commons Attribution-
NonCommercial-NoDerivatives 4.0 International licence (CC BY-NC-ND 4.0, https://
creativecommons.org/licenses/by-nc-nd/4.0/). You may re-use, distribute, and reproduce
this work in any medium for non-commercial purposes, provided you give attribution to the
copyright holder and the publisher and provide a link to the Creative Commons licence.

Bloomsbury Publishing Plc does not have any control over, or responsibility for,
any third-party websites referred to or in this book. All internet addresses given
in this book were correct at the time of going to press. The author and publisher
regret any inconvenience caused if addresses have changed or sites have ceased
to exist, but can accept no responsibility for any such changes.

A catalogue record for this book is available from the British Library.

A catalog record for this book is available from the Library of Congress.

Library of Congress Control Number: 2024933289

ISBN: HB: 978-1-3502-5782-5
PB: 978-1-3502-5785-6
ePDF: 978-1-3502-5783-2
eBook: 978-1-3502-5781-8

Typeset by Integra Software Services Pvt. Ltd.

For product safety related questions contact productsafety@bloomsbury.com.

To find out more about our authors and books visit www.bloomsbury.com
and sign up for our newsletters.

Contents

List of Figures	vii
Foreword: Early Childhood Education in Social and Political Transitions: The Legacy of the Open Society Foundations Step by Step Program	viii
Preface: The Inspiration for This Book	xii
Acknowledgments	xvi
List of Abbreviations	xviii
Introduction: Building Democracy through Early Childhood Education	1
Part 1 Why Invest in Early Childhood during a Political Transformation Process Toward Democracy	19
1 "Everything Was Planned": Early Childhood Education in Former Socialist Countries before and during Their Transition	21
2 "It Was Just a Magic Time": Investing in Early Childhood to Build Democratic Societies	41
Part 2 Inventing a Democratic Pedagogy	55
3 "Who Says We Can't Change the World?": Implementing the Step by Step Program	57
4 "The Teachers Believed in Us!" Inspiring Stories from Teachers, Parents, and Grown-Up Children Who Experienced the Programs	85
5 "Slowly We Are Getting There": Creating Opportunities for Children Experiencing Exclusion	101
6 "Don't Think That It Won't Happen": Young Children and Their Families in Times of War	123
Part 3 Extending and Sustaining Democratic Pedagogy through Civil Society Networks and Expansion to New Regions	135
7 The "Seed beneath the Snow": The Growth of Early Childhood NGOs and Networks	137
8 "Surprised and Thrilled": Rolling Out the Programs	159

Part 4 Transforming Early Childhood Education Systems 177

9   "This Is Yours": Successful Transformations of Early Education Systems 179
10 Systems Change When People Change: Lessons from Long-Term
    Investment in Early Childhood Education 201

Appendix 1: Biographies of Interviewees and Focus Group Participants 226
Appendix 2: Methodology: Oral History Interviews and Desk Review of
    Evaluations, Reports, and Documents 235
Notes 241
References 243
Index 252

Figures

0.1	Children share about feelings at a preschool in Durdevo, Serbia, on December 20, 2018	1
1.1	Children celebrate the new year in a kindergarten in the USSR in 1959	21
2.1	George Soros visits a Step by Step program in Kyiv, Ukraine, in 1993	41
3.1	Children participate in a music class for families and young children in Kragujevac, Serbia, on September 19, 2018	57
3.2	Step by Step initiatives	80
3.3	Teachers trained (cumulative) in Step by Step during the first ten years of the program	81
4.1	Children and the director of the "Junior Park" kindergarten celebrate autumn (Bishkek, 2021)	85
5.1	Child in Slovenia working on a drawing of the solar system (Murska Sobota, Slovenia, 2017)	101
6.1	Children on the playground of the "Nightingale" Preschool, which uses the Step by Step methodology, working on a paper mâché globe (Sarajevo, 1998)	123
7.1	ISSA's Annual Conference 2017, Ghent, Belgium	137
8.1	An early childhood master-trainer reads a book to kids in the LMA Waterside Early Childhood Center. In Monrovia, Liberia, on March 31, 2014	159
9.1	Professionals from Slovenia and Italy participating in a week-long training on quality-informed, non-formal early childhood education and care at the International Step by Step Association, Leiden, NL 2022	179
9.2	Step by Step Country Development Model	181
9.3	The CoRe framework and research/policy/practice triangle applied to the Step by Step program	183
10.1	Two children in a Step by Step primary program discuss the November class calendar (Chisinau, Moldova 2008)	201
11.1	Children visiting the Museum of Mining and Metallurgy in Bor, Serbia, on September 15, 2018	226

Foreword: Early Childhood Education in Social and Political Transitions: The Legacy of the Open Society Foundations Step by Step Program

Entering a Step by Step early childhood classroom for the first time, one of the most striking impressions is of young children working together in different corners of the room, busy in lively activity, talk, and games. They are relatively free to move between activities and groups. Some are dressed up and role-playing in the dramatic play corner, while others are browsing books in the reading corner. The teachers engage with the children, guiding them with open-ended questions and encouraging them to learn by exploring their environment, and collaborating on shared activities. Learning materials—arts and crafts supplies, blocks, books—are easy for children to access themselves without asking permission from a grown-up. In a room down the hall, parents meet over coffee, sharing their experiences, their hopes and concerns for their children. The preschool is a warm and welcoming space for young children and their families.

In classrooms like these around the world, Step by Step has created quality early learning environments for young children and promoted their participation in democratic, rights-respecting societies. Launched in 1994, with an initial commitment to invest $100 million, Step by Step grew rapidly over twenty years into a massive education reform focusing on introducing child-centered, democratic pedagogy across thirty countries. From 2006 onward, the scope, country coverage, and methodology of Step by Step expanded even further in locations as diverse as Liberia, Bangladesh, and Bhutan. We were privileged to have observed Step by Step classrooms, participated in professional development workshops alongside teacher trainers, and provided technical guidance to the Open Society Foundations Early Childhood Program as it expanded from Eastern Europe and Central Asia to other regions of the world.

How did this vision of fostering democracy through early childhood begin? George Soros had a long-standing commitment to investing in initiatives to combat authoritarianism and support the transition to democratic open societies, especially in Eastern Europe. He was already supporting education programs through the foundation he established, the Open Society Foundations. Then in 1993, a meeting with the eminent physician Fraser Mustard, one of the founders of the Canadian Institute for Advanced Research, led to a critical shift in his priorities. He became convinced that focusing on the very earliest years of life was crucial to achieve his vision for societies built around social justice and respect for human rights—including respect for children's rights—to enable active participation in building more democratic societies.

George Soros was ahead of his time. The Step by Step approach to early childhood education was in sharp contrast to the traditional, teacher-directed pedagogy typical of classrooms across the former Soviet region, and which is still common in many parts of the world. Moreover, in the early 1990s, international donors paid little attention to early childhood. Open Society's trailblazing investments helped to leverage support from other partners, including UNICEF, the World Bank, USAID, and the European Commission.

The authors of this book offer a fascinating account of the development of Step by Step initiatives, enriched by extensive first-hand testimony from more than forty of the key players over three decades. Offering a voice to all who care about human rights and democracy—as well as elevating the voices of children themselves as active citizens—is arguably one of the most enduring legacies of the initiative. As the authors recount the rapid expansion of Step by Step, we hear the voices of the individuals who led the scale up of quality early childhood education during this period of unprecedented change. We were moved by their enthusiasm and their achievements, as well as their unwavering optimism, even when faced with difficulties and disappointments.

Improving children's development and well-being was the first goal of Step by Step, and delivery through quality early learning programs and highly trained professionals was the main methodology. But the vision for Step by Step was much more ambitious—to nurture positive attitudes and competencies among active citizens in a democracy. This ambition drew on the motivation and skills of many thousands of (mainly) women who began as parents with small children, became qualified teachers, and went on to become trainers and often influential leaders within the International Step by Step Association (ISSA) and beyond.

Another key ambition of Step by Step—and Open Society's Early Childhood Program more generally—has been to combat social exclusion of children experiencing marginalization, especially Roma communities and children with disabilities. Step by Step recognized that the early childhood years provide unique opportunities to foster greater understanding and acceptance of children from diverse backgrounds, and among their families and communities. The authors highlight how challenging it has been to change deeply ingrained attitudes and behaviors toward these excluded groups. It demands multifaceted approaches to address disparities in access to health, education, housing, and social services. There is still a long way to go to achieve every child's right to a quality education, starting with equitable opportunities in the early years. By maintaining a focus on equity and inclusion, Open Society galvanized other donors and partners to join this effort and make progress together.

This book also offers important lessons about the contribution of early childhood education to democratic reforms during social and political transitions. What stands out is Open Society's sustained commitment to investing in people—deliberately identifying change agents in each country and then training and supporting them as leaders. These change agents, in turn, have mentored thousands of teachers, curriculum specialists, and advocates within their countries in child-centered, rights-based pedagogy. Many have provided technical support and coaching to peers in other countries through cross-country partnerships and regional networks.

Another lesson from the book is the power of civil society. Setting up independent national non-governmental organizations focused on early childhood education was an unusual decision in places where the state had played such a dominant role. Yet, for the most part, Step by Step organizations have found their way by partnering with government, securing external funding, and developing sought-after expertise in areas such as teacher training, pedagogical coaching, and inclusive education practices. The authors also caution that the establishment of NGOs took time and has not been easy to sustain in all countries given their diverse political and economic environments.

Today, Step by Step continues to be influential in Europe and around the world, not only as a model of quality, inclusive education but as a civil society movement. Over the past decade, as more actors joined the global early childhood landscape, Open Society focused on smaller, catalytic investments that have contributed to building the field. Notable examples include strengthening global and regional early childhood networks as engines of civil society engagement and expanding international post-secondary training in child development. The Open Society Foundations are widely recognized for pushing the early childhood agenda to address under-prioritized issues, such as support for young refugee children. Its departure as an early childhood funder has left a gap that will be difficult to fill. This book reminds readers that addressing inequality, discrimination, and marginalization of young children is a compelling and persistent priority in need of resources.

It is thirty years since the meeting between George Soros and Fraser Mustard that sparked the work described in this book. Open Society's investments in Step by Step have come to an end, and concerns persist about the well-being of young children globally. As we write these few words of appreciation for this book, and all the effort it represents, we are acutely aware of the continuing—and in some countries growing—threats to democracy from authoritarianism, and the pervasive poverty, violence, and social injustices felt amongst the world's youngest children and their families.

Open Society's Early Childhood Program has ended but the vision for young children and democracy has not. The legacy of Step by Step lives on, not just in this book, but more especially in the experience of so many whose lives, learning, and professional outlook have been shaped by—and will continue to shape—quality early childhood programs.

Martin Woodhead and Michelle Neuman

Preface: The Inspiration for This Book

Early Childhood Education in Social and Political Transitions explores the process through which early childhood education systems transform and adapt to new political and social contexts. It focuses on the transformations that swept across Europe and Eurasia after the fall of the Berlin wall in 1989, and the dissolution of the Soviet Union, Czechoslovakia, and Yugoslavia in subsequent years. Using the example of the Open Society Foundations flagship early childhood program, Step by Step, it explores how early childhood education contributes to the building of democratic, inclusive societies. Inspired by brain research in the early 1990s that mobilized interest in the potential of the early years to shape better futures for both individuals and societies, Open Society's Step by Step Program invested over $140 million over twenty years in early childhood education and development programs in thirty countries. The scale of the initiative was made feasible by the collaboration of Open Society's affiliated national foundations, which were based in each country, with the New York-based (and later London-based) core team leading the initiative. Its success reflects the quality of the early childhood experts selected in each country to lead the program, and their openness to implementing it appropriately within each context.

The program brought together experts from across the region and linked them with experts from Georgetown University and trainers from the US Head Start Program. This book documents their journey. Interviews conducted during the development of this book with a range of actors who had roles in the Step by Step Program, and others connected with the program and/or its offshoots in other countries, share stories about their lived experience of change. Biographies of the interviewees can be found in Appendix 1. The interviews provide an opportunity to hear the voices of the main actors. In the words of Sommer and Quinlan, such oral history offers an opportunity to discover not just what happened but how and why, to explain anomalies, to provide convincing evidence or tantalizing clues that enhance understanding of a past time and place (Sommer, Quinlan, and American Association for State and Local History 2009, 4). Readers will encounter a variety of perspectives and hear from early childhood educators and technical experts, NGO leaders, and foundation professionals. The aim is not to document every detail of this multinational reform effort but to draw out important lessons to inform future programs and inspire the next generation of educators, pedagogues, and change agents.

In addition to these interviews, the authors draw on the many reports about the early childhood and education work of the Open Society Foundations and the Step by Step Program published over the past thirty years. These include evaluations and reports commissioned by the Open Society Foundations, as well as those commissioned by independent organizations and experts. Finally, the authors had access to Step by Step program documents—reports, strategy papers, budgets, statistics, memoranda, photographs, presentations—which provided a framework for the interviewee narratives. Appendix 2 provides details about the resources used in putting together this book.

The idea of writing a book focusing on the experience of the Step by Step Program originated with Jan Peeters, upon learning that the Open Society Foundations would be discontinuing their work in early childhood at the end of 2020. He approached Sarah Klaus, the then director of the Early Childhood Program at Open Society, who readily agreed, and in the process of developing the proposal for the book, they sought out Tatjana Vonta, who was involved with the Step by Step Program in Slovenia and regionally from November 1994. In developing the book, the authors drew on their expertise in early childhood, as well as their connection to the work of Open Society, the International Step by Step Association, and the national Step by Step programs. Although the three authors started their careers in different parts of the world—Sarah in the United States, Tatjana in South-East Europe, and Jan in Western Europe—they share a fascination with early education as a space to experience democracy and as a vehicle to promote more equal, socially just, and inclusive societies. Each has set up initiatives to reform early childhood education systems. Sarah started at the macro level, coordinating and later directing the global Early Childhood Program at Open Society, Tatjana at the national level in Slovenia, and Jan at the local level introducing innovations into the early childhood sector in the city of Ghent, Belgium. Each author also brought to the table a personal history and motivation.

As director of a research center at Ghent University (VBJK - Innovations in the Early Years), Jan Peeters experimented with introducing democratic approaches in early education and care centers, first in the city of Ghent and later in the Flemish community of Belgium. With colleagues from Western Europe, he launched two European networks: the Diversity in Early Childhood Education and Training Network and *Children in Europe*, a European magazine published in nineteen European languages. In 2004, he was invited for the first time to the annual conference of the International Step by Step Association (ISSA) held that year in Yerevan. From the first moment, he was fascinated by the involvement and connectedness of ISSA's members. When he finally had the opportunity to visit Step by Step programs in several Eastern European countries the following year, he was impressed by the high pedagogical quality and intensive parent participation. Later, as a consultant for UNICEF in Eastern Europe, he observed that so many of the engaged and competent people that he encountered working in government, universities, and training institutions had links to Open Society's Early Childhood Program. Some had degrees from Central European University, others had started their careers in a national Step by Step NGO or leading an early childhood center working with Step by Step pedagogy. He became convinced of the effectiveness of Step by Step at introducing democratic approaches across different levels of early childhood systems. This included not only initiating change at the institutional level, but also success in motivating government officials and trainers to start investing in more child-centered approaches. For Jan, it is extremely important to document this large early childhood education project through interviews that capture the experiences of the main actors and to inspire new generations of innovators in countries all over the world.

As a member of the program team at Open Society, when Step by Step launched in 1994, and later as director of the Early Childhood Program, and executive director of the International Step by Step Association, Sarah Klaus worked with and later led teams in the center of the whirlwind of activity, creativity, strategy, and decision-making that brought Step by Step and the International Step by Step Association to life. The journey took her from living in New York to Budapest and finally to London, where she and a team of early childhood experts expanded Open Society's work to Africa, Asia, the Middle East, and Latin America and the Caribbean until the program closed at the end of 2020. Since then, she has joined Georgetown University as an adjunct assistant professor. As Open Society left the early childhood sphere she was keen to join Jan, and later to invite Tatjana to document the effort to build more just societies from the ground up by investing in the early years. The book offered a way to do this through thick narrative reflections that elevate the voices of participants in the programs. "For those of us involved in Step by Step, particularly in the early years, it was much, much more than a job," she commented. "It was our life. We poured ourselves into it. Intellectually, personally, passionately. We created a collaborative space where it was okay to dream big dreams, to share successes and failures and to be curious. It nourished us." One of her core motivations is to highlight the depth of early childhood scholarship, knowledge, and capacity in Eastern Europe and their leadership in building the International Step by

Step Association (ISSA), which has evolved into the leading professional early childhood network uniting professionals across Europe.

Tatjana Vonta's career in early childhood education has taken some unexpected turns, bridging experiences in East and West Europe, but her work always focused on improving practices. As an educational researcher of early childhood education at the Educational Research Institute in the 1980s, when everyone was traveling to the West, Tatjana headed for six months to Georgia in the former Soviet Union to explore how children transition to primary school. Recruited to direct the Step by Step program in Slovenia, she led the program's development for two decades, including establishing the Step by Step Centre at the Research Institute, as well as a national network of Step by Step teachers and preschools. She has been an active member of ISSA, playing a leading role in ISSA's work on quality, serving on task forces and the board. She has also been a consultant to Open Society, supporting and mentoring countries that joined the program in later years and collaborating on university projects. The invitation to work on the book came after Tatjana retired, but she joined because, in her words,

> "I felt that Step by Step, and all those who were committed to its implementation, deserved attention because of its unambiguous impact in the process of democratizing the early childhood education field at a time that was decisive for the transition processes of societies as a whole in many countries. For more than twenty years I taught students in parallel to my research work and I know how hard is for them to understand the interdependence of the various components of early childhood systems, as well as the relationship of these systems with socio-political environments. I was sure that I can bring to the book the unique perspective of somebody who was actively involved in almost all of Step by Step's initiatives on both the national and regional levels. I know all the important actors in this story, our relationships and the climate in our community."

The authors invite readers to explore how one foundation approached the introduction and scaling-up of new pedagogical approaches and reform of early childhood education systems in a region experiencing dramatic political and social changes that were largely supportive of the new approaches. From a historical perspective the Open Society investment in Step by Step, unprecedented at the time, is one of the sector's largest investments, in terms of time (spanning more than two decades), geographic reach (covering thirty countries), and funding (investing over $140 million). Thirty years has passed since Step by Step first launched in fifteen countries. It is an apt moment to reflect and take stock of lessons learned, and to gather insights from the experiences of the participants in the program to inspire new pedagogues and future initiatives.

Acknowledgments

The authors acknowledge the contributions of all of those who participated in interviews and focus groups for this book. We learned so much from the experiences that they shared. We regret not being able to interview representatives from all participating countries and have used examples from case studies and evaluations to give visibility to perspectives from across the Step by Step network, including the perspectives of teachers, parents, and children, whom we were not able to interview.

We thank the editorial team at Bloomsbury, Mark Richardson and Elissa Burns, for their support for this project. This book would not have been possible without the sponsorship of the Open Society Foundations and the support of the communications and legal teams. The International Step by Step Association (ISSA) played a critical role in sourcing images, and we thank especially Eva Izsak for her collaboration and creativity, as well as graphic designer, Judit Kovacs, who refined the charts and images. We also thank ISSA in advance for agreeing to support dissemination of the book and for their hosting of a dedicated, complementary web page, which will make available additional resources to interested readers. Ros Taylor, editor, joined the project at an important moment, as our first draft was complete, and the book is much stronger because of her insightful reading of the text, her proposals to refine the structure of the book, and her excellent edits. Hester Hulpia, Kate Lapham, Phyllis Magrab, Nora Milotay, Tina Hyder, Aija Tuna, Beka Vučo, and Martin Woodhead helped improve the text, providing comments and insights on draft chapters and sections, and Kate Lapham partnered with Tatjana Vonta to edit and refine the chapter on the history of early childhood in the region. Eliane Van Alboom provided English language editing to drafts of several chapters, and Elke De Mey provided much-needed administrative support at a critical moment.

We hope the book will succeed in bringing to life the unique role that early childhood education can play in building democratic, inclusive, and socially just societies. Step by Step was created by Liz Lorant, Pam Coughlin, and the teams that they led at Open Society, Georgetown University, and later Children's Resources International. George Soros was its strongest supporter, and Step by Step is one of Open Society's largest investments. We dedicate this book to all of the stakeholders and participants of the Step by Step Program—the children, parents, educators, country teams, Open Society national foundations, ministries, academic institutions, trainers, experts, NGOs, networks, partners—who came together to shape a better future for the next generation. With threats to democracy growing, it is even more important to amplify the voices of those seeking to build it, so future generations can learn from and be inspired by their experiences.

Abbreviations

ECD	early childhood development
ECE	early childhood education
INGO	International non-governmental organization
ISSA	International Step by Step Association
MoE	Ministry of Education
NATO	North Atlantic Treaty Organization
NGO	nongovernmental organization
OECD	Organisation for Economic Co-operation and Development
OSF	Open Society Foundations
UNESCO	United Nations Educational, Scientific and Cultural Organization
UNICEF	United Nations Children's Fund
UK	United Kingdom
US	United States of America
USAID	United States Agency for International Development
USSR	Union of Soviet Socialist Republics

Introduction: Building Democracy through Early Childhood Education

Figure 0.1 Children share about feelings at a preschool in Durdevo, Serbia, on December 20, 2018.
© Sanja Knezevic for the Open Society Foundations

In 1994, the Open Society Foundations embarked on a twenty-six-year journey into the field of early childhood, launching what became its flagship program, Step by Step. Step by Step responded to the social and political transition to democracy that was sweeping across Central and South-Eastern Europe and the former Soviet Union, evolving into one of the most extensive early childhood reform initiatives ever attempted. Over more than twenty years, Step by Step expanded from an initial cohort of fifteen countries to reach more than double that number, including nearly all the countries in Central Eastern and Southern Europe and Eurasia that were once led by communist parties, together with a handful of countries in Asia, the Americas, and Africa. Inspired by a belief in the intrinsic connection between a child's experiences in the earliest years and the health and wellbeing of open societies, the initiative supported the nurturing of skills and attitudes essential for active citizens in a democracy, among them respect for different ideas and cultures; the capacity to make decisions and think critically; and the ability to take responsibility, make choices, and resolve conflicts. It celebrated and elevated teachers' roles and emphasized their continuous professional development and collaboration; introduced child-centered, individualized teaching and learning, and social inclusion; supported children's creativity, initiative, and agency; advanced parents as primary educators of their children; and promoted community members in governance roles in early childhood institutions. From 1998 onward, Step by Step took on an equally ambitious challenge: the establishment of a vibrant, well-networked early childhood civil society in the region, through support for new professional non-governmental organizations, foundations, academic centers, and associations. Through these multiple activities, Step by Step promoted democracy on many levels. It sought to instill in children lifelong skills and attitudes; to reinforce parents' leading role in shaping young children's education; and to establish independent organizations capable of advancing children's rights, and the quality and accountability of early education services within local, national, and regional early childhood eco-systems.

Social and Political Underpinnings of Early Childhood Education in the United States and USSR: Dewey, Krupskaya, and Bronfenbrenner

The connection between education and the social and political underpinnings of society is well-established. The foundations of the early education systems that evolved in the United States and Europe, and which are the topic of this book, began in the politically oriented ideas of pedagogues and scholars from the nineteenth and twentieth centuries, several of which are summarized here.

The Step by Step program draws heavily on the ideas of the American psychologist and educational reformer John Dewey (1859–1952). Dewey, who is often referred to as the father of progressive education, captured very succinctly the central role of education in nurturing future citizens: "Democracy has to be born anew every generation, and education is its midwife" (Dewey 1993, 122). His writings emphasize education as a process of supporting children to learn to live now and in the future. In order for children to become active citizens in democratic societies, he believed education should be constructed to provide them with a chance to think, make choices, to be curious and ask questions, to negotiate and make decisions. Moreover, teachers should know the children they teach well and build learning opportunities around children's experiences and interests, while at the same time providing a strong foundation of general knowledge and opportunities to understand social relationships and the community (Mooney 2013).

Dewey's ideas influenced the progressive education movement in the United States, and nursery schools were established to support children's education and development. Supporting children's early education and development motivated just one of several strands in the history of early childhood in the United States. Perhaps more influential were childcare needs, which varied at different points in time. Beginning in the nineteenth century, childcare programs were set up as charity to enable poorer working women to keep their children, rather than send them to orphanages. There was a temporary surge of government support for childcare during wars, including the Second World War, when women took over blue-collar and agricultural jobs. But both before and after the war, arguments about the benefits for children of being raised at home superseded attempts to systematize care and/or education for young children. The numbers of children in childcare and early education rose and fell according to demand and availability, and even by the middle of the twentieth century services did not reach most children. Early childhood began to emerge as a national priority and coverage grew significantly in the 1960s and 1970s as more women entered the workforce and as political concerns grew about providing women on welfare with accessible, affordable childcare, so that they could work. Pressures to reduce inequality created additional motivations to expand free-of-charge, quality early childhood services to children and families experiencing poverty, and the US Head Start Program, the national early childhood program which launched in 1965, grew out of President Lyndon B. Johnson's war on poverty. As readers will learn, Head Start played a major role in the rollout of Step by Step almost thirty years later (Lombardi 2003; Kamerman and Gatenio-Gabel 2007).

In contrast, the Soviets, who established and inspired the early childhood systems undergoing the transformations discussed in this book, sought to align education with a very different set of political and social values. Even before the 1917 revolution, Lenin's wife, the educational expert Nadezhda Krupskaya, proposed ensuring all children receive a high-quality education to prepare them to contribute their individual talents to the emerging communist society. As the new Soviet Union began to structure its education system, Krupskaya and others helped conceptualize a strong early education component, consisting of networks of specially constructed kindergartens that promoted play, healthy living, and learning, through collective activities and connections with nature and the surrounding environment. In addition to their role nurturing future citizens, early childhood services were equally valued as essential to the liberation and emancipation of women, enabling their further education as well as their participation in work, political, and community life. A decision to build a comprehensive system of creches, preschools and boarding schools, which could provide for working mothers, was taken by the Communist party and council of ministers in 1959 (Kreusler 1970), with responsibility delegated to the ministry of education. This focus on young children as a national priority contrasts with early education in the United States, which emerged in a less consistent and intentional way.

Thus, early childhood education systems in the United States and Soviet Union developed very differently, each underpinned by its own set of social contexts and political values. A leading American developmental psychologist, Urie Bronfenbrenner, participated in two extended professional visits to the Soviet Union in the 1960s, the first supported by the American Psychological Association and the latter by the US government, both arising from curiosity about the social systems operating behind the Iron Curtain. While there, he had the opportunity to observe the raising, or "upbringing"—which is the literal translation of the Russian word associated with education and care in preschools—of young children. These visits gave him a unique perspective on how different social and political constructs influence childhood in what were at the time the two most powerful countries in the world: the Soviet Union and his home country, the United States. In *Two Worlds of Childhood: US and USSR* he conveys a fascination with the high investment in and value placed on children in the Soviet Union. Health, early education, and childcare systems sought to serve all children and were embedded in neighborhoods, creating linkages across different areas of family and community life. He contrasts this with what he describes as the neglect of children in the United States, especially those experiencing poverty, and the fragmented services that families had to negotiate. Yet the Soviet childhood he observed had distinct limitations: "Whether in creche, kindergarten, school or Pioneer palace, there was little deviation from the pattern which I had come to find so familiar—generous emotional support coupled with a firm insistence on propriety and collective conformity. In short, the individual was still very much at the service of the collective" (Bronfenbrenner 1971, x).

A further illustration of how differently politics and values influenced early childhood education in the two countries came in 1971, with the Cold War raging. In that year, President Richard Nixon vetoed a landmark piece of legislation that would have created an integrated childcare and education system in the United States. In his comments about the reason for his veto, the President outlined concerns about promoting communal child rearing over family centered care. It was understood to be a critique of Soviet values (Lombardi 2003).

Urie Bronfenbrenner's theory of the ecology of human development grew out of his observations of the multiple influences on children and their development. First published in 1979, it describes the circles of influence surrounding the developing child, providing a model that links political and social contexts to individual maturation across the life course. Early development unfolds responsively, as infants and young children interact with caregivers and the world around them. The interactions and contexts that are experienced most intensely and which are closest to the child (for instance, the relationships they have with their primary caregiver(s)) have the greatest influence. Experiences in the community such as attending preschool also have an impact, albeit a lesser one, as do contexts in which children themselves are not active, such as parents' employment, which determines family income. Local and national policies, cultural norms, political and social contexts and prejudices all play a role in establishing a child's developmental niche. In this schema the children and parents—their personalities and characteristics—are also active agents that influence the impact of the environment on their development (Bronfenbrenner 1979; Bronfenbrenner and Morris 1998).

What is interesting for the purposes of this book is how Bronfenbrenner's model situates the spheres of influence and interconnections around the child, defining the role of parents, preschool and even placing child development within a national social, political, and economic context. Politically oriented policymakers will find in his model justification for investing in preschool education (and by implication future adults) that aligns with national political and cultural values, while educators will find recognition that parents—those who are closest to the child—play the leading role in a child's development and are vital to engage in early education programs. Each child's development is unique, influenced both by national policies and values, and by family culture and the relationships that surround them in their homes and communities. This book explores what happens when national values and policies change dramatically.

Political Transformation of Early Childhood Education in Post-Second World War Europe: Democratic Movements in Northern Italy

The expansion of early childhood education from the 1960s onward was not limited to the United States and USSR. It extended across Europe and the industrialized nations. Motivated in part by the need to free women to work, the growth of early childhood programs reflected broader socio-political dynamics, including women's and civil rights movements, efforts to create more equal opportunities for people experiencing poverty, a liberalization of ideas around child rearing, and new ideas about involving communities in the development and provision of services (Singer and Wong 2021). This rapid evolution of the field of early childhood education inspired experimentation and innovation. In order to capture the richness of ideas in this period, Singer and Wong (2021) interviewed twenty-nine pioneers in the field, all born between 1940 and 1955 and professionally active from the 1960s through the 1990s. Their interviews document interesting efforts to democratize early childhood education by promoting educators' reflection and collaboration, and by shifting power and agency to the children and parents served. The pedagogical ideas of Freinet (France), Freire (Brazil), and Malaguzzi (Italy), all advocates for the creation of education spaces that promote political consciousness and democratic ideals, had a strong influence on those that were interviewed. In this overview, we focus on the impact of the innovative Italian pedagogues, led by Loris Malaguzzi and Bruno Ciari, who established the unique early childhood programs in northern Italy, including the well-known programs in Reggio Emilia and Tuscany. Interestingly, there is evidence that Malaguzzi and Ciari had access to Dewey's ideas about education and democracy through Italian translations of Dewey's works, as well as through networks of scholars, principally Lamberto Borghi. Borghi spent the Second World War in exile in the United States, where he was inspired by Dewey. Borghi returned to Italy after the war and mentored Bruno Ciari (Lindsay 2015).

The experimental early childhood programs in northern Italy (Reggio Emilia and Tuscany) that launched in the 1970s were aimed at creating democratic institutions (*democracia scolastica*) that were open to the community and organized by committees made up of representatives of staff, parents, and municipalities. In cities like Pistoia they focused on developing a culture of childhood by documenting children's experiences and projects through collaborative processes that involved children, parents, educators, and the community (Giovannini and Contini 2017). This collective activity of building a culture of childhood is an important element in the development of democratic society (Sharmahd and Peeters 2019). Peter Moss, a British scholar interested in Malaguzzi and the northern Italian approach to early childhood, uses the term "forums of democracy" to describe the role that such early childhood centers play in creating spaces where children and adults can participate in shaping decisions about things that affect them, and where a diversity of ideas, political ideals, and ethics flourishes (Dahlberg and Moss 2004; Moss 2007). Additionally, Moss has noted that when children have agency and their ideas are listened to, they gain important experiences in collective decision-making that are essential in a democracy (Moss 2017).

Imagine visiting a high-quality Soviet preschool, a Head Start center, and a program in Reggio Emilia in the 1970s or 1980s. Undoubtedly, they looked very different. What they had in common, however, is that each embodied the political and social context in which it was created. In the mid-1990s, however, following the fall of the Berlin wall, dramatic political and social changes began to influence educational policies across Eastern Europe and Eurasia, including Russia. In 1994, the deputy minister for education in Russia wrote, in a strategy paper:

> A political, sociocultural, spiritual and economic transformation is taking place in Russia, as a result of which society is changing .... This transformation can be characterized differently depending on the ideological position: from a totalitarian government to a democratic government; from a culture of usefulness to a culture of merit; from a planned economy to a market economy; from socialism to capitalism, etc ... But whatever terminology is used to describe this period, society has changed from a single monopoly on ideology to an undetermined pluralistic ideology of free choice ... The growth of a new way of life, increasing freedom of choice, weakening of the traditional system of passing knowledge and attitudes from adults to children in this dynamic unstable period in Russia has ushered in a new epoch—the epoch of alternative education.
> (Asmolov 1994, 34–5)

The change in Russia ushered in a new era whereby each preschool could move beyond the single state curriculum and choose from a group of programs approved by the ministry. The new regulations opened up the opportunity to introduce new programs. The Open Society Foundations took up Asmolov's challenge to diversify early education not only in Russia but also across the former Soviet Union and all the former socialist countries in Eastern Europe and Eurasia, many of which were already exploring more democratic approaches to early education. Step by Step offered a democratic model of early childhood education that drew its theoretical foundations from an eclectic group of American, Eastern, and Western European educational psychologists, among them Dewey, Piaget, and Vygotsky. The next section describes the Open Society Foundations and their approach to democratic education.

The Open Society Foundations and Democratic Early Childhood Education

The Open Society Foundations, a network of independent national foundations, linked initially by a regional office in Budapest and an international hub in the United States, was established by the financier George Soros in Central Europe in the 1980s and expanded across Europe and Eurasia after the fall of the Berlin wall. It aimed to respond to the revolutionary moment and to foster the transformation of closed societies into open ones. Soros established his first foundation in his native Hungary in 1984, a joint venture with the Hungarian Academy of Sciences. The Soros Foundation Hungary bought photocopying machines for libraries, translated books, supported fellowships, scholarships, and conference attendance, and provided funding for citizen-led initiatives—all activities that increased the movement of ideas and people. By 1993, the year George Soros decided to make a "big bet" investment of $100 million in early childhood, the number of national foundations had expanded, and independent, national foundations existed in a majority of countries across Central Eastern Europe and Eurasia. Each of the affiliated national foundations functioned independently, led by a board of carefully selected and trusted individuals, committed to the principles of open society. Locally hired foundation staff curated portfolios of projects, chosen for their potential to advance open society values—democracy, freedom of expression, social inclusion, and human rights—as much as for their ability to counter discrimination, exclusion, and authoritarianism.

The concept of *open society*, which underpins the Open Society Foundations, derives from Karl Popper's philosophical writings, which Soros encountered (along with Karl Popper himself) at the London School of Economics, and which explore the dangers of ideological, authoritarian societies that advance ultimate truths. Soros had experienced Nazi and communist regimes in Hungary before emigrating to the UK and then the United States and viewed truth as vulnerable to individual perceptions and perspectives. The strived-for open societies that motivate his philanthropy are democratically structured, giving equal voice, power, and inclusion to diverse ideas and beliefs, providing for protection of minority perspectives and human rights. Such societies require engaged, critically thinking citizens and a strong civil society sector, which can hold government accountable. He defined the mission of his foundation as it began to take shape in 1979 as "1) opening closed societies, 2) making open societies more viable, and 3) promoting a critical mode of thinking" (Soros 2019, 48). Over time the Foundations have increasingly focused on fighting authoritarianism and threats to open society. The Foundations support civil society organizations that hold governments accountable, while also supporting progressive governments interested in advancing open societies. For many decades the Foundations maintained a large footprint with national, regional offices and foundations across the United States, Asia, Africa, Latin America, the Middle East, and the Caribbean. At the time of writing, Open Society is consolidating its network of foundations and offices and focusing work around the themes of climate justice, equity, freedom of expression, and justice. Open Society ranks among the largest global foundations, both by endowment and by annual and cumulative expenditure (Open Society Foundations 2020).

Education has been a focus of Open Society's work since it was established, and this has continued through to 2021, when several long-standing education programs were restructured or phased out. In 2019, the foundation consolidated its approach to education in an internal paper. It emphasizes the power of education to strengthen or weaken open society, depending on how it is structured, and it promotes education as a "powerful equalizer that builds an informed citizenry committed to open society values" (Open Society Foundations 2018, 32). Education is described as a gateway right, essential to social justice and ensuring individuals can exercise their other rights. Inclusion of the most marginalized, celebration of diversity, and the teaching of critical thinking are seen as values to be embedded in education systems that support active citizenship.

These concepts of diversity, inclusion, critical thinking, and citizenship align with the progressive, democratic education movements in early education described in earlier sections of this chapter. As will be seen, the Step by Step program, which was launched by the Open Society Foundations and its network of national foundations, embodies these principles. The program promotes democratically oriented education that advances a child-centered (rather than a teacher-centered) approach. Practitioners focus on establishing a physically and emotionally safe and stimulating learning environment and community in classrooms. All children and families are welcomed, and emphasis is placed on ensuring the inclusion of children experiencing marginalization or exclusion. Teachers know children, families, and communities well and plan activities around their interests, developmental needs, cultures, and languages. Children are given opportunities to develop their unique personalities and capabilities and to appreciate the efforts and diverse perspectives of others. Classrooms offer children opportunities to make choices, to be creative, to take responsibility, to play and learn alone and together, to experience and to resolve conflicts. Parents are invited to contribute their talents to the preschool or school, to participate in governance and decision-making, and are supported as primary educators and advocates for their young children.

Visiting a Step by Step classroom, one finds a stimulating educational environment with distinct activity centers and learning materials that are carefully selected, well-labeled, and accessible to children. Children's artwork, projects, plans, and photos are visible and at their level. The day starts with a "morning meeting" to build a sense of community, providing children with a chance to share their experiences and feelings, and to introduce new ideas and plans for the day. Many programs also end the day with a community meeting to reflect on learning. Children's ideas are listened to and incorporated in the learning environment, activities, and themes. Teachers work with children to create classroom rules, which can be adapted by mutual agreement. Children are given choices about what they would like to do and are encouraged to explore and be creative, while moving through different activities and activity centers. Learning activities encourage children to explore and develop creative ways of expressing themselves and solving problems, to develop critical thinking, appreciation for diversity, conflict resolution skills, and to make choices and take responsibility. This emphasis on democratic ways of teaching and learning is a core feature of the program. Parents and families are invited into the preschool and the original Step by Step sites were required to include a room for parents in every preschool building and to designate a family coordinator to get to know parents and families and to plan ways for families and family members to participate in the life of the preschool. Teachers get to know children and their families and welcome them in classrooms to interact with children and participate in activities. Teachers observe and document children's learning and experiences to share with children and parents and they create plans that take into account the children in their classroom and the curriculum. Teachers are encouraged to develop thematic activities and programs derived from children's interests that link with the wider community. Teachers and teaching assistants take time to plan together, to reflect on their own practice, and to continue to develop their professional capacity. Planning and ongoing professional development are pillars of the program. To get a better idea of what Step by Step looks like, readers can also access this website (https://www.issa.nl/Step_by_Step_Program) which offers access to a range of pedagogical resources, photos, and films.

Interrogating Early Childhood and Democracy: Core Themes Explored in This Book

This book seeks to capture the experience of participants in the Step by Step Program and use it to better understand the impact of social and political changes on early education systems. Several hypotheses or core questions came into focus as the framework for the book was being developed, and they emerged during interviews and throughout the research process.

- *What is the role of crisis in stimulating or inspiring change in systems?* The fall of the Berlin wall and the velvet revolutions that rolled across Central, Eastern, and Southern Europe were dramatic events that created high expectations across society about a life with more freedoms and opportunities, especially for the next generation. Parents and educators alike were ready to explore and try new approaches to raising and educating children to prepare them to thrive in a different kind of society. Open Society's investment in innovative early childhood elevated democratic practices, linking education with the new political and social environment. Interviewees commented on this "magic moment" as a time when changes were possible. This book explores the role of crisis in catalyzing positive, or even negative, systems reform.
- *Systems change when people change: What motivates educators to change?* All three authors have worked on reform of education systems at local and national levels. One observation or bias that all brought into the process was a conviction that changing systems is about much more than changing legislation, policies, and curriculum, though international development agencies often assess impact through these kinds of structural changes and through the number of teachers trained in cascade trainings. Real changes for children and families can only happen when practitioners gain new attitudes, skills, knowledge, and experiences and when professional

environments encourage reflection and provide opportunities to question and adapt attitudes and beliefs and to experiment with new approaches and behaviors.

- *Crossing boundaries: How does the exchange of educational theories, practices, and experiences across borders contribute to building democratic education systems?* Open Society drew on expertise from the United States, rather than from democratically oriented programs that originated in Europe. The authors marveled at how Vygotsky's ideas were conceived in and permeated practices in Eastern Europe, and how well they were received in the West (Europe and the United States), though early education systems behind the Iron Curtain were established on the basis of very different social values. Several interviewees noted the hesitancy in some countries to engage with "American" programs, while others remarked on the positive influence that the Open Society Foundations enjoyed at the time, as an American donor which was both established by a founder from Eastern Europe and operated through legally independent and distinct national foundations. Of equal interest is the role Step by Step has played in establishing a strong practitioner and expert community across Europe and Eurasia.
- *Reform of education systems takes time: What are the advantages of long-term, flexible investments?* Open Society implemented Step by Step in a large number of countries over a long period of time. The program started as a two-year initiative for preschool and ended up lasting more than two decades. The interviews explore how participants in the program made use of the opportunity to participate in an operating program led by a strong, locally grounded donor, and to what extent Step by Step teams were able to shape the program collaboratively with Open Society Foundations, adding many initiatives and expanding not only the reach (number of families participating), but also the programmatic scope and age range of beneficiary children. Long-term investment enabled the Step by Step program and later the new early childhood professional organizations that were established with funding from the program to become part of the early childhood ecosystem in each country and regionally. In the interviews we asked the stakeholders who were active at different levels of the program how they perceived the effects of the funder's long-term investment.

Insights into these challenging questions about the process of change came out during the interviews and in the authors' discussions and we have reflected what we discovered across the chapters in this book. We return to these three themes in Chapter 10, which draws together lessons learned.

Key Terms Used in This Book

To guide the reader, brief definitions of several key terms used in this book are provided below.

Early Childhood Education: The core Step by Step program—training for center-based early childhood—was aimed at reforming practices in preschools and primary schools. Step by Step was also introduced in infant and toddler programs, and complementary initiatives include cross-sectoral parenting programs that are more accurately described as early childhood development initiatives. The term *Early Childhood Education (ECE)* is used throughout this book to refer to preschool and primary programs, which provide formal educational and development services. It eschews several terms that have wider usage, but more limited meanings. The term used by the European Commission and the Organisation for Economic Co-operation and Development (OECD)—Early Childhood Education and Care (ECEC)—is avoided as it refers exclusively to pre-primary years, and Step by Step spanned preschool and primary.

Child-Centered Approach: This term, used widely in early childhood, describes education that places the child at the center of their own learning process and teaching and learning that prioritize children's needs and interests. Child-centered is sometimes confused with allowing children to do what they choose at all times without providing any structure. In this book, and in the Step by Step program, *child-centered* is used more flexibly to include approaches to teaching and learning that prioritize children's agency, holistic needs, and interests within an organized learning environment and classroom community. Staff in an excellent child-centered program will observe children and speak with parents in order to understand each child's strengths, interests, characteristics, and personalities and will coordinate the learning environment to establish a balance between children's self-directed activities, classroom community activities that are guided and shaped by children's interests, and activities that help children to develop in areas where they benefit from additional support and opportunities.

Preschool and **Kindergarten:** The terms *preschool* and *kindergarten* signify early childhood programs for children of different ages in different countries. Throughout this book the terms are used interchangeably to refer to center-based services for children before primary school.

Roma: This book follows the widespread practice across the European Union and uses the term "Roma" to refer collectively to Roma, Sinti/Manush, Calé, Kaale, and related groups in Europe, including Travellers, to cover the wide diversity of ethnic communities concerned, including persons who identify themselves as "Gypsies" in the UK, for instance. Roma collectively make up the largest minority and are amongst the most disadvantaged citizens in Europe. Due to under-reporting, stigma, and mobility, estimates of the total population are widely contested (McDonald and Negrin 2010); however, the most widely accepted estimates from the Council of Europe indicate that there are approximately 10–12 million Roma living in Europe and approximately half are citizens of the European Union (European Commission 2020).

Disabilities and **Special Educational Needs:** This book uses the term "disabilities" in line with the definition in the United Nations *Convention on the Rights of Persons with Disabilities* to refer to persons "who have long-term physical, mental, intellectual or sensory impairments which in interaction with various barriers may hinder their full and effective participation in society on an equal basis with others" (UN General Assembly 2007). The term "special educational needs" is used when referring to all children who need support to fully access education on an equal basis with other children. This includes not only children with disabilities, but also children who need other kinds of support (e.g., financial assistance, transportation, language support) to fully access education on an equal basis with other children.

An overview of the organization of the book follows.

Organization of the Book

This book is divided into four parts each consisting of one or more chapters and a conclusion. Each chapter is written by a lead author with contributions from the other two and readers who endeavor to read the entire book may notice slight stylistic variations across chapters. Several chapters, including this one, have been co-created.

Part One, **"Why Invest in Early Childhood during a Political Transformation Process Toward Democracy?"** establishes a historical framework for the book. Chapter 1, *"Everything Was Planned": Early Childhood Education in Former Socialist Countries before and during Their Transition*, describes early education in the region from the establishment of the Soviet Union, through the fall of the Berlin wall and the collapse of the Soviet Union and dissolution of Yugoslavia and Czechoslovakia and into the period of transition. It offers a rare glimpse into the dynamics of early education in a region about which relatively little has been published for international audiences, providing personal narrative accounts about the experience of attending preschool to complement a general historical overview. In Chapter 2, *"It Was Just a Magic Time": Investing in Early Childhood to Build Democratic Societies*, readers will learn what motivated the Open Society Foundations to launch what became its flagship early childhood program, Step by Step, how the US Head Start program influenced its design, and how Step by Step was received and shaped by Open Society's affiliated national foundations.

Part Two, **"Inventing a Democratic Pedagogy,"** tells the story of how the Step by Step program introduced child-centered, democratic pedagogy across thirty countries over a twenty-year period. Chapter 3, *"Who Says We Can't Change the World?": Implementing the Step by Step Program*, presents a consolidated history of the program through the eyes of the change agents who developed and implemented it, including program directors and NGO leaders, early childhood experts and staff of the Foundation, and other international organizations. Chapter 4, *"The Teachers Believed in Us!": Inspiring Stories from Teachers, Parents, and Grown-Up Children Who Experienced the Programs*, elaborates the teacher professional development framework adopted by Step by Step and includes testimonies from educators in preschools and schools who share their experiences. Educators also describe the role of parents, and readers will find reflections from children who were in the first Step by Step cohorts. Chapter 5, *"Slowly We Are Getting There": Creating Opportunities for Children Experiencing Exclusion*, describes the successes and challenges faced as Step by Step reached out to families with children experiencing poverty, children living in remote areas, Roma children, and children with disabilities to advance their rights to inclusive early education and development. Chapter 6, *"Don't Think That It Won't Happen": Young Children and Their Families in Times of War*, provides testimonies from educators about their efforts to use early childhood programs to bring together communities during the war in the former Yugoslavia and to rebuild society in Tajikistan. Initially drafted before the war in Ukraine, the authors revisited this chapter to include material that is both chilling and hopeful from Ukraine and countries that are hosting refugees.

Part Three, **Extending and Sustaining Democratic Pedagogy through Civil Society Networks and Expansion to New Regions,** describes new directions that were never imagined when Step by Step was established in 1994. Four years into the implementation of the program, to sustain its momentum and promote its independence, Open Society began to "spin off" the program in each country and supported the development of a regional network of national organizations. By the time the first Eastern European countries joined the EU in 2004 and 2007, there were almost thirty national associations linked together through a regional umbrella organization, the International Step by Step Association (ISSA). ISSA expanded to invite members from Western Europe and evolved into the leading network for early childhood professionals in Europe and Eurasia. Chapter 7, *"The Seed beneath the Snow": The Growth of Early Childhood NGOs and Networks*, describes the challenge of building up an early childhood civil society across the region. Open Society implemented initiatives derived from Step by Step in different countries and regions, including in Haiti, Liberia, Bangladesh, and Bhutan. Chapter 8, *"Surprised and Thrilled": Rolling Out the Programs*, describes the process and challenges of adapting Step by Step to these vastly different political and social contexts and explores whether materials developed initially for Europe and Eurasia have relevance in low-income countries.

Part Four, **Transforming Early Childhood Education Systems**, uses a systems perspective, the Competent System of Early Childhood, to assess the extent to which the Step by Step program created lasting changes in early education systems. A single consolidating chapter, Chapter 9, *"This Is Yours": Successful Transformations of Early Education Systems,* invites program participants to reflect on how Step by Step projects impacted national early childhood policy and practice, created change, and were able to transform all levels of the system by introducing new methods, new tools, new resources, and, most importantly, new values of inclusion and equity.

The book ends with a **Conclusion** that reflects on the regional and international impacts of Step by Step that emerged and what they teach us about making changes in early education systems and society. Chapter 10, *Systems Change When People Change: Lessons from Long-Term Investment in Early Childhood Education*, draws together reflections and insights from Step by Step, highlighting what has been learned and what could be done differently to be more effective. It revisits the four themes that emerged through the interviews and research and looks forward to think about the role of democratically oriented early childhood in the future.

The Appendices contain a summary of the methodology that guided the research for this book, together with brief biographies of the educators who were interviewed for this book. Documents and resources from the Step by Step program, along with a Russian language version of this text, are available to interested readers on the website of the International Step by Step Association (https://www.issa.nl/Step_by_Step_Program).

Part One

Why Invest in Early Childhood during a Political Transformation Process Toward Democracy

1

"Everything Was Planned": Early Childhood Education in Former Socialist Countries before and during Their Transition

Figure 1.1 Children celebrate the new year in a kindergarten in the USSR in 1959.
Credit © Juriy Alexandrov/Alamy

Introduction

Early childhood education was a strong component of the education systems across the Eastern Bloc,[1] and it had multiple functions in a socialist society. Preschools and nurseries provided children with health care, social protection, child development opportunities, socialization, and preparation for school. By offering low-cost childcare they gave mothers the opportunity to work, and through community-focused cultural activities, preschools promoted social transformation and patriotism. This chapter explores the policy motivations for establishing these systems, and provides an overview of the ways that preschool education developed across the region from the 1920s onward, with an emphasis on the systems in the former Soviet Union and Yugoslavia. Although these countries were governed by one-party political systems in which communist parties ruled in the name of the working class, and planned economies prevailed, ECE was not a homogeneous field, and access to preschool education has varied widely in different sub-regions. The chapter closes with a description of what happened to early childhood systems during the economic, political, and social crisis in the region after the Berlin wall fell and in the period immediately before the Step by Step program was launched.

Motivations for Establishing Early Childhood Education Systems

There were a number of motivations for launching early childhood education in socialist countries, which shifted over time. Chief among these were the evolution of new concepts of citizenship and collectivism; the need to free parents, and especially women, to work and participate in civic and political life; and preparation of children for school. These motivations are set out in the section below, which uses the trajectory of preschool education in the former Soviet Union to illustrate how they played out.

Following the upheaval of revolutions and the First World War, early childhood education in the USSR was seen as a way of instilling collective and social values and building skills for a socialist (and eventually, communist) society. A department of preschool education was established in the new education ministry immediately after the October Revolution. Nadezhda Krupskaya, Lenin's wife, who was both heavily influenced by and critical of the bourgeois values of ECE systems in Europe and imperial Russia, played a key role in this process. She understood children's play as an important learning process that should allow children independence, without inhibiting their self-initiative or imposing content. She thought that "preschool institutions would serve the dual purpose of freeing the mother for work and giving a child useful knowledge and pleasure" (Weaver 1971, 57). Collectively organized ECE was in tune with the needs of the new society to nurture a citizen whose private aims would reflect the common aims of the collective. Makarenko emerged as one of the central theorists and scholars of education in the Soviet Union and his ideas infused the entire education system, starting with preschool education (Halvorsen 2014). A devout communist, he believed building a socialist state required a new kind of education focused on collectivism, altruism, discipline, and morality. As a result, character education became embedded as a strong pillar in preschool education across the Soviet Union. Children were taught self-reliance, obedience, to love their country, to cooperate, and to love work (Kreusler 1970).

ECE policy, like broader education policy, remained heavily influenced by ideology and politics well beyond the early days of socialism. Expanding education and literacy served as a form of nation-building for the Soviet Union. The new Soviet state built pedagogic institutes, schools, and kindergartens, and pushed a centralized curriculum in the new republics in Central Asia and the Caucasus, leaving limited space for native languages and cultures, with the result that efforts to expand early education sometimes met resistance (Kreusler 1970; Shakira Mukashovna 2013). Though preschool education had taken hold early in the Soviet Union, civil war, famine, and lack of funding between the two world wars meant the system initially grew slowly.

New values of women's equality also motivated ECE policy, because kindergartens freed women from what a well-known campaign called "kitchen slavery" (Shegal 1929) to participate in civic life and to work outside the home. Women were encouraged to take up roles in industry, on farms, in politics and to enter professions such as science and engineering. Following the Second World War, countries needed to rebuild and recover economically, including the Soviet Union, which is understood to have lost 19 million men and incurred a birth deficit of 8 million (Riazantsev, Sipos, and Labetsky 1992). As a generation of men returned from war with injuries or did not return at all, women entered the workforce in greater numbers and the need for childcare grew. During the 1950s and 1960s, the Soviet Union needed to increase its workforce to maintain recovery and return to growth rates as high as 7 percent per year by 1967 (Riazantsev, Sipos, and Labetsky 1992). In 1959, the Soviet Communist Party called for the opening of preschool institutions for children from two months to seven years of age and they commissioned a detailed preschool program, which was grounded in political values with detailed educational objectives and daily activities. In only three years, the number of children involved in ECE increased from 8 to 12 million, but even this expansion did not meet all needs (Kreusler 1970).

> *For Ukraine in Soviet times the 1960s was actually the most flourishing stage. It was official Soviet policy to support the development of this system for children between two months and seven years old. Women had to have time to work and places to leave their children.*
> (Natalia Sofiy, Borys Grinchenko Kyiv University, Ukraine)

The state financed the majority of this huge ECE system. Only a small part came from local enterprises and parents' fees. In the early 1970s, as economic logic shifted with slowing economies, some advocated unsuccessfully for mothers staying at home until their baby's third year, arguing this would be less expensive and better for the child (Weaver 1971). In the Soviet Union kindergartens were available to children of working parents and employment was something to be taken for granted. If children were not in kindergarten, grandparents or other family members took care of them. ECE was organized in institutions sometimes connected with factories or cooperatives to meet the needs of children whose parents worked there. Such kindergartens were an important perk for enterprises to offer because they often had better access to furniture and learning materials and lower child-to-staff ratios than public kindergartens (Bodrova and Yudina 2018). Some enterprises, like collective farms, organized ECE for children with parents involved in seasonal or occasional tasks in cooperatives. In rural environments in Tajikistan:

> *… We actually had kindergartens in cities, towns and jamoats [groups of villages] because parents had to go to work. … It was more about childcare than teaching. All these kindergartens were founded by the government, trade unions and factories to support parents who could not have afforded them. The fees were ridiculously small: the parents would pay five roubles a month.*
> (Zuhra Halimova, former executive director
> (Tajikistan) and advisory board member, OSF)

Finally, preparing children for school was used as a policy justification for early education in the Eastern Bloc. Historically, the ECE field is among the last in the education system to develop and it has had to prove its relevance for the next stage of education rather than focusing on its own intrinsic value. Nationally, education was an important component of the competition with the West for scientific discoveries and economic development. For families and children, focusing on a better future was woven into the culture of raising children. Goodness, diligence, and obedience in preschool would make a child successful in school, and success at school assured a decent job and happiness in adult life. The relationship between ECE and primary education began in the 1930s with the first national curriculum in the Soviet Union. Bodrova and Yudina (2018, 60) noted that preschool "teachers follow scope and sequence for specific skills and concepts thought to prepare children for school."

An additional motivation came into play in some countries, where alternative part-day or reduced frequency programs were introduced to provide opportunities for children, where there was insufficient space for children in kindergartens, including, for example, in Yugoslavia. This trend began in the 1960s and 1970s.

> *Over time state kindergartens offered programs of different lengths. You could stay three hours, five hours, an entire day, there were different options. …. Kids and families were getting diverse services, but unfortunately only a limited number benefited. One of the most inspiring programmes, "Školigrica" (playschool) was established in 1981 with state funding. It was not part of the regular preschool system, but the Centre for Culture "Stari Grad". It was the most innovative preschool in Serbia, and their work has a great impact even today.*
>
> *(Zorica Trikić, senior program manager, ISSA)*

Children across the region were portrayed as something that adults must care for and protect to assure a better future. Investments in preschool education varied across the Eastern Bloc. Some countries, as we will see in the upcoming section on access, attained high percentages of participation, while in other countries preschool still had low coverage in the 1990s. In many countries, though, ECE was not a high budgetary priority after the initial large investments of the 1950s and 1960s. In documents and political speeches children were mentioned as a treasure, the future of society, and that society must strive to provide better conditions for their wellbeing now and in the future.

> *(Childhood) was valued in words but not necessarily in reality. The slogan was that children are our treasure, but preschool teachers were very poorly paid and funding preschool education was not the top priority. During the school reforms (during the late 1980s) when we were interviewed by the media we would tell the correspondent that if you divide the spending on preschool education by the number of children, it was equivalent to one half of a teddy bear per child. That would be the actual money spent per child. There were some good things but in general, it was not high priority.*
>
> *(Elena Bodrova, Tools of the Mind, US)*

Though there was a great deal of motivation early on to establish early education, as time went on a dichotomy emerged between rhetoric and investment. The expansion of early education happened in bursts in response to a variety of motivations. In many countries the system never reached a majority of children, while in others it succeeded in reaching almost all of them.

Life in the Preschool

What was life like for children, teachers, and parents in preschools in the Eastern Bloc? This section draws together insights from interviews and research as well as the personal experience of the lead author of this chapter, Tatjana Vonta. It is divided into four sections: buildings and structural issues, a child's day at preschool, curriculum and the role of the teacher, and the role of parents. The aim is to explore some of the distinctive features of the early education systems across the region, which were connected with the social and political systems and values that underwent sharp transformations in the 1990s. As researchers we recognize the limitations of presenting an overview that generalizes across classrooms, preschools, municipalities, districts, and countries and acknowledge the important efforts of scholars to rethink, reconstruct, and make visible the diversity of perspectives and narratives about childhood and education and to elevate the experiences of participants from socialist countries (Piattoeva, Silova, and Millei 2018). To help mitigate this challenge, we draw attention in the descriptions below to differences within and among early education systems and include quotes from interviews that highlight these variations.

Buildings and Structural Issues

Preschools were set up to take care of children while parents worked. Schedules were adapted accordingly, and many preschools operated extended hours. Some children in the USSR spent weeknights in preschools, coming home on weekends to live with their families. Kindergartens could exist independently, or they could be attached to a larger preschool institution (which was typical in former Yugoslavia, where a number of preschool buildings formed a single institution) or they could be attached to primary schools, factories, collective farms, or other enterprises. Few private kindergartens existed, if any.

Buildings shared a familiar architecture across the Soviet republics and in much of the Eastern Bloc. Children were grouped into classrooms by age. Each class had one or two rooms.

> *The buildings would typically have two rooms for each class, one being the common room and playroom, and the other one being a bedroom that was always a separate space, typically a separate room where children would take a midday nap. There would be stationary beds ... so children would have a nap on those beds and use the playroom for the rest of the day ... again in small villages or small towns maybe there were different kinds of buildings but in a typical building, there would also be a large room for music classes and big performances ... it could also be used as a gym.*
>
> (Elena Bodrova, Tools of the Mind, US)

Large preschools in the Soviet Union had swimming pools, gyms, and dining rooms as well as rooms for medical treatments. Typically, each classroom also had its own playground outside, which was thought to be more sanitary than shared outdoor equipment. In contrast, the majority of preschools in Yugoslavia had only one room per class and no large multifunctional room, but there were big differences among and within the republics.

> *... at some (textile and tobacco factories with a traditionally female labor force), there were huge kindergartens that were for workers' children ... The kindergarten at the textile factory in Štip worked in two shifts because the women worked in three shifts .... The kindergartens were built in the 1970s and 1980s according to national standards. They were buildings with big classrooms, with additional spaces for teachers, for parents, for celebrations, and with a huge outdoor area.*
>
> (Suzana Kirandžiska, Foundation for Educational and Cultural Initiatives, Step by Step, North Macedonia)

Training and staffing varied across the region, but in general each group had at least one preschool teacher and one teaching assistant (or "nurse") who was responsible for cleaning tables, serving food, and putting things in order. Teachers worked in two shifts and overlapped during the middle of the day to ensure more staff were on hand to manage the transitions connected with lunchtime.

> *There were two educators for a classroom, who worked in shifts, from 11:00 to 13:00, they would work together to take children to wash their hands to prepare for lunch, have lunch and that part before the children would go to sleep. The first teacher started from 6:30 or from 6:00, as the factory employees started work incredibly early.*
>
> (Hašima Ćurak, advisor to the Ministry of Education and Science, Bosnia and Herzegovina)

Teachers finished secondary vocational education (pedagogic high school) or higher education at a pedagogic institute or university. The American Step by

Step trainers, who visited preschools and worked with teachers and assistants, were impressed with staff knowledge of child development, and their training and talents in music and the arts. Creative teachers used their skills to personalize and decorate classrooms. Many teachers stayed in their jobs for years and had excellent classroom management skills and created a warm, professional atmosphere in their classrooms. Most teachers spent six to seven hours in the classroom each day and had an extra hour for planning, documentation, and activities with parents. Refresher trainings were required.

The number of children and staff in the classroom depended on the age of the children being served. However, due to the shortage of places, classrooms were often overcrowded.

> *There could have been up to fifty children in groups. My first day at work was meeting with forty-five children in the group.*
> *(Hašima Ćurak, advisor to the Ministry of Education and Science, Bosnia and Herzegovina)*

Let's explore what a typical day might look like for children in a preschool.

A Child's Day in Preschool

For children, a day in the classroom usually started with free play. Each classroom was equipped with chairs and tables, cabinets, toys, and materials and the walls were decorated with pictures and illustrations created by adults. Though some children's artwork was also hung on the walls, not infrequently their pictures were the result of whole group activities, a display of nearly identical drawings, copied from the teacher's example. In each classroom there were several permanent activity corners (e.g., a family corner) equipped with toys and materials for play. Toys and materials were also on shelves and in cabinets out of reach, sometimes intentionally to teach asking for help, or so that staff could keep track of who was requesting a certain toy.

> *It was not out of malice, but because teachers were really afraid of what would happen if children took toys for themselves. They were afraid of losing control over the toy cupboard. It shows the lack of trust in children's ability to act in a logical and responsible way. It was also a reflection of what was happening in wider society. Everyone had to be told what to do and was checked up on.*
> *(Aija Tuna, former program director, International Step by Step Association and Soros Foundation Latvia)*

In Yugoslavia teachers used the time when children were having free play to work with individual children, who needed additional support. But it was different in the Soviet Union:

> We didn't talk about individualisation because to be different and individual wasn't supposed to be a good thing under the communist system. We all had to be similar and not distinguish ourselves. We didn't talk about choice because everyone had to obey the adults. Communist values did not disappear in a single day. You could still see them in practice.
>
> (Natalia Sofiy, Borys Grinchenko Kyiv University, Ukraine)

Children received two or three hot meals and snacks during the day, all prepared in well-equipped preschool kitchens. If there was only one room in the class, the teacher and assistant rearranged the tables for mealtimes. Eating routines were established by the teachers and efforts were made to create a pleasant atmosphere. While waiting for meals or while transitioning from one activity to another the teacher usually engaged the whole class in group exercises, songs, and dances. Children visited the toilet and washed hands as a group, and waiting in line was part of the daily routine.

The daily schedule, regardless of the weather, also included outdoor activities such as playing in the playground or walks and excursions to nearby places. Finally, after lunch the children took long naps. In many preschools in the Soviet Union each classroom had a separate room with beds, but where space was limited, for instance in Yugoslavia, teachers put out folding beds. Usually, all children were supposed to rest until a specific time when, again, they were allowed to play until parents picked them up.

The most important times during the day, however, were lesson times, which were built into the schedule and through which the all-important national curriculum was fulfilled.

Curricula and the Role of the Teacher

Curricula from the Soviet Union initially had a significant impact on how early childhood programs developed both in the Soviet republics and across the region. The field of educational psychology, in particular, has a rich and deep history grounded in the work of scientists active before the Soviet Union was established, and which has continued across generations of scholars through to today. Some of this work, like the work of Vygotsky, has subsequently been embraced in the West, but streams of work in areas such as the development of mental activity and play have had relatively limited exposure outside the countries of the former Eastern Bloc. A number of these scholars—Zaporozhets, Luria, Elkonin, Davydov, Galperin, Venger—built on Vygotsky's original research. In their introduction to a volume that compiles translated works by Soviet psychologists, the American scholars Michael Cole and Irving Maltzman praise their colleagues in the USSR: "Much of the Soviet research is marked by a high degree of ingenuity and an innovative character that outstrips its Western counterpart" (Cole and Maltzman 1969, xii). Lab preschools piloted some of the innovative ideas of these educational psychologists, and their work has influenced some practices, but the majority of preschools during the Soviet period followed guidelines and scripted lessons that were put out by various regulatory educational agencies.

> *The preschool department of the ministry of education USSR and Institute for Preschool Education of the USSR Academy of Sciences prepared a federal preschool program (tipovaja programa) with a curriculum that strictly defined the objectives, the requirements for each age group, and the schedule of activities to enable the prescribed goals to be achieved. The* tipovaja programa *for preschools was in fact a federal curriculum for all republics, one framework with some adaptations for local cultural differences like language, music, poems, dance, games.*
>
> (Elena Bodrova, Tools of the Mind, US)

Across Eastern Europe there were similarly strong scholars, psychologists, and educators, engaged in introducing innovative practices, but these new approaches were often limited to a small number of experimental schools and were slow to transfer into the system.

There was virtually no flexibility in the Soviet Union in implementing the compulsory program. However, over time some variation emerged across the region as well as between individual educational institutions, particularly regarding planning and implementation of lessons. Some variations had historical origins. For example, the Baltic states had established early childhood education systems well before they were taken over by the Soviet Union. In Latvia prior to the 1940s kindergartens had been free to choose curricula, including those of Froebel and Montessori, which supported children's development and preparation for school. The exposure to different methodologies continued to influence practices long after the Baltics became part of the Soviet Union, though this was not discussed openly.

Other variations were inevitable, simply because people, including teachers, are so different.

It depended so much on just the personality of the teacher. Teachers were the executors of pre-established and prescriptive programs, and they had to implement it. It was also a kind of control all over the country as the authorities knew what was happening in every kindergarten in the whole Soviet Union at a certain time.
(Cornelia Cincilei, Step by Step Moldova)

I think that any totalitarian system has flexibility because of human nature. Flexibility was on a personal level as usual but not on an official level for sure.
(Elena Yudina, expert, Russia)

In Yugoslavia each republic developed its own curriculum, with similarities as well as differences. Curriculums were based on normative psychology and age appropriateness. They were relatively detailed and divided into goals, tasks, and content for each age group. All of them stressed the comprehensive development of children with a recommended number of activities from each developmental domain or curricular area each week. Control over implementation varied across the republics and mostly depended on personal and professional skills, knowledge, and the values of the people in control. The two quotations below illustrate the differences in the level of control in two republics, Bosnia and Herzegovina and Serbia.

…. everything was planned. It is known that at 9:00 children do directed activities, which is a "lesson" and you are with children right outside, and as much as you want to change that, you can't change that because some excessively strict inspector is coming and he'll say, "Where is your preparation?"
(Hašima Ćurak, advisor to the Ministry of Education and Science, Bosnia and Herzegovina)

… this part of the educational system was not really in the focus of policymakers. They gave us a huge degree of freedom. You just had to dare to do something innovative. It was completely different from schools. The idea was to have as many kids as possible.
(Zorica Trikić, senior program manager, ISSA)

Teachers in Yugoslavia had a lot of autonomy around how and when they realized the objectives in the curriculum, and teachers were required to adapt activities to children's interests and to the local environment. Yet children did not have many opportunities to influence what they would learn or how they spent a day, and teachers were not trained to support and challenge children's free play or to build developmental activities into child-initiated activities. Children's ideas were redirected unless they were connected with the teacher's plan; otherwise, children's ideas were postponed and seldom realized. The teacher set classroom rules. Trust in children's abilities depended on the level of trust supervisors had in their teachers.

Lessons and routines were teacher-directed and collectivist. Teaching approaches were still based on behaviorism and results were valued more than the process of learning. Educational processes during lessons were almost completely teacher-directed regardless of children's preferences for play, lessons, work or eating, sleeping, toileting, etc. Teachers transmitted knowledge, set the emotional tone, and promoted the values of collectivist routines. When children mastered a routine, there would be fewer directives from the teacher, and it would look as if everything was running very smoothly. Children's individual interests and learning needs during lessons were of less importance than the teacher's plan. Lessons were given by the teacher to all children at the same time and teachers often struggled to motivate children to engage in group activities. In Yugoslavia, constructivist ideas sprung up in the 1970s, and despite overcrowded classrooms, some teachers managed to create an environment that challenged each child to develop and learn in his/her own way.

Ideological beliefs, values, and goals were incorporated into the curricula, some of them in daily routines, some in content, and some through the collective approach to children's learning. In the Soviet Union ideological symbols like pictures of past and current communist party leaders, and symbols of the homeland could be found in each preschool and classroom. In the case of Yugoslavia, these kinds of symbols were present only around national holidays.

> ... *Ideology in ECE was very clearly seen, even if we did not talk about it.*
> *(Natalia Sofiy, Borys Grinchenko Kyiv University, Ukraine).*

The political goals of ECE were apparent in the way that systems were centralized from the top down to meet the communist parties' goals and need for control. For practitioners in kindergartens, professional support staff played a dual role of both support and monitoring through inspections. In the Soviet Union kindergarten teachers were given pedagogical support from a designated professional staff member, the methodologist. Methodologists were based in large preschools or hired as staff by the municipality, providing support to several preschools. They developed lessons and activities and worked together with teachers on methodological planning. Not infrequently, this created situations where the same activities and materials were being used by all the preschools covered by a particular methodologist.

For example, when Tatjana Vonta spent half a year in Georgia in the late 1980s, methodological specialists in the methodological department prepared manuals outlining working methods, collected statistical data, and worked directly with preschool directors, teachers, and staff through meetings, seminars, tours, and presentations of good practice from experienced teachers. They connected ECE practitioners across the district. Each of the methodological specialists covered kindergartens in up to ten districts in Georgia. This structure gave them power to influence the learning processes across all kindergartens. Similarly, the ministries of education in the Republics of Yugoslavia set up special pedagogical services in the 1960s and 1970s. The role of this service included inspection, monitoring, implementation of social goals, and directing and accelerating educational activities, which was remarkably like the role of the methodological centers in the Soviet Union. New school-based consulting services combined with more ambitious requirements for teachers' pedagogical training in the 1980s brought about significant improvements in the professionalization of the field in most of the country.

The Role of Parents in the Preschool

Parents usually left and picked up their children in front of the classroom door, as they were not welcome to enter the classroom. In the Soviet Union, parents were invited to meetings and common holidays where children demonstrated their achievements with performances. According to one interviewee, the most talented children were always selected for leading roles with minimum attention to equitable participation and development of all children, and parents never questioned the system.

> *The role of parents in the previous format was just to bring children to the kindergarten clean, and in good health and stay at the door, not come into the classroom. They must follow the teachers' instructions, who would tell them whether their child had been well-behaved, and share work they had done on class assignments.*
>
> *(Cornelia Cincilei, Step by Step Moldova)*

The development of the ECE system in Yugoslavia experienced major changes in the 1960s and 1970s as a result of constitutional reforms supporting decentralization, and this impacted parents' roles. Self-governing bodies were set up in kindergartens (Dolanc et al. 1975). Parents, together with kindergarten staff, participated in governing kindergartens. Their representatives voted at the municipal level on decisions about preschool programs, fees for parents, criteria for enrollment, and even the number of children in the classroom. Kindergarten staff also played a role in building awareness in the community, and they presented their plans and engaged parents as supporters with varying degrees of skill and success.

Despite the evolution of the role of parents and communities on paper, most often they had little impact on the education of their children. Parents were usually still not permitted to enter classrooms and did not play an active role in the functioning of kindergartens. Everyday communication with parents consisted of sharing information about children's nutrition, rest, or daily activities. Teachers held individual meetings with parents to discuss their child's progress and to offer advice, although teachers' observations were not always underpinned with evidence. Teachers also provided three or four full classroom parent meetings annually about the health, care, and education of children.

Despite the ideological underpinnings of ECE systems and the regimented nature of teaching and learning, life in classrooms was enjoyable for many children. Children moved as a group through most activities and the maximum number of staff were on hand to manage transitions in the middle of the day. Fewer staff were in classrooms when learning activities were taking place. Play was a part of each day and children had access to interesting materials and opportunities to learn and make friends. The day included meals and naps and children had access to health services. Many adults have fond memories of their experiences in ECE.

> *I cannot articulate if they valued me as a personality or if that approach was child centered. No, I just remember that I was happy. I was really happy. I liked my teachers. I liked the environment. I had good friends. This is about what I remember from my childhood, in terms of personal experience.*
>
> (Ulviyya Mikayilova, ADA University, Azerbaijan)

Access to and Availability of ECE

Access to early education varied widely across the region with spending on social programs, including education, peaking in the 1970s. Disparities of access to ECE mirrored disparities in housing, healthcare, and other social protections.

This section explores the access to and availability of ECE in the region in the period from 1989 to 1994, immediately after the fall of the Berlin wall, at the outset of the massive social and political transformation that followed. It provides context about the ECE systems across the region before the Step by Step program was introduced and describes large differences in coverage that existed in different sub-regions.

Data about early childhood education systems in transition are challenging to collect, particularly given the dramatic geopolitical changes that took place across Europe and Eurasia at the start of the 1990s, as Yugoslavia, Czechoslovakia, and the Soviet Union all split into multiple countries. We draw our data from papers compiled by UNICEF's Innocenti Research Centre in Italy (Riazantsev, Sipos, and Labetsky 1992; UNICEF 2001) and from UNESCO's Global Monitoring Report (UNESCO 2006), which focused on early childhood care and education, to draw out trends and provide a snapshot of early education systems in the region at the moment of transition and in the five years that followed.

What is clear from the data presented in this paragraph is that coverage of early childhood education in 1988 and 1989, as outlined in a UNICEF report (Riazantsev, Sipos, and Labetsky 1992, 27) focusing on the economic situation in the USSR before the transition, was dramatically different in different sub-regions. Though coverage in the Soviet Union as a whole for children between three and six years old was 58 percent, across all fifteen republics, the republics (and later countries) in the European region (the Baltics, Russia, Belarus, Ukraine, Moldova) had much higher rates of participation, ranging from 61 percent to 72 percent, while Central Asia and the Caucasus had significantly lower rates of participation, ranging from 16 percent to 53 percent. At the low end were Tajikistan and Azerbaijan with less than 20 percent participation, reflecting low levels of investment. The majority of countries in Central Asia and the Caucasus—Kyrgyzstan, Turkmenistan, Uzbekistan, Armenia, and Georgia— had relatively modest coverage rates, in the range of 30 percent to 49 percent. Among the republics in the Caucasus and Central Asia, only Kazakhstan (with its large share of oil production and kindergartens attached to enterprises) approached enrollment levels (53 percent) consistent with USSR averages and the gains made in the European republics, which included Russia. Inequity in access to ECE programs reflects the social context overall in the Soviet Union and, to some extent, the colonial history of the Caucasus and Central Asia.

UNESCO's EFA Global Monitoring Report (UNESCO 2006, 135–7) tracks trends in preschool coverage of children between three and six years of age in the transition countries between 1989 and 2003, and we draw data from this document to illustrate the context in Yugoslavia and Central Eastern Europe.

Preschool access in Yugoslavia was at the low end (between 20 and 40 percent in Croatia, Slovenia, Serbia & Montenegro, Macedonia[2]) and the lowest numbers in the region were found in Bosnia, where only around 10 percent of children had access to preschool education. At the other end of the scale, Bulgaria, Romania, Hungary, the Czech Republic, and Slovakia had coverage rates for children between three and five years of age of 72 percent to 99 percent, with the Czech Republic topping them all with nearly universal coverage. Poland, with rates just under 50 percent, was similar to the average coverage rates in the USSR, but it joined the European Union with the lowest rates of coverage among member states in 2004.

ECE access also varied within countries, often further entrenching existing inequity. For example, in the USSR in the late 1980s, there was an average of 107 children for every 100 kindergarten spots available, but in Central Asian republics this average climbed to 128 children (Riazantsev, Sipos, and Labetsky 1992). Investment in early education did not always match demographic changes. For example, in 1980 Ukraine had the lowest fertility rate in the USSR (2.03) and Tajikistan the highest (5.35), widening the gap in child welfare between the European and Asian parts of the USSR that already existed (Riazantsev, Sipos, and Labetsky 1992). Services were generally prioritized (and subsidized) for parents who were working, creating greater inequalities both between families where both parents worked and parents who did not, and between regions with high and low unemployment. Riazantsev, Sipos, and Labetsky (1992) draw attention to greater access in urban environments where more family members worked outside or away from home. Lower access in rural areas stemmed from lower budgets for ECE, but lower demand for services also played a role.

To overcome social differences, legislation in Yugoslavia from the early 1970s gave enrollment priority to children identified as educationally, economically, and socially disadvantaged. Some shorter, non-obligatory programs were also opened to address the need for more places. Kindergartens started to be more open to all children and not only to those of working parents. Fees for parents were based on the social situation of families, reflecting the principles of solidarity and social responsibility, but there was often not enough funding or spaces available to implement progressive policies fully, fairly, or transparently.

> [Kindergarten] ... was not only for privileged children, ... there was a scale for parents who were not employed or who had a low salary. The government, the state paid for those children to go into the kindergarten.
> (Suzana Kirandžiska, Foundation for Educational and Cultural Initiatives, Step by Step, North Macedonia)

Immediately after the transition coverage fell across the region, though this was hardly noticeable in the Czech Republic and Belarus, and coverage began to grow steadily, but slowly, in the countries of former Yugoslavia, and by 2003 had recovered or exceeded original levels in the Baltics and across Central Eastern Europe. The transition was devastating for Central Asia and the Caucasus, where rates plummeted and did not recover. In Kazakhstan, which had relatively high coverage rages in 1989, because of its many enterprise-owned kindergartens, coverage fell by as much as 40 percent, dropping from over 50 percent to less than 20 percent between 1989 and 2003 (UNESCO 2006). This was an indirect effect of the privatization of industries, as privatizing enterprises shed preschools and sold off the buildings.

Finally, it is important to draw attention here to the accessibility of preschool and early primary education across the region for children with disabilities. For the most part, even those with moderate disabilities were not able to participate in mainstream education. Instead, they were educated at home or segregated into special classrooms and schools, and in some cases, they lived in institutions, which were governed by special departments in the education system. Many Roma children and other minorities, who were disproportionately assessed as having disabilities, ended up in special schools as a result of biased school readiness testing and structural racism. Chapter 5 delves into the education of these children.

Collapse and Transition

The system of ECE in the Soviet Union in the 1980s was huge and expensive to maintain, let alone expand. Although the 1990s brought cataclysmic economic and political changes with the disintigration of the Soviet Union, Yugoslavia and Czechoslovakia, changes in ECE had already begun in the 1980s, paving the way for some of the policy decisions of the 1990s and beyond. In Romania, Ceausescu's strict austerity measures in the 1970s affected all citizens, including services for children. Enrollment rates slowed in all parts of the Eastern Bloc and Soviet Union from 1985. New kindergarten capacity dropped by 16 percent between 1988 and 1989 (Riazantsev, Sipos, and Labetsky 1992, 26). The collective "one size fits all" approach began to shift after the political developments in 1989.

> *I was in a group formed from several institutes under the All-Soviet Academy of Education that started to develop an innovative, new framework for preschool*

> education, defining what had to be changed, from philosophy to legal issues. We met with local and federal ministers of education and held workshops and seminars for preschool directors from different regions of the Soviet Union. We were trying to change their mentality and it was very hard to do. They were used to old ways of thinking so just lecturing wouldn't help. We used all kinds of trainings to try to reduce their defences and change their beliefs.
>
> Our Institute was very much Vygotsky-oriented and some innovative curricula that our institute developed was very strongly based on Vygotsky, but when it came to implementation, there was a conflict between Vygotskian philosophy and authoritarian education traditions. Our curricula were implemented in lab schools, but when it came to implementing them all over the Soviet Union, it was not the case.
> (Elena Bodrova, Tools of the Mind, US)

In Yugoslavia, the breakdown also started long before it began in earnest. After Tito's death political struggles that had been brewing for years came to the surface. The Balkan wars started in 1991, with dire consequences for ECE.

> The war [in Sarajevo] stopped at the end of 1995. By that time, all kindergartens and all, at least primary schools in Sarajevo, which was under siege, were completely destroyed, physically destroyed. Unfortunately, there was also a lack of teachers because out of four million, one million people left the country and were refugees.
> (Dženana Trbić, former education program coordinator,
> Open Society Fund - Bosnia and Herzegovina)

Even countries not embroiled in violent conflict faced challenges in establishing new state structures and systems as the geopolitical map changed dramatically in the early 1990s. Reformist movements swept across all the countries of the former Eastern Bloc. Poland held its first semi-democratic elections, and Hungary removed controls on its border with Austria, allowing people from the East to travel to the West. A velvet revolution took place in Prague and ultimately divided Czechoslovakia into the Czech Republic and Slovakia. In Romania, violent protests removed the Ceausescu dynasty. The early transition brought decreased financing and the decentralization of ECE systems from national governments to local authorities. If a cooperative, factory, or company that operated a kindergarten closed, they transferred ownership to the municipality in hopes that it would continue to provide services. Many municipalities did not have the resources to maintain these buildings and services.

> *After preschools came under the authority of local municipalities, because they no longer had legal responsibility, the ministry of education did not pay any attention to the field, up until a few years ago. After the collapse of the Soviet Union, there was no financing of these schools. The ceiling, walls and the floors of the classrooms were destroyed, windows broken. There was no heating, no sanitary system, no toilets. That's why people stopped sending their children to kindergartens.*
> *(Eteri Gvineria, Center for Educational Initiatives, Step by Step Georgia)*

Unemployment among parents, low birth rates, and mothers taking longer maternity leave meant that there were not enough children to fill classrooms, or children stayed in "grey market care" as the fees in formal kindergartens grew too high. Donors and advisors insisted that firms shift kindergartens off their balance sheets. In countries where they were not protected, municipalities sold off the buildings. Consequently, kindergartens closed.

> *Early education infrastructure collapsed first, the salaries of teachers started to be so low that they had to switch jobs. Most of the kindergartens at that time collapsed but the buildings remained. When the Soviet Union collapsed, all of these social welfare systems also collapsed automatically. In majority of the cases, donors did not target early childhood at all, because that was not their priority.*
> *(Zuhra Halimova, former executive director (Tajikistan) and advisory board member, OSF)*

The disorientation of the economic and political crisis also brought conservative social values to the forefront in some communities, in contrast to the progressive or revolutionary goals of the first ECE systems in the 1920s and 1930s. When mothers stayed at home, those who understood kindergarten as childcare saw no reason to continue sending their children.

> *During Soviet times women achieved a level of autonomy and emancipation through their employment and economic liberty as at least childcare services and kindergarten were running for their children. After the collapse so many of them just had to go back home behind the stove.*
> *(Zuhra Halimova, former executive director (Tajikistan) and advisory board member, OSF)*

Independence gave rise to nostalgic ideas and unrealistic political and economic proposals around ECE and kindergartens from parents, teachers or experts, and politicians alike.

> *The idea was connected with a wish to go back to wonderful old times and then normal life will take place, as we are free from Soviets, and we have our own state. In this old, nice, normal life—actually the life of people in West—women stayed at home and took care of their children. The number of preschools dramatically decreased.*
> *(Aija Tuna, former program director, International Step by Step Association and Soros Foundation Latvia)*

Meanwhile some kindergartens continued operating, mostly with the old curriculum. Some teachers were full of expectation for new things—but not all of them, as changes could be painful. Parents were cautious and mostly they trusted old models, as the majority were unfamiliar with anything else. Still, the evolution of ECE continued, creating new curricula and new opportunities.

> *One of the biggest changes in the ECE system according to the new law is that every kindergarten has the right to elaborate its own curriculum, so we can have as many curriculums as we have kindergartens. They can use any materials available on the educational market. Usually, they continued to use the program from the Soviet period because it was easy for them, so it was popular. This was because the in-service training system and institutions didn't change a lot and remained traditional. They didn't have competition and were funded regardless of the quality of their work, according to the number of participants who attended trainings.*
> *(Elena Yudina, expert, Russia)*

The Baltic countries and Central European countries started to harmonize their legislation and regulations with the European Union. Many innovative ideas emerged at that time.

> *It was also a time when more literature about different pedagogical approaches and self-improvement programs and how to start your business came in. Everything that came from the West was so important, so new, so necessary although it could be also very questionable.*
> *(Aija Tuna, former program director, International Step by Step Association and Soros Foundation Latvia)*

In practice, new approaches took root but stayed within an extremely limited range, as there was no appropriate strategy for expansion. Liberalization brought private kindergartens which did not receive much attention or support from the education system. At the same time, as education reforms started to take shape, ministries gradually began to allow preschools more flexibility. This created an opening for the Step by Step program.

2

"It Was Just a Magic Time": Investing in Early Childhood to Build Democratic Societies

Figure 2.1 George Soros visits a Step by Step program in Kyiv, Ukraine, in 1993.
© Open Society Foundations

Global Early Childhood and Donor Engagement in Central Europe and Eurasia in the 1990s

In stark contrast to the declining conditions in preschools across Central Europe and Eurasia, described in Chapter 1, the field of early childhood was gaining traction globally. This was a result of what Sheila Kamerman has described as a set of "remarkable developments culminating in the explosion of attention to Early

Childhood Education and Care in the 1990s" (Kamerman 2006, 2). The fall of the Berlin wall in 1989 coincided with the approval of the Convention on the Rights of the Child by the General Assembly of the United Nations, which most countries in the region signed, bringing the wellbeing and rights of children to greater attention. This was followed in 1990 by the World Conference on Education for All, which put early childhood on the international financing and development agenda and incorporated early education and care into basic education. Extraordinary developments in the field of neuroscience accelerated interest in early childhood.

Though the attention of some donors was shifting to include early childhood, it was not yet prominent in their portfolios, and this was true for donors present in the transition countries in Europe in the early 1990s. Education reform initiatives in the newly independent countries in the region first paid attention to higher education and only later addressed high schools and primary education. In their chapter on the post-socialist education reform in this region, Silova and Steiner-Khamsi (2008) describe how, globally, support for education from the World Bank and UN agencies was structured around the Millennium Development Goal of achieving universal primary education, which was not relevant for this region as participation in primary education was already high. Instead, efforts focused on transforming systems to meet the standards and ideologies of Western neighbors. Education assistance tended to support a formulaic set of reforms, including the introduction of a new curriculum, student-centered approaches, student outcomes and standardized assessment, and decentralization of funding and governance. Little attention was initially paid to inclusive practices, teacher training, and participatory governance. Neither the countries nor the donor agencies were homogeneous. Reinforcing national cultures was important to the newly independent countries, a number of which were leaning toward autocracy rather than democracy. The result was that the financial and technical resources on offer to countries and what they actually needed and wanted were not always aligned. Where mismatches occurred, reforms were either not implemented, hybridized—sometimes with positive effects—or negatively compromised (Silova and Steiner-Khamsi 2008).

Open Society Foundations' Decision to Launch an Early Childhood Program

The work of the Open Society Foundations in education and early childhood did not fall neatly into the prevailing categories described above. A private operating foundation, its work was tied neither to the Millennium Development Goals nor to the formulaic reforms on offer from the main international donors. With its network of independent foundations across the region, Open Society could both tailor educational initiatives to country priorities and launch large-scale single and multi-country initiatives.

By 1993, the year George Soros decided to make a "big bet" investment in early childhood, independent, national foundations existed in most countries across Central Eastern Europe and Eurasia. The New York office of Open Society was at the time largely administrative, though several multi-country, centrally run thematic projects supported scholarships, English language teaching, contemporary art centers, and an adolescent health education initiative (Sudetic 2011). Activities in the sphere of education emphasized transforming social sciences to fit the new political ideology, replacing or at least augmenting the teaching of Marxist theories. Efforts were made to enlarge library holdings, bring scholars together, translate previously censored works, and create new academic programs. Reform of preschool education was on no-one's mind.

In 1993, things were going well for Open Society. George Soros's investments were thriving, and the footprint and reputation of the foundation network were growing. The optimistic political mood in the region encouraged bold initiatives. One of Soros's top priorities was to establish a university dedicated to fields of study connected with open society and founded on principles of excellence, freedom of expression, and collaboration to motivate the future leaders of an open society. In pursuit of this aim, he met with leading scholars around the world, including Dr. Fraser Mustard, a physician and scientist and founding president of the Canadian Institute for Advanced Research, a novel academic institution bringing together leading scholars from across Canada to engage in cross-disciplinary work on challenging subjects.

Mustard told Soros that if he wanted to create citizens who would build an open society, he must start with young children. The encounter is referenced in Open Society, Canadian and World Bank publications as an example of the extraordinary influence that a single meeting can have on donor funding. In the words of George Soros:

> My encounter with Fraser Mustard in the early 1990s was one of the factors that led me to invest, over time, nearly $100 million in Step by Step—an early child development program in 28 Eastern European countries. The approach will take hold in some countries and will have a significant impact on the emergence of democratic, prosperous societies. It was a risk only a living donor could take.
>
> (McCain, Mustard, and Shanker 2007, 157)

A deeper look into Mustard's numerous speeches and writings on the topic offers insight into the scientific and historical detail that he used to advocate for investment in the early years. His work, which was featured at an historic international conference on early childhood organized by the World Bank in 2000 and captured in a follow-up publication, brings together outstanding research and evidence from numerous fields. His arguments extend well beyond the often-discussed finding that infants are born with partially developed neurological systems that undergo profound development in the first few years of life, when provided with nurturing care. Mustard starts with studies from the last century that correlate declines in adult mortality and, in parallel, increases in economic growth, with improvements in the health and wellbeing of populations starting with children. He elaborates with accompanying charts and graphs how the complex interaction of genes and environment, particularly exposure to stress, influences the development of the biological-hormonal, stress-response, and sensory pathways that impact lifelong cognitive, emotional, and biological health, creating protection from or predisposition toward coronary heart disease, high blood pressure, diabetes, immune function, obesity, emotional responsiveness, self-control, executive function, and intelligence. He draws on animal studies to illustrate the impact of nurturing parenting on later health and status; from human cohort studies to illustrate the impact of socio-economic status on lifelong education attainment, employment, and health outcomes; and from longitudinal evaluations of successful programs to illustrate the potential gained from intervening early. Finally, as an example of how to put it all into action, he shares a concept he developed with colleagues to implement coordinated services for parents and young children across Ontario (Mustard 2002).

One can imagine it was a long discussion, and that Mustard was convincing. Soros intimates as much:

> He showed me very extensive research, which showed conclusively what happens in the first years of life has a disproportionate effect in later development and that investment and effort in early years pays off disproportionately in later years.
> George Soros, founder, Open Society Foundations
> (Soros 2007)

Designing an Early Childhood Program for Eastern Europe

It fell to Liz Lorant to develop a program for "minus one to plus six," George Soros's suggested name for the program. Lorant, a Hungarian émigré and executive director of the Soros Foundation Hungary in NY, had been with the foundation since 1981 as preparations were underway to establish the foundation in Budapest. She had recently extended a successful health education program for adolescents from the Czech Republic to interested Soros national foundations across the region. Lessons learned from implementing the health education program, a teacher training initiative in multiple countries, had a bearing on how the early childhood program was ultimately shaped. One of the most important reflections from the health education program was the eagerness of teachers in the region to embrace new teaching methodologies.

To help develop a program Lorant turned to Dr. Phyllis Magrab, Director of Georgetown University's Center for Child and Human Development (GUCCHD). She had met Magrab serendipitously on a metro in Budapest. A number of factors made Georgetown a good potential technical partner for the initiative. Firstly, staff had visited the region and were familiar with the health, education, and social care systems serving young children with disabilities and developmental delays. Secondly, GUCCHD, based in Georgetown's Medical School, was renowned for expertise in early childhood, including early education, early intervention, infant mental health, and cultural competence and had extensive experience implementing collaborative projects. Thirdly, Georgetown was institutionally connected with the Head Start program, serving as a regional center of technical assistance, with a number of leading experts and trainers on faculty and staff. As ideas for a large-scale program in the region began to take shape, the then director of Head Start's national technical assistance department in the federal government, Pam Coughlin, arranged to be seconded to Georgetown to lead the initiative.

Though the identification of Head Start as the guiding framework for the Open Society early childhood initiative did not follow an extensive assessment of options in the United States and Europe, it turned out to be a strategic choice, aligning well with the broader social issues that interested George Soros. Established in 1965 through President Johnson's "war on poverty," during the height of the civil rights movement, Head Start put into practice emerging findings from research by leading academics and implemented these within a social justice framework, targeting the program to reach children experiencing poverty, especially those who did not have access to early childhood programs as a result of exclusion and discrimination. To address the wider social issues that underpin poverty, Head Start is designed as a comprehensive program, providing educational, health, and social welfare services, focusing as much on parents as it does on their young children. Beyond providing young children with quality center-based programming, nutrition, health and social services, Head Start offers parenting classes, links parents with social benefits and continuing educational opportunities, and even trains and employs interested parents as child development associates in classrooms.

Joan Lombardi, who served as the first associate commissioner of the Child Care Bureau in the US Department of Health and Human Services, which had oversight over the Head Start Program, emphasized several features that made Head Start a great fit for the Open Society Foundations initiative:

> *It is an approach that seeks to break the cycle of poverty. It supports democratic principles, because it is based on maximum participation of the poor. It is about parents making decisions about their own children. Head Start was the original program to really focus on using early childhood programs as a gateway to parents, and their own wellbeing and creating an enabling environment for their parenting.*
> *(Joan Lombardi, Georgetown University and Stanford University)*

Head Start provides participating US states with co-funding, technical assistance, and quality standards to support services for children and families with household incomes that meet a poverty threshold. The guidelines mandate that funds be used for high-quality play-based, parent and child-focused, culturally and developmentally appropriate inclusive programs that support children's development and readiness for school. Programs are required to meet minimum structural standards (staffing ratios, staff training and professional development, class size, etc.), must link with health, social service, and welfare programs, and must include parents and communities in governance structures. What Head Start does *not* do is dictate detailed content or a specific curricular approach to use in center-based programs. Head Start-funded programs can use any developmentally appropriate curriculum, for instance Montessori, the Creative Curriculum, High Scope, or Reggio Emilia, and can be either publicly or privately owned as long as they meet the framework criteria and quality indicators set out in the guidelines.

> *Head Start is constantly evolving. There are performance standards, but the actual service delivery model can vary based on the needs of the community. There are requirements about teachers having to reflect the languages and cultures of children served. It sounds like Step by Step kept those principles but contextualized them.*
> *(Joan Lombardi, Georgetown University, and Stanford University)*

> *I think, frankly, it was a very fortunate serendipitous choice, even though it was not chosen by an evaluative approach. I think it was a terrific choice, not because it is American and not because it is Head Start but because, as I said earlier, it is not*

a dogmatic prescribed program. If you look at High Scope, Montessori, all of these programs, they are very defined.

(Phyllis Magrab, Georgetown University, former board chair,
Early Childhood Program Advisory Board, OSF)

Lorant joined early childhood experts convened by Georgetown to plan a rapid, multi-country initiative to introduce democratic reforms in early childhood education in Central Eastern Europe and the former Soviet Union. Head Start's comprehensive approach inspired the framework, which also drew on Lorant's experience implementing the multi-country health education program in the region.

Less than a month later, Soros reviewed a concise summary of the well-elaborated plan, which Lorant had prepared.

It set out the idea of training trainers, that we're going to work with experts from the region, and bring in early childhood programs from the West. When I walked into his office, he was on the phone. When he hung up, he asked for the piece of paper. I handed it over and he read it, front and back. He said, "Okay, go ahead." I said thank you and got up to leave. Halfway out the door, he called after me and said, "I want to spend $100 million on this." .... To this day, I don't know what came over me in a split second and I said, "I will only spend as much as I can spend well." I never told anybody not even Sarah Klaus, about that part of the conversation, because I wanted everyone on the project to feel tested every single year at budget time. As a result we were able to develop strategies based on the needs as expressed by the Step by Step teams and the Soros Foundations, not around that very intimidating number. At the tenth anniversary celebration with George Soros in attendance I finally told everyone. By then we had spent well over $100 million in nearly thirty countries and it was all very carefully and well spent.

(Liz Lorant, former director, Children & Youth Program, OSF)

The plan relied on Head Start's wealth of expertise and trainers, hiring more than thirty leading consultants during the first year of implementation to support and mentor program teams in participating countries.

What we really used from Head Start were the resources of the trainers and the people who knew how to create developmental classrooms and experiences. They were all different, but they all had a common philosophy and a common way of thinking about how you prepare an experience for a child. What we got from Head Start was a capacity ... That capacity ... was a group of people who were committed to inclusion, who were committed to developmental approaches, who definitely

> *had tools and defined approaches. But it wasn't a rigid lockstep approach. We just all happened to be Americans, but the way the program ended up it was not at all American. It was Central and Eastern European. It fit within the culture of each classroom.*
>
> (Phyllis Magrab, Georgetown University, former board chair, Early Childhood Program Advisory Board, OSF)

Next, a comprehensive information package was sent to each national foundation affiliated with Open Society offering them the opportunity to participate in what was initially intended to be a two-year initiative. The package contained an introductory memo, a four-page description of Head Start, job descriptions for the leading expert roles to be hired in each country (country director and master teacher trainer), two research articles analyzing the economic benefits of early education (Barnett 1985; Barnett and Escobar 1987), and a three-page questionnaire requesting information about early education in the country.

> *George made absolutely sure that it was up to the foundations if they wanted to participate. He definitely checked up on us but in a very casual way. If the foundations had not been happy with us, they would have told him for sure because they had the final say, not us, so we had to be pretty good.*
>
> (Liz Lorant, former director, Children & Youth Program, OSF)

Following a local assessment by experts, staff, and boards, national foundations in fifteen countries signed up to participate in the first year. Over the ensuing two decades that number grew to thirty.

The Experiences of the National Foundations

National contexts across the participating countries were diverse and evolving. Many did not have enabling environments to implement a democratically informed early education reform initiative. War was still raging through former Yugoslavia and in the early years of the program authoritarian regimes came to power in Slovakia, Croatia, and Serbia and took hold in some countries in the former Soviet Union.

> *These were post-communist governments that were emerging. In some countries, the people who had been dissidents became the leaders in the government … There were other places in which right-wing forces came to the fore in Eastern Europe. The foundation tended to have friendly relations with the governments that were emerging in some countries and rather contentious or hostile relationships*

with the governments that were emerging in other countries ... I saw the early childhood program as something that would be relatively acceptable to the different governments in the region. This was something that they tended to regard as a benefit that was becoming available to the country, even if the government, as a whole, was somewhat antagonistic to the foundation.

(Aryeh Neier, president emeritus, Open Society Foundations)

Education reform was high on the agenda of the Open Society Foundations in these early years and education-related initiatives made up around a third of the budget (Silova and Steiner-Khamsi 2008). The national foundations—even those based in challenging environments—grasped the potential of the proposed early childhood initiative as an entry point to support the evolution of open societies. Two former directors of national foundations and several former Open Society staff members were interviewed for this book. These conversations reveal insights into the high expectations for early education as a strategic entry point to use to leverage broader social transformation. Slovakia was one of the first countries to join Step by Step. At the time the country was under the authoritarian regime of Vladimír Mečiar.

We were convinced that it was important to work on education. When the Step by Step program came, it was a big chance to work in a different field and to help change attitudes and the situation of education in Slovakia. It was not only about segregation and Roma. It was an overall effort to change the direction of education in Slovakia because here, before, as in many other countries the education system was not directed towards the interests of the child.

(Alena Panikova, former executive director, Open Society Foundation—Bratislava)

The foundation in Tajikistan was established in 1996, following a civil war. Education was a priority in their first comprehensive strategy in 1999:

Restoring education was one of the highest demands of all the people we met ... It was always a very strategic aim in a post-conflict country, as a country which is going through a transition, as a country which is not necessarily very democratic ... you have to have a very good entry point and that entry point is always education, programs related to children. Reform in any one part will trigger reforms in the other parts. Education is usually taken, especially by authoritarian regimes, as not very serious or apolitical ... A government will not be afraid of reform unless it is higher education ... everyone has grandkids and everyone wants to have a better education for them no matter who they are.

(Zuhra Halimova, former executive director (Tajikistan) and advisory board member, OSF)

The Tajik foundation director negotiated a launch of Step by Step at a time when programs in the original countries were already becoming independent of Open Society. She was challenged to find co-funding, a process which revealed the lack of donor interest in early education. Her fundraising quickly refocused on donors interested in democracy building.

> [Soros] said, "if you find another donor, I will give you 25 percent." Basically, between me and George Soros, it was a business deal about Step by Step ... Sarah and I and Liz, we drafted a short document and I started working through all the donors I could. I met with UNICEF, I've met with, I don't know, Save the Children, UNESCO, USAID, I've met the Asian Development Bank, World Bank, you name it. I also started meeting them in their regional offices, not only in Tajikistan. The problem was that early childhood was not a priority for almost all donors ... Even if they do education, early childhood was never a part.
>
> Every donor had to be approached their own way. When you talk about early childhood and Step by Step, you had to learn what it is they want to hear from you. We had several roundtables [with donors]. We immediately made the point that education starts from early childhood, not secondary school.
>
> Our first proposal was to the US State Department Democracy Fund. We named our proposal Learning Democracy from Childhood, considering that Step by Step was about bringing up resilient citizens from childhood. This was our first message. That was the first proposal, which immediately got through. It was around $200,000 for two years.
>
> (Zuhra Halimova, former executive director (Tajikistan) and advisory board member, OSF)

Fostering Allies and Hiring a Program Team

Once the decision was made to launch Step by Step, the national foundations had the critically important task of gaining local support and hiring a professional team to lead the program.

> I immediately contacted the Soros Foundation offices in the region and told them that there was only one condition attached to receiving full funding for the project—they had to find the very best early childhood professionals in their country who also understood Open Society's philosophy underscoring this approach to early childhood development. They managed to find and send us truly unique, creative individuals with endless energy who became the pioneer Step by Step teams. From the very first day they instinctively and deeply understood the very direct

relationship between Step by Step and the building of open societies—to them it was always very clear and very simple—always.

(Speech at tenth anniversary Liz Lorant, former director,
Children & Youth Program, OSF)

Implementing Step by Step required more than early childhood expertise. Candidates had to be committed change agents with the ability to work at all levels of the early education system: family, classroom, preschool, pedagogic institutions, local and national government. In Slovakia, the national foundation hired Eva Končoková, who was *"able among the enemies to find allies."* The former director of the Open Society Foundation—Bratislava explained:

> We had the contacts with some enlightened people at the ministry who really wanted to change the situation. They cooperated with the foundation from the very beginning and helped us in the official way to work with Step by Step like a pilot, which can be used in future as an official system. I would stress the personalities of people who were involved in the program from the very beginning because they came from the teachers' community. They were methodologically strong and also had special, I would say, diplomatic talent to be able to involve people. There were individuals who really were interested in the serious changes in the Slovak educational system. In spite of the general situation, you could find the individuals who were open to cooperation and very helpful. Also in the Institute of Pedagogy, we had some allies there, many methodologies, but many teachers who are interested in changes in the educational system.
>
> She [Eva] stubbornly worked on the development of the program in Slovakia. I would say that [working with parents] was her talent and it's probably the approach of the program itself because it involves parents. If you have parents, then those parents can influence representatives from political circles. Eva really used the involvement of parents to push the local government representatives to donate to the kindergartens and to preserve them because the program brought also money. For the first time in history it brought people inside the kindergartens. They could see how it worked with the children and there were many aspects which persuaded parents to cooperate and to push. Also, the teachers were eager to learn how to work differently with the children.

(Alena Panikova, former executive director,
Open Society Foundation—Bratislava)

The National Foundations cultivated shared ownership of the initiative in the country in order to get the program on track and off to a good start:

It's a matter of how you actually talk to people, decision makers, everyone, how you find co-thinkers. How you actually involve them in the conversation even if they are opponents, to really talk things through so that at the end of the day, they say, "Oh, yes, we think the same and this is our idea." It is about how you actually create ownership.

In the end, as soon as you reach this point, things become easier. I wouldn't say absolutely easy, but easier and smoother because you actually put down the rail and now you're putting your train on the rail and what you need is a little push. The little push is actually quite a big push but this little push is actually a combination of funding, expertise and other factors, which will make this train move slowly in the beginning and then faster and faster and faster.

(Zuhra Halimova, former executive director (Tajikistan) and advisory board member, OSF)

Chapter 3 serves as a reference for the rest of the book, describing the rollout of Step by Step and Open Society's Early Childhood Program—"the train journey" that Halimova describes—between 1994 and 2020. The next section returns to the importance of timing in reform processes.

"It Was Just a Magic Time"

An unique set of factors came together around the design and launch of the Step by Step program. Two serendipitous encounters—of George Soros with Fraser Mustard, and Liz Lorant with Phyllis Magrab—catalyzed its creation, and inspired an approach modeled on Head Start. Aryeh Neier, then president of Open Society Foundations, noted in his interview: "I think the $100 million was his single largest commitment. Proportionate to the purchasing power of the dollar, far larger than it sounds today."

I think it was just a magic time, really, and there were very good people from very good foundations. Just the fact that we were there when the Berlin wall fell and provided incredible opportunities and George was ready to give the money. It is just a wonderful thing that we already had our feet on the ground, and everybody came to us and we were able to send them to the local foundation. It wasn't just Step by Step. We were the only game in town when the Berlin wall fell ... We were the first stop to get to the next place because the foundation was so strong and so respected across the region.

(Liz Lorant, former director, Children & Youth Program, OSF)

The Open Society network between and among the national foundations and New York provided a sense of excitement and whole-organization commitment based on mutual respect:

> *In those days, really, you could rely on the people there and the system there [at the Open Society Foundations]. It was like a plate with many delicate foods. It was always offered every year, and almost every month, there was a new approach to changing something. We were really lucky to have this opportunity ... There were several programs in those days which were led by people . . who really started working for Open Society because they wanted to change the world. It was a unique opportunity where the money, knowledge and devotion to make change simply came together. It was a unique chance to create something good ...*
>
> (Alena Panikova, former executive director,
> Open Society Foundation—Bratislava)

> *Because of the availability of funding and the expertise of the Step by Step network, because of this whole combination—it's like the opportunity of a lifetime. You have everything at one time.*
>
> (Zuhra Halimova, former executive director (Tajikistan)
> and advisory board member, OSF)

The crisis in the region created momentum for change. Looking back, the deputy director of the Early Childhood Program and board chair commented:

> *If there was a driver within Open Society, there were also drivers in broader society as well.*
>
> (Tina Hyder, former deputy director, Early Childhood Program, OSF)

> *It was a very chaotic time in the countries, and that made it challenging because there wasn't a lot of bureaucratic clarity about what was happening. On the other hand, it was a time of change and everyone was looking towards transformation—not everyone, but most people in the countries were hopeful that this transformation would create a better life for them and their families.*
>
> *If you tried to do this ten years earlier or five years earlier, there would not have been receptivity for change. You couldn't have created change, because a curtain would have dropped down in front of it. At this moment in time there was great receptivity, and a lot of hopefulness. I think that really helped us a lot; there was a lot of energy.*
>
> (Phyllis Magrab, Georgetown University, former board chair,
> Early Childhood Program Advisory Board, OSF)

In later years, Open Society scaled back funding and shifted away from multi-country demonstration programs, like Step by Step, to focus on mega-education projects in a handful of countries and on advocacy for policy change. The Step by Step programs that had operated initially out of the national foundations were "spun off" with some support and the majority became independent non-governmental organizations, challenged with both expanding and sustaining the Step by Step program.[1] Together, the new national NGOs established a network, the International Step by Step Association (ISSA), in the Netherlands. Significant programmatic funding to the national Step by Step NGOs was scaled down as Open Society's global footprint expanded. The Early Childhood Program expanded internationally to Latin America, Asia, Africa, and the Middle East. These initiatives drew in part on the capacity developed through Step by Step, but also hired in new expertise and created new resources. The Early Childhood Program established new focused programs addressing Roma, children with disabilities, and migrants and refugees and provided core support and capacity development to new regional networks in Asia-Pacific, Africa, and the Middle East. Ultimately, the Early Childhood Program closed at the end of 2020 as Open Society entered a multi-year strategic and structural transformation. Key partner organizations were provided with tie-off grants and a library of resources is now available on ISSA's website (https://www.issa.nl/Step_by_Step_Program). The final Early Childhood Program grant was made to establish the Early Childhood Regional Networks Fund, a collaborative donor fund to help secure for the early childhood field the sustainability of these vital professional networks. This book provides the reader with participant insights into their impact.

Part Two

Inventing a Democratic Pedagogy

3

"Who Says We Can't Change the World?": Implementing the Step by Step Program

Figure 3.1 Children participate in a music class for families and young children in Kragujevac, Serbia, on September 19, 2018.
© Sanja Knezevic for the Open Society Foundations

Introduction

In 1993, the Open Society Foundations took the bold decision to invest $100 million in democratic reform of the early childhood education (ECE) systems in Eastern Europe and Eurasia. What was initially envisioned as a two-year initiative ultimately extended over two decades. This chapter traces the progression of the core program: reform of preschool and early primary education. The first sections focus on the launch of Step by Step in preschool and primary school and its expansion and replication across the region and within countries. Next, it introduces the complementary initiatives and partnership projects that extended the reach of the original program. Finally, it discusses the scale of the initiative and its impact, including the program's commitment to promoting quality, access, and equity. Subsequent chapters will explore the extent to which key components of Step by Step became embedded in early education systems, as well as the critical role and prospects for sustainability of the civil society organizations and networks it created.

First Steps: Launching the Step by Step Program in Preschools

Preparing the Methodology and Training Country Teams in the United States

With the partnership of Open Society Foundations and Georgetown University established in the fall of 1993, and the first cohort of fifteen countries signed on, Georgetown experts began to draft a methodology and an accompanying training package. Drafting a new manual—as opposed to purchasing rights to an existing curriculum—ensured countries would have flexibility to adapt the resource to local needs and cultures without encountering copyright issues. The manual drew inspiration from the comprehensive approach, standards, and parent engagement found in the Head Start Program. Its learning perspectives were grounded in theories of social constructivism (Vygotsky), developmentally appropriate practice (Piaget, Erikson), and progressive education (John Dewey) (International Step by Step Association 2019).[1]

> *It happened so fast. We were really excited, and we were really scared because it was an awesome responsibility. We had developed lots of training materials, and we had done lots of training, and we were steeped in our beliefs about what was important around early childhood education, but how could we put this together? We didn't know these countries. Writing the curriculum was the easiest part of it all.*
> *(Roxane Kaufmann, US Step by Step expert team)*

On the other side of the ocean, fifteen national foundations—all affiliated partners of Open Society—were busy assessing early childhood education systems, meeting with ministry officials, and recruiting two leading early childhood experts, a country director, and master teacher trainer to staff the program. These two national experts (thirty in total) subsequently flew to the United States in February/March 1994 for six weeks of training, program visits, and strategic planning. Each country team was paired with two American experts, who would regularly visit their country and provide training and mentoring over the next two years, starting with introductory training in summer 1994, for educators, local government, and academic partners involved in launching the program.

For both trainers and participants, the visit of country teams to the United States in early 1994 was a watershed event. Formal and informal activities fostered strong bonds across the group and created the trust and relationships the country teams needed to be able to lead reform initiatives in their countries.

> *We met everybody at the airport individually, so they would feel welcome. This was absolutely the best experience of my life. Everybody came to my house for dinner. By the end of the evening, they were all sitting on the floor in our downstairs family room with a fire. They were singing. It was a wonderful bonding experience. The energy that this all created, was incredibly contagious, and I think we all felt it, such an opportunity.*
>
> (Roxane Kaufmann, US Step by Step expert team)

During the meetings, the module that would be used in the summer trainings in each country was piloted. US trainers intentionally modeled democratic principles, while building on the strengths of the early childhood education systems in the region.

> *[In the training] they were experiencing what we wanted the kids to experience. They got to vote on things. They got to prioritize things. They had to negotiate certain things. They had to collaborate to build something together. We used a lot of techniques and training that we wanted the kids to be able to use. All of these voices are listened to, and then you come to some consensus. We did that through lots of interaction and small groups, and then coming together to share your opinion with your colleagues and learn from each other. Everything in that regard was purposeful in terms of the way we set things up.*
>
> (Roxane Kaufmann, US Step by Step expert team)

> *We wanted to add democratic philosophies, we wanted to add problem-solving, and we knew [education] was somewhat didactic there. We wanted to have it more child-centered, the things that we believed in. The democratic principles, working together, active learning, child-focused learning, child decisions.*
>
> (Kirsten Hansen, US Step by Step expert team)

They [European colleagues] knew educational theory and they were very well educated in the academic realm. The difference was, "Okay, so what does that really look like? What's it sound like in a classroom? How do you put legs on that and make that real and concrete?"

(Kate Burke Walsh, US Step by Step expert team)

European experts interviewed for this book reflected on the impact of that first training:

We learned so much in the trainings because they were somehow participant-centered. So they tried to motivate us to share what we already know, to share our ideas, to participate in creating common understanding. There were a lot of different strategies in those trainings, definitely. How they treated us, we try to treat our teachers in our schools. It is a kind of modelling democracy at the training. You try to model this to teachers, and teachers then try to model this kind of work with the children.

(Tatjana Vonta, co-author and former director, Step by Step Slovenia)

Those trainings were so eye-opening because both the trainers and the practices that we saw were quite different from what we had in the country. They showed us what is meant by child-centeredness.

(Cornelia Cincilei, Step by Step Moldova)

At this initial and at subsequent trainings over the next twenty years, the translators' roles turned out to be vital, too:

The role of the interpreter at such meetings is as a cultural facilitator. Just seeing is absolutely not enough. What you come and see needs contextualizing. During all these dinners, during coffee breaks the participants would sit together discussing what they saw, and there you, as interpreter or you as a person who understands, could intervene and really guide people a little bit to see it in a different way or to interpret it in a different way.

(Sergei, interpreter and translator)

Following the two-week induction and training in Washington DC, participants were sent to cities in the United States to observe child-centered, inclusive practices and parent involvement in preschools. Everyone returned to Washington DC for the final week to develop country plans before returning home.

Back in their countries, the country director and master teacher trainer, who had received training in the United States, were employed full-time as staff of Open Society's national foundations, which provided administrative and logistical support.

> We had support from the central office of the Soros Foundation in Kyiv. We didn't think about accountancy, organizational issues like booking tickets because their department took care of these things.
>
> (Natalia Sofiy, Borys Grinchenko Kyiv University, Ukraine)

The "to do" list for country teams between the return from the United States in March and the launch of the program in September was phenomenal. It included setting up a program office; securing agreements with education authorities; raising awareness and building allies at national and local levels; selecting, renovating, and equipping pilot preschools; introducing the program to preschool staff and parents; recruiting and enrolling children; hiring additional staff (family coordinators and assistants) at each site; adapting, translating, and preparing the manual and training package for the local context; and organizing a summer training for around fifty participants to be conducted with the support of the US trainers.

Designed initially as a two-year program, each country signed formal agreements with the appropriate ministry, usually the Ministry of Education, and presented the program to academic and training institutions and local governments to raise awareness and gain support. The national foundations helped create these links.

> The director of our Soros Foundation had already established the connections with the ministry of education because he knew that it was important. He helped us to build those relationships, and we had to establish relationships with the city, with the local educational authorities, with our Ukrainian Academy of Pedagogical Sciences because we understood that in order to go into state kindergartens you have to have good relationships with the state agencies.
>
> (Natalia Sofiy, Borys Grinchenko Kyiv University, Ukraine)

The program was to be launched exclusively in state kindergartens (not private services) with the aim of reaching children and families from excluded and vulnerable groups. Countries used different approaches to strategically select up to ten pilot sites in the first year, and to ensure the most vulnerable children were included. In Romania, competition was fierce, while in Azerbaijan, which launched the program several years later in 1998, it was difficult to recruit kindergartens willing to take the risk of working with an American program:

> It took three months to arrange the partnership agreement with the ministry of education. We opened the application process to all forty-two county inspectorates, announcing that we would only start in nine counties. There was huge interest in Step by Step. I remember chief inspectors coming to our office and telling us that they would sleep in front of our office door just to make sure that they will be part of the program. After an extensive selection process we identified the nine counties, ensuring national coverage of the program. Those families registered with social services and who had children of the correct age were eligible to be part of the program. We had poor children, Roma children, and children with special needs also.
>
> (Carmen Lica, Centrul Step by Step Romania)

> The plan for the first year of program implementation was ten kindergartens. We could not find ten; the majority of kindergartens refused to participate in the Step by Step program. We started with nine. Probably they were afraid because someone from an American Foundation would be coming and doing some reform. We never focused on the capital, Baku. We were trying to have this regional outreach. The regional population's socioeconomic status was lower than in the capital. I'm very proud about this, we specifically were trying to provide access to all ethnic minorities living in Azerbaijan, even those in small villages: Georgians, Jews, Lezgins. Another focus coming from New York was to focus on disadvantaged populations.
>
> (Ulviyya Mikayilova, ADA University, Azerbaijan)

The idea of selecting kindergartens ready to change and serve as model sites factored into these decisions:

> When we were speaking about the kindergartens to be chosen for the program, [the authorities] said, "Take very poor kindergartens because these would benefit mostly from the program." For us, the strategy was different. We were saying that we need open-minded teachers, the teachers who would understand the essence of this change because they need to become the pioneers. The idea was to establish models of new practices that would be attractive for the others, be persuasive. If you just pick teachers who are reluctant to change, nothing would happen.
>
> (Cornelia Cincilei, Step by Step Moldova)

Most countries combined strategies and selected a few kindergartens convenient to larger cities and pedagogic institutions, and others located in villages, targeting areas with high minority populations. The selected kindergartens needed material support.

For the first three months before we travelled to the US, we visited the kindergartens in Macedonia to see what kind of condition they were in. We made one simple questionnaire. We visited about thirty kindergartens. [They were] nothing like child-centered classrooms. Some classrooms only had tables and children had very little to do.

(Suzana Kirandžiska, Foundation for Educational and Cultural Initiatives, Step by Step, North Macedonia)

We went and saw places that had no electricity usually outside of the big cities. They had no money either, the toilets weren't working. It was freezing. It was amazing because the Soros Foundation said fine, we'll fix it. There was that structural piece, they had to rebuild these classrooms to make them habitable.

(Roxane Kaufmann, US Step by Step expert team)

Step by Step supported renovation of the buildings and purchase of child-centered furniture and materials for the pilot classrooms. Initially, two classrooms at each site would introduce Step by Step.[2] Working with a few classrooms in each kindergarten ensured that teachers in the pilot classrooms had colleagues to work with in the same building, and it enabled those parents wary of the pilot program to keep their children in traditional classrooms.

However, the decision to start with two classrooms in each preschool backfired in some cases.

There were quite substantial differences in the physical equipment that was available. I felt something of a sense of resentment from the people who were not in the early childhood program while others in the school were getting this additional help, which was not available to them. I remember thinking that was a problem in that period.

(Ayreh Neier, president emeritus, Open Society Foundations)

I'm thinking about the beginning. Parents whose children were in other groups, in poorly equipped classrooms really reacted. It was so big a difference. The [Step by Step] teachers were not accepted by their colleagues, because of their different approach and the environment. They had better classes and more equipment and everything.

(Nives Milinović, former director, Open Academy Step by Step, Croatia, and former board president, ISSA)

Each kindergarten was required to organize one room for parents and to welcome and encourage parent involvement and parent associations. A parent coordinator was hired at each site to link with families and coordinate activities, and additional assistants were provided to bring down child/staff ratios in classrooms. Program teams could also plan into site budget funds to support excursions, parent involvement, and children's health, such as dentist visits, antibiotics, eyeglasses, vitamins, and nutritious snacks. Prioritizing the engagement of parents drew on the best of Head Start.

> *Head Start has a lot of problems, but one of its great strengths is family involvement and engagement. We think family engagement and involvement is something that makes a huge difference because it translates to the child's important life, the one that continues, which is within their family.*
> *(Roxane Kaufmann, US Step by Step team expert)*

Once the classrooms opened in September, the country director and master teacher trainer provided intensive onsite mentoring and support, spending at least one day per month at each site during the first year of the program. In large countries like Ukraine, this meant flying to some sites. National foundations provided the team with transportation, in many cases a designated car.

> *I remember maybe first two or three years of my life, my life was in the roads, in the car, and eating in canteens in the roads. That was my life for two or three years because we visited almost all the kindergartens in country.*
> *(Ulviyya Mikayilova, ADA University, Azerbaijan)*

> *We even had to organize the logistics to buy materials, to furnish classrooms, to support teachers, and arrange the materials inside. Then to do training, to visit the kindergartens and monitor the teachers. For a few years, it was really a huge job that we did to establish the program. Every day, we went from one place to another place visiting one kindergarten, another day another kindergarten.*
> *(Suzana Kirandžiska, Foundation for Educational and Cultural Initiatives, Step by Step, North Macedonia)*

The intense mentoring proved to be essential, and ongoing professional development became a hallmark of Step by Step as it expanded.

> *One training was still not enough for [teachers] to change completely and understand totally how to translate the principles into practice. Gradually, they really succeeded, and they got, as I said, parents to go along with them in this.*
> *(Cornelia Cincilei, Step by Step Moldova)*

> Those kindergartens which we had more opportunities to visit, I think they were more successful. They were more successful because they had more support and they had this external observation, and more opportunities to ask questions and to share their experience.
> (Natalia Sofiy, Borys Grinchenko Kyiv University, Ukraine)

American trainers and Open Society staff who visited programs in fall 1994 were astounded by the changes.

> So much was implemented, and so many changes had been made. It was just the most rewarding and shocking, actually, a thing to see.
> (Roxane Kaufmann, US Step by Step team expert)

> I started worrying about what's going to happen when we go back to check on this. When I went back to check I saw, universally, that the Eastern Europeans got it, and they were doing their best to make it come to life. There was a huge interest in the program, and everybody wanted it.
> (Liz Lorant, former director, Children & Youth Program, OSF)

The First All-Program Meeting

In December 1994 the core team (country director and master teacher trainer) from the first cohort of countries and staff from Georgetown University and Open Society reconvened in Budapest to reflect and plan. The new methods had been piloted now in kindergartens for nearly four months. Teams discussed successes, problems, and creative ideas in roundtables, shared classroom videos, toys, and materials, and planned next steps. Additional training was provided on areas identified for development. Plans got underway to develop a companion guide to the original methodology to deepen understanding of democratic practices in areas such as children's agency and choice, initiative, individualization, managing challenging behaviors, cultural competence, and communication with children and parents.

Such annual program meetings were a crucial part of the initiative. They offered opportunities to share what was working and—even more importantly—what was not working, to create a shared vision of the future and for each country to meet and plan with the US technical assistance and Open Society teams.

I appreciate the huge support from Open Society bringing knowledge, people, and also continued training, tutoring and international cooperation. For us, it was equally important that we were in touch with other countries in our environment, including neighbouring countries with which we could compare our work and cooperate.

(Alena Panikova, former executive director,
Open Society Foundation—Bratislava)

Step by Step adapted quickly to address what was happening on the ground. This responsiveness and flexibility were motivating—opportunities and problems could be aired—and addressing them generated new trainings, manuals, and initiatives.

The December 1994 meeting was no exception. Multiple countries came with urgent requests to rapidly expand the program to more classrooms. Parents, even those in countries where the idea of implementing an American program initially raised concerns, started pushing for the program to expand within the pilot kindergartens as well as to new kindergartens.

Parents were the main group vouching for Step by Step, because they immediately called Step by Step an American program. Those kindergartens which were implementing Step by Step, they immediately became the most popular in the location. Many parents wanted to place their children in Step by Step kindergartens.

(Ulviyya Mikayilova, ADA University, Azerbaijan)

The program started planning for a massive replication in new classrooms.

Planning the First Expansion to More Preschool Classrooms

Extending Step by Step to the remaining classrooms in the pilot sites was prioritized in order to address the stark differences noted earlier between pilot and traditional classrooms in the original pilot preschools. Additional kindergartens also signed up to start Step by Step in fall 1995. A second cohort of countries, Kazakhstan and Slovenia, launched pilot classrooms in September of that year. The 252 original pilot preschool classrooms in 120 kindergartens in the first academic year (1994/5) quickly mushroomed to 980 classrooms in 298 kindergartens in the second (1995/6). Open Society had provided the first round of classrooms with salaries for additional teaching assistants and a family coordinator for two years, renovation, building maintenance, furniture, educational materials, medical/dental and nutrition supplements, parent involvement activities, and ongoing training and mentoring for staff. Expansion classrooms received less financial support. Parents and local governments organized furniture to support child-centered learning at activity centers, and secured salary support for additional staff up front from local sources or by leveraging parent volunteers. Open Society rewarded this community mobilization with funds for modest renovations, educational materials, support for parent involvement activities, and ongoing training and mentoring. The average cost per classroom fell from \$33,600 (pilot classroom)[3] to \$3,300 (expansion classroom).

The first program countries each started with between ten and twenty program classrooms. Expansion plans, which were drawn up by each country team in collaboration with national stakeholders, Open Society and Georgetown, varied enormously with most countries at least doubling the number of classrooms. The team in Serbia, which faced political opposition from President Milošević's government, halted plans for expansion in state preschools and instead established kindergartens in Roma settlements, while Romania used the political and social capital they had fostered with parents and the ministry of education (local and national) to establish an application process and secure memorandums of understanding with successful expansion preschools and local education authorities.

> We had annual meetings with all the school principals and school inspectors, and they participated in the trainings and were very familiar with Step by Step. The parents were very pleased with what was happening in Step by Step classrooms and pressured the county school inspectorate to expand them.
>
> *(Carmen Lica, Centrul Step by Step Romania)*

The National Foundation in Macedonia funded a massive expansion of Step by Step, multiplying the reach of the program by a factor of ten.

> The [second] year in Macedonia, the Macedonia National Foundation decided that they would like to spread the program in all kindergartens in Macedonia. The national foundation was willing to give \$1 million from their national budget. We expanded the Step by Step Program, adding an additional 200 classrooms in all kindergartens in Macedonia.
>
> *(Suzana Kirandžiska, Foundation for Educational and Cultural Initiatives, Step by Step, North Macedonia)*

Countries could be opportunistic where there were opportunities to partner and grow the program rapidly. Where there were political or capacity challenges, they could adopt an expansion strategy that made sense in constrained contexts.

Assessing the Impact of the Preschool Program

Plans for a longitudinal evaluation were abandoned during the first year because of time constraints. Perhaps because the program was envisioned as a two-year initiative, a two-year study did not appear to be as critical as it does now, twenty years later.

At the end of the second year of Step by Step (1996), the Open Society's national foundations each appointed an independent national expert to visit and observe preschool sites and to conduct interviews with the ministry, Step by Step staff, teachers, and parents. This internal review drew conclusions from the thirteen completed national reports:

> All thirteen Step by Step evaluations indicated that the program met their goals and was received positively by program staff, administrators at all sites. Children were observed to be actively engaged in this new learning environment and parents took on unprecedented active roles in their child's education. This new educational model was seen to provide a framework for necessary educational and social reform that was initiated by recent political changes in the region. The major challenge to sustainability of the program was the lack of financial resources to continue, expand and replicate Step by Step.
>
> (Open Society Foundations 1996, 8)

In 1998, the US Agency for International Development funded an impact study of Step by Step preschools in Bulgaria, Kyrgyzstan, Romania, and Ukraine. The quasi-experimental study, conducted over the course of an academic year, compared developmental outcomes of children in Step by Step and traditional preschool classrooms and collected qualitative information from parents and teachers and classrooms. Children in Step by Step classrooms performed as well or better than children in traditional classrooms on tests assessing literacy, creativity, and especially in mathematics. Importantly, the results consistently showed that Step by Step provides greater support than traditional programs to children who enter with less developed academic skills, likely because teachers were individualizing teaching and learning to children's developmental levels. USAID, like Open Society, was interested in the extent to which Step by Step changed behaviors in classrooms to promote more democratic environments and to support children in learning the skills needed in a democracy. Here the differences between Step by Step and traditional classrooms were profound. Step by Step was found to encourage children's initiative, questioning, experimentation, expression, and problem-solving skills. Step by Step children, in contrast to children in traditional classrooms, were observed making choices, taking responsibility, and setting rules (Brady et al. 1999).

Step Two: Expanding to Primary Schools and Infant/Toddler Classrooms

The expansion was not only horizontal. From the start, Step by Step provided transition training to primary schools that would enrol Step by Step children. This proved necessary to introduce teachers in receiving primary schools to the kinds of teaching and learning Step by Step children were used to.

> *Teachers from elementary schools would say, "The Step by Step kids are the worst because they walk around all the time, they ask questions all the time, they want to take everything on their own," and so on.*
> *(Hašima Ćurak, advisor to the Ministry of Education and Science, Bosnia and Herzegovina)*

> *Teachers said that children from Step by Step were very different emotionally and much more ready to learn. They were not afraid to communicate with new classmates or tell the teacher if they had a problem.*
> *(Zuhra Halimova, former executive director (Tajikistan) and advisory board member, OSF)*

The national evaluator hired in Macedonia at the end of the second year of the program offered a similar assessment: "There's a real chance that these children would not be able to cope with the regime that dominates in the first grade ... not the learning problems, but the traditional relations in the primary schools" (Open Society Foundations 1996, 5).

Parents with children in the oldest preschool groups advocated for the program to continue in nearby primary schools to provide continuity for children learning in exciting, new democratically oriented environments.

> *The parents were the ones who advocated for the extension of the program, beyond preschool, ensuring the transition to primary school. They were the advocates of the success of the program and its lasting effect.*
> *(Cornelia Cincilei, Step by Step Moldova)*

The primary school initiative unfolded at a scale similar to that of the initial program for preschools. Kate Burke Walsh, an experienced teacher and principal, was hired to lead the initiative. Because children start first grade at different ages in different countries, Step by Step manuals and training were developed for teachers working with children aged between six and seven years, and eight and ten years of age. In January 1996, Belarus and Romania piloted the new approach in a few primary classrooms, and the first primary school manual and training were rolled out to all interested countries in September 1996. Each participating national foundation selected a master teacher trainer to lead work in primary schools, and the new trainers visited the United States in 1996 for several weeks of training, site visits, and planning. Implementing the program in primary schools introduced a new level of complexity and constraints.

> *I think one of the most significant differences is that we were working with countries and systems that had a national curriculum. We did not have that in this country [USA]. How much freedom and flexibility classroom teachers had in those countries was a big question for us and it varied country to country, and even within countries. It was much more restricted as we got into the schools.*
>
> (Kate Burke Walsh, US Step by Step expert team)

In 1996, fourteen countries launched programs in 211 first-grade classrooms in primary schools near the original preschool sites, and this number grew annually as additional countries, primary schools, and classrooms joined. Annual trainings from visiting US trainers were provided for the first four years of the primary school program in each country.

The infant and toddler program was planned in 1996 and launched in 1997, with a new manual and trainings. It was equally popular with country teams, as many kindergartens included infant and toddler classrooms. Caregivers of infants and toddlers had not been included in the initial training programs, which were designed for staff working with children between three and five years of age.

At the annual program meeting in 1996, program teams adopted the slogan, "Who says we can't change the world!" and voted to use the name "Step by Step."

Step Three: Replication through Institutions of Higher Education and Model Sites

The initial two-year strategy of the Step by Step program had envisioned linking program kindergartens with universities and pedagogic institutes to enable in-country replication. Starting with the earliest trainings in summer 1994, experts from institutions of higher education were invited to participate in Step by Step trainings.

By the second year of the program it was clear that targeted training and support would be required to make meaningful changes in pre- and in-service training programs. The national evaluator hired in Hungary in the second year of the program summarized the challenge:

> The methodologies currently taught in the teacher training institutes or employed at schools are mostly teacher-centered. What is taught is what and how the teacher should teach to the average child, and not what he/she should do so the child might engage in activities which are developmentally appropriate and are in harmony with the child's needs, personality and background.
>
> (Open Society Foundations 1996)

A "Higher Education Initiative" was developed and launched in 1996 to institutionalize Step by Step in teacher training systems, building on the relationships that had been forming with pedagogic institutions and universities. The initiative would support institutions of higher education to develop linkages with Step by Step teachers and classrooms and involve them in research and student practicum, to add additional courses and content to existing teacher training curricula, and to alter the methodologies used to train teachers.

Faculty from across the region were invited to a three-week seminar in Lake Balaton in Hungary in summer 1996. This first seminar focused as much on how to teach as it did on what to teach. On the "how to" side, sessions focused on creating an environment for change, effective course design, best practices in early education, and adult learning concepts and their practical application in teacher training. A full-developed, semester-length course on *Individualization* was presented, along with course outlines on *Learning through Play* and *Family/Community Participation*. New courses for three or four faculty from each country were introduced each subsequent summer at follow-up seminars. These were replicated for larger groups of between ten and fifteen faculty members from each country at sub-regional seminars organized for clusters of countries. Over the course of the Step by Step program, the Higher Education Initiative developed and disseminated eight semester-length courses and a practicum guide to nearly 2,000 faculty from almost 500 institutions, potentially reaching tens of thousands of aspiring educators. These courses were later adapted and revised for use in postgraduate programs in Russia, Bangladesh, and Myanmar (see Chapter 8).

The training of new teachers via reform of higher education could not keep up with the demand for Step by Step. In the first place, in many countries few newly trained teachers were securing teaching positions, particularly in the

1990s, given falling birth rates and the closure of many kindergartens (UNICEF 2001). Secondly, making changes at universities and pedagogic institutes is slow.

> The Step by Step program developed several university courses for all of the countries and the training was really good, but it was just with one or two people from universities in each country. You cannot change universities with such a small investment.
>
> (Suzana Kirandžiska, Foundation for Educational and Cultural Initiatives, Step by Step, North Macedonia)

The results of the Step by Step higher education initiative were mixed and they are discussed in Chapter 9, which explores systemic change.

The most promising route to scaling up the program to meet immediate demand turned out to be by transforming the best preschools into model training sites and cultivating networks of highly skilled trainers and mentors in each country. This eliminated the need for travel to the United States to see excellent practice, as well as the need for US trainers to travel to the region to conduct trainings. Instead, capacity was built locally. Country teams selected model centers and Open Society provided funding for training equipment and materials and in some cases for a part- or full-time training coordinator.

> When we had those large numbers, big numbers of trainings across the country, we were relying on the resource centers. These are the kindergartens that were [in the program] from the very beginning, and that benefited from material support from Open Society. They were meant to become model centers and we relied on them for trainings in the region.
>
> (Cornelia Cincilei, Step by Step Moldova)

> We set up model sites that people could visit, and I think this was the best thing we did there. Step by Step trainees said they now understood what to do and how to do it.
>
> (Eteri Gvineria, Center for Educational Initiatives, Step by Step Georgia)

To build capacity in adult learning, Step by Step rolled out beginning and advanced training for trainers, as well as training on mentoring.

> Introducing training of trainers put another layer on the program by making it possible for people to train more teachers locally, not just in the capitals, once a year, or twice a year, when the American trainers visited. Developing local trainers was a huge step and it was requested by the country teams. We hired the American

team to do training of trainers. That's when [Step by Step] really made it into the small cities and the villages and so on.
> (Liz Lorant, former director, Children & Youth Program, OSF)

I mentioned capacity building, and human capacity among other things, and the training of educators. From the inside, they built the core groups. In 1999 there was a training for coaches. Among the groups of professionals, they found people who had a certain way of taking over and spreading the idea of Step by Step.
> (Hašima Ćurak, advisor, Ministry of Education and Science, Bosnia and Herzegovina)

Strategies for expansion were unique to each country. Step by Step teams could leverage all the ingredients needed to support scale-up of the program in preschools and primary schools. Collectively, these assets included networks of highly skilled trainers and mentors, model preschools and primary schools, and extensive intellectual resources in the form of training modules and teacher manuals adapted to the national context. Where required, ministry approval either of the methodology or trainings for preschool, primary or both, was secured in some form in all countries that launched the program, and a group of higher education faculty were knowledgeable about the program and its philosophy. Countries were supported by their peers in the network that was forming across the region and with the US technical assistance teams. New trainings and manuals were introduced each year and adapted by national experts to respond to cultural differences and curricular requirements.

> Every year, we had training sessions and part of the content was predefined by our team based on what we saw during our visits in the classrooms, as well as requests from teachers and preschool principals.
> (Carmen Lica, Centrul Step by Step Romania)

Now we have a core team of trainers, mentors, who are also developers of materials, developers of modules, and a more extended team of trainers, like a pool of trainers. They're still practitioners and this is an added value that they bring as trainers and mentors, because they have credibility. It's not just do like I do, but, "Yes, I also have similar challenges and let's see how this may be solved." The fact that they are reflective practitioners is the key thing. The system needs to maintain the system of mentoring, and also opportunities for these mentors to continuously grow.
> (Cornelia Cincilei, Step by Step Moldova)

These networks of trainers have persisted to the present day.

> *I think Step by Step does have a future because we still have the trainers. Some of them have now retired but the network still exists and we have a few institutions where we can model the program.*
>
> *(Éva Deák, Partners Hungary Foundation)*

Step Four: Expansion through Partnership Initiatives

Just as the program expanded within countries, it also expanded to new ones. The first fifteen countries were joined by Kyrgyzstan and Slovenia in 1995. This was followed in 1996 by Bosnia and Kazakhstan; in 1997, by Haiti, Latvia, and South Africa[4]; in 1998, by Armenia, Azerbaijan, Georgia, and Mongolia; in 1999, by the newly independent Montenegro and Kosovo; in 2003, by Uzbekistan and Tajikistan; and in 2004, a modest program was launched in primary schools in Argentina. Trainers and mentors from the first countries supported introduction in new countries. For example, the Kosovo team was paired with country directors from Albania (Gerda Sula) and Slovenia (Tatjana Vonta), when launching the program in 1999.

> *When Tatjana and Gerda were introduced to us as mentors it was easier for us because they speak our languages, because we could invite them here more often, and because both of them know the context. Tatjana is also familiar with those small kindergarten buildings that we have, how they are built and what they look like inside, while Gerda knows the language.*
>
> *(Hana Zylfiu-Haziri, Kosovo Education Center)*

Strategic partnership projects accelerated scale-up in specific countries. In Russia, where around one third of preschools under communism were operated by factories and agricultural facilities, the World Bank Privatization Project worked with the government to transfer the operations and management of enterprise-run kindergartens over to local governments (Commander, Lee, and Tolstopiatenko 1996). Step by Step expanded to kindergartens in five of the nine cities receiving World Bank funding to mitigate the impact of privatization. In concrete terms, the World Bank funded renovation, furniture, and operating costs (including teacher assistant salaries) of former enterprise preschools joining Step by Step, and the Foundation provided training and ongoing technical assistance to hundreds of classrooms. Twelve training centers were established across the country at model sites.

In Moldova, a multi-year partnership with the World Bank Social Investment Fund transformed preschools and primary schools in rural areas. Launched in 1999, the initiative offered interested, rural communities support to introduce Step by Step to preschools and primary schools. Like the arrangement in Russia, the World Bank invested in renovation and equipping of the preschools and schools, and Open Society provided, via the national foundation, teacher training, ongoing professional development, and monitoring to ensure quality implementation of Step by Step. Communities were required to mobilize 15 percent of the costs, which they fulfilled through in-kind support for renovations, volunteering, and by supporting classroom assistants. The establishment of active Parent Teacher Associations at participating preschools and schools was a hallmark of the program. The initiative, which helped more than 200 village schools across the three years of the program, became a catalyst for democratization.

The expansion of Step by Step in Central Asia was facilitated through a USAID-funded initiative: the Participation in Education and Knowledge Strengthening (PEAKS) program (2003–7), which was implemented by a coalition that included Open Society Foundations, Save the Children, and Abt Associations, and which was led by the Academy of Education Development. The initiative aimed to improve in-service teacher training to support active learning, refine the curriculum, increase parent and community involvement, strengthen government capacity to support innovation, and upgrade school infrastructure. By activating Step by Step's resources and trainers, Open Society Foundations in New York and the national foundations in Central Asia played a leading role in designing and delivering teacher training components; establishing model schools, learning communities and networks; and fostering parent and community involvement. With significant co-funding from USAID, Step by Step was launched in Tajikistan and Uzbekistan and expanded in Kazakhstan and Kyrgyzstan.

Each of these partnership projects, in Russia, Moldova, and Central Asia, facilitated a dramatic expansion of Step by Step.

Building Quality, Equity, and Access

From 1998, Step by Step programs began to "spin-off" from Open Society's national foundations, becoming independent and seeking independent sources of funding, a phenomenon that will be covered in depth in Chapter 7. As a consequence, programs needed to offer a greater variety of training packages to adjust to national teacher professional development systems and donor requirements.

Teacher retraining systems varied greatly by country. For instance, in Slovenia, schools had funds to purchase teacher professional development from a long list of ministry-accredited courses. Typically, these courses were one or two days long. The team in Slovenia divided their foundational Step by Step trainings into shorter trainings, but now needed a system to differentiate between teachers implementing child-centered Step by Step practices at a high level of quality in their classrooms, and those teachers who had completed a one- or two-day course. The ministry in Hungary certified courses of 120 hours (three weeks), and Step by Step succeeded in gaining accreditation for a substantial package of training and mentoring. The Step by Step NGO in Moldova even succeeded in gaining accreditation as a training institution.

> *We tried to develop modules that would be interactive, that would develop teachers' reflective skills and enhance their creativity. We saw our role as an NGO as providing changes to in-service teacher training. We're on the list of training centers at the Ministry of Education. Last year, we even got accredited by the national authority on quality and education.*
>
> *(Cornelia Cincilei, Step by Step Moldova)*

The drive to replicate and scale up Step by Step created concerns that quality would suffer. The Step by Step network turned its attention to this challenge in 1999, and opted to create a new instrument that would be flexible and fit—for purpose. The development of program standards and principles is discussed in Chapter 4, which focuses on the experiences of teachers, parents, and children.

Democratizing early education systems involved prioritizing equity and social inclusion of excluded children and their families, including Roma and minority children. This guided the selection of pilot and expansion classrooms, and inspired initiatives to address biases in teachers, amongst parents, and in society. Roma initiatives sought to expand the Roma early childhood workforce, to advance Roma rights, and to include Roma culture and language in education systems. Step by Step also introduced the inclusion of children with disabilities in mainstream preschool and primary school classrooms. As teachers became comfortable with developmentally appropriate practices and individualization, Step by Step introduced trainings and initiatives to support inclusion of children with very diverse abilities. Chapter 5 elaborates the efforts to break down barriers and push to respect the diversity and inclusion of all children, while Chapter 6 describes the experience of implementing Step by Step in times of war.

A major development in 2002 was the introduction of resources to strengthen parenting, as well as to reach children who do not attend preschool.

> Step's kindergartens were always oversubscribed. Everyone wanted to get into them. [Step by Step] developed a lot of materials to help parents work with children, who may not be able to afford a kindergarten, who don't have access, or if they're in a smaller community where there's no kindergarten. I know they developed a lot of materials to help parents work with children.
> (Hašima Ćurak, advisor, Ministry of Education and Science, Bosnia and Herzegovina)

Comprehensive sets of materials were developed by consultant Cassie Landers and disseminated to the Step by Step network. *Parenting with Confidence* provided parent facilitators with flexible resources to use to design and implement multi-session group programs for parents, addressing a wide range of topics. A set of ten parent pamphlets, training manuals, and facilitator guides rounded out this resource. *Getting Ready for School* (GRS) was created for children who did not have access to preschool, but the resources have also been used widely by preschools to guide work with the parents of children attending them. In addition to a training manual and facilitator guides, GRS also provides activity books containing educational games and stories and ideas on how to adjust activities to each child's developmental level and interests. Open Society funded an evaluation of multi-year pilot initiatives of GRS in Armenia, Bosnia, Kazakhstan, and Tajikistan. Qualitative results indicated positive impacts in parental interest in children's education, in parents' communication with their children, and in children's social-emotional development (American Institutes for Research 2012a, b, c, d).

Step by Step also piloted part-day and community-based programs in some countries. These alternatives to formal full-day preschool education were not always understood.

> In many cases, reopening the kindergartens, or creating some alternative programs was hard to do because people were still relying on their memories of kindergartens, and they were not expecting community centers or something like that. Alternatives were not so easily accepted.
> (Cornelia Cincilei, Step by Step Moldova)

> When [the program brought] senior people from the ministries to London, we took them to see kindergartens and playgroups, some of which worked for a couple of

> hours each day. The people from Central Asia said "It's much worse. They operate shorter programs simply to save money." Me, as somebody who is not teaching them, can finally start making the point that kindergartens do not exist only to take care of children for eight hours a day, but much more important to increase the outreach of early learning programs. That all people, particularly those with lower incomes who do not have access to full-day kindergartens, could be developed and their lives could be changed simply because they have access to early learning programs for two or three hours a day when they are three, or four, or five years old.
>
> (Sergei, interpreter and translator)

Over the course of the intervening years, through the efforts of UNICEF, the World Bank, European Commission, and national governments, many more countries have now implemented a half-day preparatory program, often based in schools, and Step by Step teams in EU member countries are striving to increase the participation of children in early care and education programs in line with European Commission goals. As this book was being written, plans to introduce early childhood education as a statutory part of all education systems are being advanced by a multi-agency coalition led by UNESCO (UNESCO 2022a, b).

Step by Step teams found other innovative ways to reach more children. In Lithuania the program worked with a women's prison to enable prisoners with young children to spend time together in a nearby kindergarten. Step by Step in Macedonia established a children's museum in 1997, in the Youth Cultural Center in Skopje, inspired by the museums the country director visited during her trip to the United States. The Children's Creative Center, which still operates today, is the first of its kind in Macedonia. It advances multi-ethnic tolerance, and promotes the central role of parents and families in children's development, offering exhibits, cultural events, and activities to more than 3,000 young visitors monthly. Low entrance fees and income from catered birthday parties subsidize the participation of families experiencing poverty, Roma and refugee children, and children from rural areas.

Macedonia also published a set of children's books to introduce literature relevant to children's lives.

> We started an initiative for publishing new picture books, because the ones that were available were just fairy tales. We had a competition for local authors and illustrators, and we were pleased to create appropriate books for children that went along with the curriculum.
>
> (Suzana Kirandžiska, Foundation for Educational and Cultural Initiatives, Step by Step, North Macedonia)

This evolved into the Reading Corner Project, initiated jointly by Open Society Foundations and the new regional Step by Step network, the International Step by Step Association. The project fostered emerging writers and illustrators of children's books from across the region, providing training and mentoring from leading published international authors. The most promising stories were illustrated and shared across the region for publication in local languages. Accompanying resources encourage children's engagement with the books in classrooms and at home. The books are constructed so that text in different languages can be easily substituted, and several countries have printed dual or tri-lingual versions, for instance in Serbian, Romany, and English. The books continue to be available worldwide (print on demand) and have been used in multiple projects, most recently to make available Ukrainian language books to refugees across Europe and to support parents and young children in Macedonia during COVID.

Assessing Scope, Scale, and Impact

The original concept of introducing democracy into preschool education through intensive training and mentoring, accompanied by provision of educational resources, furniture, additional staff, and in some cases physical renovations, became a platform for a breath-taking set of linked initiatives that reinforce quality, social inclusion, and continuity across early education settings for children from birth through age ten and beyond. Each initiative was made available to interested Step by Step teams with manuals, training, and mentoring to support quality implementation. Over time, peer groups and learning communities have evolved in each thematic area. The menu of Step by Step initiatives is set out in Figure 3.2.

Calculating the geographic and thematic scope of Step by Step is easier than, for instance, the number of teachers or children reached. During the first years, when the Step by Step program was funded and operated through Open Society's affiliated national foundations, it was relatively easy to track sites (creches, preschools, primary schools, institutions of higher education), classrooms, and children as well as the number (and type) of trainings and trained teachers and educators. However, as the programs "spun off" from Open Society's national foundations into independent organizations, trainings were adjusted to meet the accreditation and funding requirements of diverse re-training systems and new donors. Furthermore, as the program grew, trainings

Step by Step Initiatives

Within the context of child-centered learning and family participation, the Step by Step Program supports a wide range of programs.

When implemented together, these initiatives provide a comprehensive foundation for reform of education and care for children from birth throung age 10.

Programs can also be implemented individually.

Early Childhood (birth age 6)
- Parent Education Programs
- Early Childhood Development Community Centers
- Preschool
- Center-based Infant and Toddler programs

Primary School
- Grades 1–4
- Creating Democratic Schools. (School Improvement)
- Community Education
- Transition to Middle School

Equal Access
- Education for Social Justice
- Inclusive Education
- Roma and Minority Education

Teacher Education
- Courses for Teacher Training/Re-training Institutions
- Student Practica
- Training for Adult Trainers
- Teacher Certification

Civic Participation in Education
- Parent Advocacy
- Early Childhood Non-Governmental Organizations

Professional Standards and Assessment Instruments
- Pedagogical Principles
- Trainer Standards
- Preschool and Primary Observation and Assessment Instruments

Figure 3.2 Step by Step Initiatives.
@International Step by Step Association

began to be provided by the decentralized model sites based in preschools and primary schools and through re-training institutions and, in some cases, pre-service institutions. As a result, the delivery and dosage of trainings were no longer uniform, prompting the development of standards and principles to support teachers' professional development.

Open Society collected and analyzed program and budget statistics annually, a task that eventually transitioned over to the International Step by Step Association. The tenth anniversary of Step by Step in 2004 was celebrated at an event in Budapest attended by representatives from all countries, global experts, and Open Society staff and Board Members, including Aryeh Neier, the president, and George Soros, founder and chair. A curated volume of narrative case studies, covering the thematic and geographic breadth of the program, was commissioned from national experts (Open Society Institute 2008).

Statistics collected that year provide an excellent gauge of the scale of Step by Step, at time when it was still possible to gather accurate information about the reach of the program model in its original form. Reports from 2004 show Step by Step had been implemented in 24,172 classrooms, almost equally split between preschools and primary schools. An estimated 600,000 children were directly benefiting from the original model, including approximately 15,000 children with disabilities and 15,000 children of Roma origin. Vastly more were benefiting from teachers who received training through model sites and institutes of higher education. The rapid increase in training capacity is captured in Figure 3.3, which tracks the cumulative number of teachers trained during the first decade of the program.

Data supports the assertion that the program was having a systemic impact. During the first decade of Step by Step, nearly 1,800 faculty from 291 universities and 192 training institutes participated in Step by Step's Higher Education Initiative, and 328 preschools and primary schools—centers of excellence—were operating as model sites hosting observers and trainings. In nearly all Step by Step countries[5], Step by Step was approved as either an alternative or official methodology, available for any preschool to adopt. The situation was similar for primary school, though in some countries the program was still classified as an experimental model approved for specific sites. This is both because the primary program was launched a few years after the preschool program, and it also reflects the greater difficulty in gaining approval for a novel methodology in statutory education provision.

Between 2006 and 2008, Open Society hired RAND Education to conduct an independent assessment of the capacity and scope of the national Step by Step programs and to explore the impact on teachers and the potential to sustain the program and the national NGOs. RAND worked from existing secondary reports supplemented by the results of a self-reported survey of country directors. As

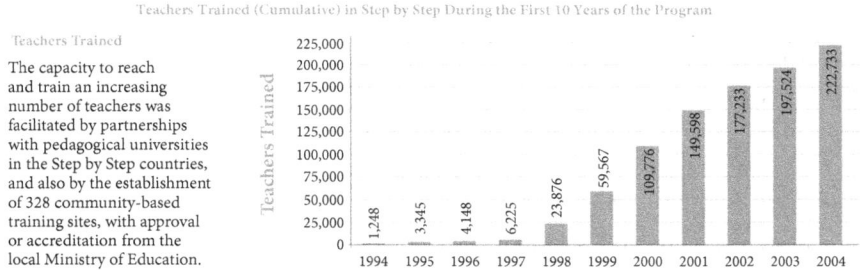

Figure 3.3 Teachers trained (cumulative) in Step by Step during the first ten years of the program.

@ International Step by Step Association

noted earlier, data became more difficult to compile as the program began to expand through multiple mechanisms, not all of which were directly managed by the Step by Step program offices. Their report finds that by 2006 the program had reached at least 68,000 teachers and 1.5 million children, including more than 18,000 Roma children (Stasz et al. 2008). It acknowledges data is challenging to collect, suggesting this is an undercount, particularly given the number of teachers and student teachers participating in trainings through training centers and institutions of higher education. The report is clearer about the impact on education systems. Twenty-seven of the surveyed country directors noted that Step by Step programs had achieved ministry approval while two indicated ministry approval was not applicable in their country.

> Step by Step programs have been successful in attaining Ministry of Education endorsement in their country and have been involved in developing policy, curriculum, and standards at the national level.
>
> (Stasz et al. 2008, xvii)

Over twenty-six years, the Open Society Foundations invested more than $175 million in early childhood programs reaching more than eighty countries, including, but in no way limited to Step by Step. The program, implemented in thirty countries, including Argentina and South Africa, made up approximately $140 million of the total funding invested in early childhood. It was more than the $100 million that George Soros initially pledged for the initial two-year initiative but spread over ten times as many years. Funding from Open Society makes up only part of the resources invested in Step by Step. Large partnerships, such as those with the World Bank and USAID that were highlighted earlier, brought co-funding into the program with support from Open Society's New York office. The majority of co-funding, however, was generated in-country, and grew as national programs became independent of Open Society and began to actively seek and apply for funding from other donors. Step by Step teams launched income-generating initiatives, for instance, selling trainings, publications, and expertise. Step by Step training began to be funded by resources from within education systems in many countries; local governments, businesses, and parents provided in-kind goods and services; and the newly established Step by Step NGOs and the International Step by Step Association leveraged funding from the European Union, UNICEF, World Bank, bilateral donors, and international NGOs and foundations. In 2010, Open Society funding made up approximately one quarter of the Step by Step program and ISSA budgets; however, dependency on Open Society in individual countries ranged from 10 to nearly 60 percent.

At the time of writing, Open Society funding to the program as a whole has wound down. The Early Childhood Program closed at the end of 2020, but the regional network, the International Step by Step Association (ISSA) established by the Step by Step program, has grown. Collaboratively with other funders, Open Society established the Early Childhood Regional Networks Fund to secure and grow the capacity of regional networks, including ISSA, over the next five or more years. In the intervening period (1994–2020), twenty-nine countries in Europe and Central Asia, including Haiti and Mongolia, had launched and nurtured national Step by Step programs. Additionally, between 1997 and 2001, South Africa introduced Step by Step in a limited number of preschool sites, and beginning in 2004, an NGO in Argentina piloted the program in primary schools in Buenos Aires and Misiones.[6] As will be seen in Chapter 8, Open Society later drew upon the training modules, teacher manuals, and university courses developed through the Step by Step program when designing programs in Bangladesh, Bhutan, Liberia, Myanmar, and Peru, and included experts from the original Step by Step countries in international technical assistance teams supporting early education initiatives in these countries.

Step by Step Arrived at the Right Moment

The Albanian expert tasked with evaluating Step by Step in 1996, two years after it was launched, commented on the timing of its launch:

> In this context, Step by Step has arrived in the right moment in Albania and is taking the right place. The Step by Step philosophy contains a relevant methodology for Albania because of its commitment to an open and democratic society.
> (Open Society Foundations 1996, 3)

Step by Step may have started out as an "American" program, beholden to Head Start, but it was to a great extent warmly welcomed, adapted, and absorbed across the region. The USAID evaluation conducted in four countries in 1998 found evidence of strong local ownership and adaptation of the program among teachers, parents, ministry, and program staff, and noted the alignment of Step by Step with the social and political context in the region. Both the local ownership and alignment were viewed as indicative of sustainability (Brady et al. 1999).

Those early evaluators were not wrong. Nearly thirty years later, Step by Step not only survived, but grew into an extraordinary network uniting early childhood professionals from Western Europe to Eurasia, dedicated to democracy and the values of open society.

4

"The Teachers Believed in Us!" Inspiring Stories from Teachers, Parents, and Grown-Up Children Who Experienced the Programs

Figure 4.1 Children and the director of the "Junior Park" kindergarten celebrate autumn (Bishkek, 2021).
@Irina Loboda

Toward a More Democratic Approach: From Teacher-Centered to Child-Centered

The first chapters of this book describe how early childhood education under communist-led governments was characterized by a teacher-centered approach, and how Step by Step sought to introduce a more democratic child-centered pedagogy after the collapse of the Soviet Union. It is interesting to see how the transition from teacher-centeredness toward a child-centered approach was perceived by teachers and parents. Early childhood education in the former Soviet Union and the Central, Eastern, and Southern European States was largely characterized by an authoritarian approach:

> *Teachers knew what to do, when to do, how to do it and there was very little attention to the interests or the wishes of the child. Teachers knew the pedagogy developed by the government and were sure that they were doing the right things with children. The most important thing was strict discipline and obedience.*
> (Eteri Gvineria, Center for Educational Initiatives, Step by Step Georgia)

There were also differences between the countries; according to Tatjana Vonta teachers in Slovenia had much more autonomy, and Aija Tuna had a similar experience in the Baltic states. But in most former communist-led countries, the introduction of the Step by Step program meant the whole system of early childhood education had to be questioned. There was a need to introduce a more democratic approach at all levels of the early childhood education system. The methodology emphasized new ideas like family participation, classroom community, children's agency, choice, independence, decision-making, and responsibility. The program introduced morning circle time, activity centers, and thematic projects.

In this chapter, we give a voice to the people the Step by Step programs aimed to impact. How did the teachers, parents, and children who were involved in Step by Step programs experience the Open Society programs? What kind of influence did Step by Step have on them?

How Teachers Fueled the Transformation[1]

The move to a more child-centered approach is not only about program components, but also about the change agents themselves: the Step by Step teachers and parents who fueled the engine of the transformation (Open Society Institute 2008, 5). The Step by Step approach supported teachers to transform their orientation from teacher-centered to a more child-centered professional identity. One of the Step by Step master teacher trainers from Russia described the magnitude of this challenge:

> The change is so profound that it cannot but affect the goals, values, methods and means of education. It inevitably has to do with a restructuring of teachers'

professional mentality, as most teachers were professionally trained within a totally different education system and naturally have certain pedagogical attitudes and stereotypes.

(Zaitsev 2002, 11)

This transformation process was quite complex because, in a teacher-centered professional environment, the teacher had a very technical task. He or she had to follow daily schedules, methodologies, and in some cases detailed programs developed by the education authorities. In a democratic child-centered form of professionalism, the teacher has to question beliefs they have taken for granted. He or she has to become a reflective practitioner who understands that knowledge is contestable (Peeters and Vandenbroeck 2011; Urban and Dalli 2008). But practitioners are often virtually absent from research discussion about their reflective professionalism. The result is that, paradoxically, the literature on reflective practitioners risks reducing the practitioners to objects, rather than including them as reflective and agentic subjects (Peeters and Vandenbroeck 2011). According to Wittorski and Sorel (2005), it is essential that the individuals "professionalizing" themselves are not reduced to the role of a "consumer" of the knowledge presented to them. This is why the teachers' testimonies that we use in this chapter are so important, since they give a voice to practitioners in these emerging transformations of their role, with their new emphasis on negotiating and networking competencies. The narratives will also provide insights into how such a transformation process works in practice and what other projects can learn from it.

Teachers as Change Agents

We start with an interesting testimony from Yelizaveta Bubenova, an experienced and dynamic teacher from Kyrgyzstan. Her story illustrates how the Step by Step program was in complete contradiction with the dominant teacher-centered professional identity.

> I was horrified, I have to confess that my heart was crying. The vibrant, colourful room seemed noisy, disorderly, and confusing when I saw it for the first time. Frankly speaking, my eyes popped up from my sockets when I saw children during the lesson go and sprawl out on the sofa to have some rest! Where is the order, the clear sequence, the beginning and end, the teacher's authority? I lamented.

(Open Society Institute 2008, 55)

Bubenova followed Step by Step training and gradually her impression of the Step by Step approach changed. Five years later she was a trainer herself in the Step by Step approach:

> The training developed my ability to be self-sufficient. In the past, other people did everything instead of me. Now I know I am perfectly capable of making my own decisions.
>
> (Open Society Institute 2008, 56)

This story of teachers gradually becoming the actors of their own change process through the Step by Step program is heard in many interviews. Olga Panaite, a teacher from Moldova, formulates it like this:

> I liked the possibility to create, and change, the environment, and the new psychological climate in the classroom. I enjoyed the children's lively discussions. But all these came gradually. In the beginning, it was not easy.
>
> (Open Society Institute 2008, 139)

Encouraging children's preferences and adapting learning to their individual learning styles, interests, temperament, and family culture was one of the biggest changes.

> *Kids do things themselves, but at the beginning of Step by Step, that was the biggest fight.*
>
> *(Aija Tuna, former program director, International Step by Step Association and Soros Foundation Latvia)*

> *That a child can choose what they want to do. That a child can reach a toy they want at any time. That was something completely new. There was a bit of fear, "And how are we going to control all that? Will there be anarchy?" That no one would want to put things back. That our cleaning ladies would be mad at us. However, that didn't happen at all.*
>
> *(Hašima Ćurak, advisor, Ministry of Education and Science, Bosnia and Herzegovina)*

While in some countries there was initially some resistance to introducing this approach, in other countries teachers welcomed the introduction of a child-centered approach that responds to each child's unique needs and potential, and encourages innovation, creativity, and self-reflection.

> The first time I came in touch with this pedagogy was in the kindergarten next door. When I saw how the children worked, how free they were, how they used materials and then the meeting area, everything was a revelation. The way the

children began the day by thinking, and talking to each other, all of it excited me! I then started to read books to understand it and learn how to do it.

Amira Sehić, Bosnia and Herzegovina
(Open Society Institute 2008, 49)

On the other hand, some professionals seemed to resist changes more strongly than others, and a minority never accepted the changes. Gerda Sula, country director of the Albania Step by Step program, mentioned in her case study written with colleagues about working in childcare centers (for 0–3-year-olds) that it was difficult for nurses who had always used a medical-hygienic approach to adapt to the child-centered pedagogical approach (Open Society Institute 2008, 103). This can be explained by the fact that nurses have a strong professional medical identity. This is also seen in other countries where the childcare system was transformed into a more child- and parent-centered approach. For some nurses in Western European countries it was also difficult to make the shift toward a pedagogical professional identity (Peeters and Vandenbroeck 2011).

When the Step by Step program started in the mid-1990s, some teachers in kindergarten and the first years of primary education had many questions.

> *Some were confusing child-centred with an anti-authoritarian, permissive approach. It took some time before they understood what child-centred actually means. Teachers in kindergarten had problems with the activity corners, they thought the classrooms were too small for so many different corners. What helped a lot were visits to child-centered classrooms. Teachers could see that it worked in practice, and they could observe the opportunities that a child-centred approach provided for children and parents. During the visits, the children were so involved in their activities that they did not even pay attention to the visitors, and this was very convincing.*
>
> (Tatjana Vonta, co-author and former director, Step by Step Slovenia)

Also, the introduction of a democratic approach of openness, reflecting on practice, and the active participation of the teachers is strongly appreciated by the teachers who started to use the Step by Step approach.

> It would be easier if you only had to take ideas from books, but these ideas have to be studied experientially. The trainees need time and more experience in Step by Step classrooms. Sharing ideas with their colleagues and mentors, asking questions, and expressing doubts—characteristics of reflective practice—are the best ways of improving personal teaching.
>
> Jeni Batiste, Teacher, Romania
(Open Society Institute 2008, 67)

This openness and critical thinking required that teachers take important decisions themselves about how they wanted to work. They started to reflect on their own practice. Dawn Tankersley, one of the US Step by Step trainers, noted that through reflection teachers gained ownership of the child-centered approach (Open Society Institute 2008, 11). Planning lessons and assessment of children remained challenging for many teachers, and it was reflected succinctly by one Romanian teacher:

> How to plan a lesson that takes into account all children's needs?
>
> (Open Society Institute 2008, 68)

Providing practical support to newly trained teachers to help them plan activities taking into account the diverse needs of the children was an important issue in the Step by Step training and mentoring. Mentoring time during child-free hours is essential to support teachers to create a climate of change in the early childhood education institutions and schools (Eurofund 2015) and it was provided by the Step by Step program and trainers.

But budget constraints in some countries meant teachers did not always get the mentoring they wanted to improve their pedagogical practice (Open Society Institute 2008, 68) and not all teachers had that same predisposition to being flexible, being aware of changes that were happening and why they were happening. Some teachers could not grasp the basic concept of the Step by Step approach as reflected in the Step by Step standards and principles.

> *Trainers mention the problems many teachers had with the Parent Participation Standard. For instance, having parents in the classroom was a surprise for some teachers.*
>
> (Kate Burke Walsh, US Step by Step expert team)

Other interviewees describe the chaotic situations when they invited parents for the first time into the classroom.

> For parents and teachers, parent participation in the classroom was the most innovative aspect of the Step by Step program. Russian teachers are not used to having their classroom work observed or participated in by parents.
>
> (Open Society Institute 2008, 146)

A very important condition for the implementation of the child-centered Step by Step approach was the opportunity to share ideas among colleagues and the active participation of practitioners in professional learning communities. The participation of the practitioners in professional learning communities that is so crucial in the Step by Step approach is also found in other programs such as the North-Italian pedagogy of Pistoia (Giovannini and Contini 2017) and Reggio Emilia and is an important factor supporting a child-centered form of professionalization: *"The staff member should be the first to nurture the pleasure of participation, to draw meaning from meetings, and find the opportunity to qualify and enrich his/her professionalism through participation"* (Rinaldi 2005, 51).

Step by Step nurtured the kinds of strong relationships that Rinaldi describes across staff at all levels. The very first international meeting of core team members from the first fifteen countries in Washington DC in early 1994 set the tone for these kinds of professional relationships and networks that the program needed to build.

> *Pam [Coughlin] felt very strongly about building networks and building relationships.*
>
> *(Kirsten Hansen, US Step by Step expert team)*

As the program unfolded in each country, interactive trainings for teachers were organized in comfortable places, away from everyday environments, combining hard but interesting work with some social activities. Evening tasks required participants to work together in teams on joint activities. The training quality was exceptionally high. Only leading American trainers were invited to serve as international Step by Step mentors and trainers, and they presented new knowledge and skills that engaged participants in reflection and active, autonomous participation, always recognizing and appreciating their efforts. The national training teams modeled this approach as they replicated and developed new training in their countries. Interactive training was new for teachers, who were used to listening to lectures. Another new practice was introduced: inviting teacher assistants and other educational staff to join training and team meetings at preschools and schools, recognizing the important role they play in classrooms. These experiences of having fun together, sharing ideas, and receiving appreciation from colleagues, stayed with participants for years and had a positive impact on their work.

Between training sessions, the Step by Step national teams supported the newly trained educators. They visited and observed preschools and schools, provided additional workshops, and developed and disseminated new educational resources. Beginning in 1998, national Step by Step teams began "spinning off" from national Open Society foundations. The connection between the new organizations and centers was strengthened by the establishment of the International Step by Step Association (ISSA) in the Netherlands in 1999.

I think the fact that they were part of the network allowed and supported them to continuously reinvigorate their work around this mission and these values.
(Liana Ghent, executive director, ISSA)

Assessing Teacher Quality in the Step by Step Program

One of the first activities ISSA embarked on was to bring together the network's experience of implementing Step by Step across an entire region to create a common understanding and definition of key pedagogical concepts. This was an important process to ensure that the scale-up of the programs in countries would adhere to a common framework. In essence, ISSA took on the task of defining excellence in early childhood teaching that was both child-centered and which emphasized democratic approaches. An ISSA taskforce with members from eleven countries was created and with the support of the US experts they set out, through multiple intensive meetings, the following domains of quality: Individualization, Learning Environment, Family Participation, Teaching Strategies for Meaningful Learning, Planning and Assessment, and Professional Development. The standards were validated, then piloted, and they were used initially to support the professional development of individual teachers and to certify those that achieved threshold scores.

In 2005, when initial implementation demonstrated a shortcoming in measuring teacher performance in managing diversity, a new standard was added: Diversity, Inclusion, and Democratic Values. It includes three key competencies: 1) providing equal opportunities for every child and family to learn and participate regardless of gender, race, ethnic origin, culture, native language, religion, family structure, social status, economic status, age, or special need; 2) helping children understand, accept, and appreciate diversity; and 3) developing children's understanding of the values of civil society and the skills required for participating (International Step by Step Association 2010). Making inclusion, diversity, and democracy a required component of quality was entirely new in countries that were implementing Step by Step.

One important validation of the ISSA standards was provided through a research study in Slovenia, which involved a representative sample of twenty teachers selected from 124 preschool classrooms where Step by Step was implemented. A small team of five reliable observers and mentors (Step by Step master teacher trainers) were recruited and trained to support teacher development over a six-month period and to collect data on teacher performance using both the ISSA standards (International Step by Step Association 2001) and the well-known, internationally used Early Childhood Environmental Rating Scale (ECERS) (Harms, Clifford, and Cryer 1998). The instruments were applied to measure teacher quality at the beginning and end of the quality improvement process, which involved teacher observation, review of the scores on the ISSA standards, development of a personal improvement plan by the teacher, and ongoing mentoring. Importantly, the results showed a high correlation between scores on the ISSA standards and ECERS. The research confirmed that the ISSA standards can be used as an effective tool for professional development when combined with constructive feedback, reflective conversation, and the creation of a quality improvement plan and active participation of the teacher and the mentor (Vonta 2004).

Over time, the goal of ISSA's work on quality has evolved from certifying Step by Step teachers to creating pathways for professional development and influencing national early education standards and quality systems.

> Good documents have been developed at that point, like the standards for child development, and the learning and development standards for children from zero to seven. Although the word standards sounds a little bit scary, it depends how you use them. These were promoting a holistic approach to child development.
> (Cornelia Cincilei, Step by Step Moldova)

ISSA later conducted a set of multi-country case studies on the impact of the teacher standards, which illustrated how the core principles had the most sustainable impact. It concluded:

> [The Standards] provided a way to measure and evaluate highly effective classroom practice and they are based on a set of foundational principles that can help guide a number of efforts both programmatic and systemic. At the same time, such an international document can have only an advisory capacity in most cases, as local context, educational traditions and national requirements are crucial in developing ownership and meaningful commitments from all stakeholders.
> (Howard et al. 2010, 12)

Responding to the results of the study, ISSA published a revised version of the document and a set of educational resources to support implementation. The new documents focus on strengthening "principles" of quality to encourage their wider use in influencing quality systems, teacher training, policies, and academia and to underscore their connection to the underlying values of a democracy. They offer indicators of quality practice for use by any child-centered program, including, but not limited to Step by Step (International Step by Step Association 2010).

A Democratic Culture toward Parents Increases Hope and Self-Confidence

The program gave parents a new role in preschools, and they played an interesting role in the change process.

> *The program, actually for the first time, introduced the philosophy that parents are of the same value as preschool teachers, because, actually, they are teachers for their children from birth.*
>
> *(Natalia Sofiy, Borys Grinchenko Kyiv University, Ukraine)*

> *In some places families hadn't even been allowed to come into the school. It was a new concept for them. Some people found it difficult, but once they got going, they had family meetings, they had family policy councils, they had the parents coming to volunteer. It turned out to be very freeing. I went to many, many family meetings and saw what they had done and saw the families and their faces. They were just so happy to be there.*
>
> *(Kirsten Hansen, US Step by Step expert team)*

The family coordinators, hired by the program at each kindergarten, had a role in developing closer relationships with parents and families and they got to know each family's unique circumstances. The expectation for parents to become partners and play an active role in the kindergartens and schools was initially challenging for parents, but gradually parents came to enjoy participating in Step by Step class activities. Each preschool was required to set aside one room for parents and to encourage their participation in classrooms and governance roles. In the early years of the program, Open Society provided preschools with small funds to support parent engagement activities. This even included, for instance, in Slovakia and Kyrgyzstan, purchasing sewing machines for the parent rooms that parents could use to create and sell handmade goods to benefit the preschool. An example from Estonia and Kyrgyzstan:

> Unfortunately, we had no systematic work with parents before. Sites were not open to them. They could only visit kindergartens on special occasions. Now parents are full of ideas and enthusiasm to be involved in the Soros Preschool Project.
>
> (Country director, Kyrgyzstan, Open Society Foundations, 1995)

> We can feel the parents' support everywhere. It's a miracle! Every time the teaching staff attends training, the parents have voluntarily worked in the classrooms.
>
> (Site manager, Estonia, Open Society Foundations, 1995)

After two years of Step by Step, the Albanian country team could already see a change in the relationship with parents.

> The impact this program has had on families is very exciting. Families feel welcome in the classroom; they were never allowed in before. Parents have commented that they see a change in their children's behaviour. They are more independent and make decisions more easily. They comment about how their children's social skills have changed.
>
> (Albania Country Team, Open Society Foundations, 1995)

> But children played also an important role in getting their parents involved. When a child can see his or her parent in the class, he or she is happy and tries to be active. Children were proud of their mothers when they see them helping other children.
>
> Jamilla, Teacher, Tajikistan
> (Open Society Institute 2008, 154)

Last but not least, parents became advocates for implementing the Step by Step approach on a larger scale within the school and in other locations. Together with preschool staff, parents played a critical role as advocates for implementing Step by Step beyond the original preschools, including extending Step by Step into the early years of primary school. Their success in achieving this offers a positive example of the impact that citizens can have on the evolution of education systems.

From excluding parents under communist-led governments, preschools shifted toward inviting parents to actively participate to increase children's wellbeing. These narratives of teachers and parents demonstrate that being actively involved with Step by Step's process of change gives hope and self-confidence and increases teachers' job satisfaction.

The Voice of the (Grown-Up) Children: Individualization and Autonomy: "The Teacher Believed in Us!"

> My school is great because we learn in a Step by Step classroom where I feel happy.
>
> (Mariam (9), Georgia)

For the tenth and twenty-fifth anniversaries of the Step by Step program, children were interviewed about it. In 2004, young children between four and fifteen years were asked several questions about their Step by Step schools, and in 2020 nineteen adults from different countries where the program was implemented were interviewed and shared reflections about their experiences as young children in the Step by Step classrooms (Magrab 2004). In this chapter, we also hear from teachers and trainers with their reflections on the effects of the program on children.

Tanja is now a teacher herself in Croatia and describes the positive approach she experienced as a child from the Step by Step approach:

> The teacher approached all of us individually and at the end of each school period she wrote a note about us, our character, and about how we worked. These notes were very positive because the teacher wanted to let us know that she believed in us.

Shavkhat from Kyrgyzstan testifies that the teachers in the Step by Step program believed in the talents of each child.

> Our teacher made a lot of effort to help us develop the skills that she saw we could be talented at. I liked mathematics a lot and logical thinking, which I learnt to develop in my early years at school.

These testimonies are confirmed by several trainers and teachers in the case studies. According to teachers from Lithuania, Step by Step is tailored to look for potential in every child (Open Society Institute 2008, 65).

Narratives from adults illustrate that Step by Step is an approach based on individualization that responds to each child's unique needs and potential.

> The Step by Step program taught me to study, to get knowledge and to take responsibility.
>
> (Veronika, Czech Republic)

The Step by Step program also strengthened the self-direction of young children. Vivien was a young child in a Step by Step kindergarten in Croatia:

> I had a lot of freedom but also knew my boundaries. I had a very warm and loving teacher. It was a very nice experience for us because we felt that we always had a choice and that our opinion mattered.
>
> (Vivien, Croatia)

> Since my early childhood education, I was taught that I will not be judged and that I can say what I think. Our teacher was also our friend, we were not afraid to share our thoughts.
>
> (Perizat, Kyrgyzstan)

The perspectives of a teacher from Lithuania on the effect on children also confirm this:

> The children are active in the classroom, brave and possess self-confidence. They are not afraid to ask questions, and they are not afraid to stand up in front of the class and present and defend their own opinions.
>
> (Open Society Institute 2008, 65)

According to teachers, children from Step by Step classrooms appear to show more empathy toward their peers (Open Society Institute 2008, 129).

> We understand each other, listen to, and hear each other.
>
> (Ina (9) Moldova)

> The program taught me how to make decisions and make choices; how to solve problems by myself; how to achieve my goals and correct my faults.
>
> (Narmin, Azerbaijan)

Dodo Tavedze, a teacher from Tbilisi, puts it succinctly:

> When the children are given an opportunity to explore what they are interested in, they can achieve amazing results.
>
> (Open Society Institute 2008, 38)

But parents, too, see the benefits of a learning environment that facilitates their children taking learning risks and practicing democracy:

> I believe that children benefit a lot when they get a chance to look at a problem or event from different perspectives and learn by practical

involvement. The teachers have also changed, and this makes us parents closer to the preschool.

Nina Metreveli, parent, Georgia
(Open Society Institute 2008, 39)

For Yulia from Kazakhstan:

> The Step by Step kindergarten taught me how to think critically and how to work hard. It also encouraged creativity and leadership in me.

The most important change was that children were seen as active citizens who could make decisions about important aspects of daily life and their learning process. One child in an Estonian primary school, who had attended Step by Step preschool, wrote a letter to a new teacher and criticized her way of teaching:

> "You could teach us in another way. If you do not know how you could do that then go to my previous teacher and ask her. But if you don't want to do it, then it would be better if you were not a teacher." The new teacher could have been offended but in fact, she asked a colleague to help her improve her practice towards a more child-centred approach.

(Open Society Institute 2008, 29)

Results of a Longitudinal Study of the Effect of the Step by Step Program on Children

A longitudinal child outcomes study of Step by Step was planned, but never implemented. However, a study funded by the US Agency for International Development (USAID) in 1998 explored child outcomes in four countries. It demonstrates that Step by Step supported children's development, even exceeding levels achieved by children in traditional programs, and that it promoted democratic behaviors and practices in classrooms (see Chapter 3) (Bradly et al. 1999).

There are numerous examples of national studies about the impact of Step by Step on children, parents, and teachers. To close this chapter, we provide information from one of these national studies, a three-year longitudinal study conducted by experts in the Czech Republic. The Step by Step program was introduced there in 1994 and brought child-centered educational practices into preschool and primary school classrooms. Teachers and parents from the start were interested in its effectiveness. Would the use of a pedagogy based on individualization and meaningful learning meet the program's aim to positively influence the social and personal development of children? And parents wanted to know if the replacement of teacher-centered, traditional didactic approaches with child-centered approaches put the Step by Step children at a disadvantage when they transitioned to elementary school. Would they have gained the necessary skills and knowledge to succeed in primary school?

To address these questions, an independent research team was asked by the Open Society Fund—Prague to measure the impact of the Step by Step program for kindergartens on children's psychosocial capacities (Havlinova et al. 2004). The research sample included 821 children aged three to seven. Four hundred and nine children attended classrooms in ten Step by Step kindergartens, and there was a control group of 412 children that attended classrooms in twelve "mainstream" kindergartens without any special program. For three years all the children were tested every six months using a variety of internationally validated scientific scales measuring problem-solving, creativity, language, and social-emotional capacity. The results of the research showed that the Step by Step program succeeds in promoting children's emotional, intellectual, social, and personality development. Children in the program acquire a wide range of psychosocial skills, which align with the values espoused by Open Society and ISSA and are embedded in the ISSA principles. At the same time, this does not weaken the acquisition of skills required by mainstream schools at the time of primary school entry. This study demonstrates how child-centered methodologies like those promoted through Step by Step (learning through play, cooperative work, thematic projects that build on children's interests, and the opportunity for children to engage in self-selected activities in a stimulating environment) have beneficial effects on young children (Havlinova et al. 2004).

Conclusion

The narratives of teachers, parents, and children and the results of a study on the implementation of the ISSA standards and the longitudinal study in the Czech Republic bear witness to the important changes that the Step by Step approach has had on the lives of children, parents, and teachers. They illustrate a notable evolution in the way teachers view children. Teachers who once viewed the child as an object that needed to be instructed gained an appreciation for them as subjects and actors in their own learning process. Interestingly, this shift coincides with a second evolution: a shift in how these teachers themselves are treated. The rigid hierarchy of the settings under most communist-led governments stopped professionals from speaking up and banned parents or "experts" from addressing the professionals directly.

The interviewees describe the important effects of these transformations. The teachers learned through continuous professional development, organized within the Step by Step program, to create a warm, democratic, and stimulating environment for children and parents and this had beneficial effects on their emotional, intellectual, social, and personal development (Havlinova et al. 2004). It also had a positive effect on parents. Teachers began to conceptualize the education of the child as a shared responsibility between parents and teachers. The Step by Step approach motivated them to become involved in activities for their children and gave them tools to support them.

5

"Slowly We Are Getting There": Creating Opportunities for Children Experiencing Exclusion

Figure 5.1 Child in Slovenia working on a drawing of the solar system (Murska Sobota, Slovenia, 2017).

@Aljoša Rudaš

Open Society Responds to the Exclusion of Young Children

Embracing inclusion and diversity is fundamental to the concept of open society and essential in a vibrant democracy. The political and social transitions in Central, Eastern, and Southern Europe and Eurasia disrupted the status quo and created spaces for new voices and groups that have historically experienced marginalization to participate and influence policies and practices. The role Step by Step was able to play in promoting equity for populations experiencing exclusion captured the attention of Open Society's leadership.

> *I was very concerned with the equality issues so far as the Roma and disabled children were concerned. The fact that [Step by Step] was addressing those issues made the program particularly attractive to me.*
>
> (Ayreh Neier, president emeritus, Open Society Foundations)

The intensification of the exclusion of Roma and people with disabilities in the mid-1990s also motivated the interest of the Open Society's national foundations in the Step by Step program.

> *The political and economic situation brought problems with employment especially in a segregated community. Poverty was increasing. People in Roma communities were excluded from official life and illiteracy was growing. One of our biggest goals was to include Roma people in the mainstream community. [Step by Step] was the first time handicapped [sic] children had a chance to enter the common school or kindergarten and to be integrated. People and parents and teachers appreciated that.*
>
> (Alena Panikova, former executive director, Open Society Foundation—Bratislava)

Open Society's emphasis on human rights aligned with the rights and equity focus of the US Head Start program, which was a model for Step by Step.

Exclusion and Segregation of Children with Special Educational Needs

Step by Step encountered education systems in Eastern, Central, and Southern Europe and Eurasia that had long histories of segregating and excluding children who require additional support. A good framework for inclusion and inclusive education can be found in UNESCO's 2020 Global Education Monitoring Report. It discusses inclusive education as education that overcomes barriers to participation, such as "gender, age, location, poverty, disability, ethnicity, indigeneity, language, religion, migration or displacement status, sexual orientation or gender identity expression, incarceration, beliefs and attitudes." Inclusion is seen as a process that overcomes discrimination and includes "*actions that embrace diversity and build a sense of belonging, rooted in the belief that every person has value and potential, and should be respected, regardless of their background, ability or identity*" (UNESCO 2020, 10–11).

At the time Step by Step was established, education systems in the region excluded many children from mainstream education and segregated them in special schools or classrooms. Decisions about where to place children (in mainstream or special education) were all too often made through high-stakes assessments of children by local committees, using inappropriate testing methods and influenced by prejudices. For children with medically diagnosed disabilities and learning difficulties, institutionalization, segregated education in special schools or classrooms, or home-based learning was common. Roma children, who spoke a different language at home, frequently ended up assigned to special education settings because of their lack of fluency in the majority language and low expectations of their capabilities. These practices, where they continue, remain a profoundly disturbing and unacceptable abrogation of the rights of Roma children based on their ethnicity. This challenge also motivated Open Society's interest in Step by Step.

> *There had been a tendency in Europe and the US to consider minority children, the Roma in Eastern Europe, Black children in the US, as in need of special education. They were very often taken out of mainstream education and sent to separate schools or separate classes. These special education programs, in effect, rigidified the disadvantages of the minority children. I think that is a huge part of the overall issue of equality. I think offering high-quality education at the earliest possible age is the antithesis of that special education approach.*
>
> (Ayreh Neier, president emeritus, Open Society Foundations)

The first challenge involved introducing new words into local languages to align them with the idea of equity and inclusion of Roma children and children with disabilities. The translators struggled to convey new concepts.

> *How do you explain to people [the US trainers] in other languages where the [Russian] word, for instance, "invalid" comes from? It simply denotes a group of people who have certain disabilities. A bit later, people in our countries started hearing that you have to eliminate the word "invalid," but the term they came up with in Russian means "children with limited ability," and that's exactly what in English they tried to avoid. I translated an article into Russian and used the word "Roma," but the editor without notifying me changed it to "gypsy." So this rigamarole goes on. Somehow you have to educate people, to explain it.*
>
> (Sergei, interpreter and translator)

US trainers were shocked to learn that the field of special education in the countries of the former Soviet Union was known as "defectology."

> *When I first heard "defectologist" I was so alarmed. I thought, "Whoa, we have a steep hill to climb." This deficit model it seems was more prevalent in Eastern Europe than other countries. There was a lot of that type of thinking, and those were some of the initial attitudinal barriers that we had to overcome, as we moved towards looking at children as individuals, at their strengths and how we could teach to them. The Step by Step leadership shifted toward a new paradigm over time.*
> *(Deborah A. Ziegler, US Step by Step expert team)*

In the 1990s separate streams of expertise in special education, or "defectology," existed in ministries and permeated down through all levels of education. Special educators completed higher education courses that prepared them to work with children in segregated institutions, schools, and classrooms. Conversely, mainstream teachers did not acquire the knowledge, skills, or experience to work with children with disabilities and their families. Inclusive practices were not taught in pedagogical institutions. Professors in Mongolia, who were part of a Step by Step initiative to introduce inclusion into pre-service courses for future teachers, expressed frustration with their own lack of experience.

> About the practice we are not sure. If someone brings a child with special needs into the room I will be very nervous because I have never had direct interaction with such a child.
> (Open Society Institute 2008, 94)

Real problems emerged after the dissolution of the Soviet Union, as many of the newly independent countries did not have universities and pedagogic institutes capable of preparing special educators. The language of special education was Russian.

> *In Central Asia this system had a particular layer of cruelty where the defectologist and the specialists were mostly from Russia and they were Russian-speaking. For a Kyrgyz or a Tajik family who sent their child to a special school, it meant that child would be brought up in Russian by Russians. It represents an additional layer of separation from your family because if you can come home for a school vacation, you no longer speak the same language, particularly if you're from a rural area and your family is not a Russian-speaking family. It also meant when the Soviet Union fell apart all of those specialized teachers could get jobs in Russia. In the 2000s when Russia's economy started turning around they left and there was a huge vacuum of professional knowledge.*
> *(Kate Lapham, former deputy director, Education Support Program, OSF)*

Vice Minister Victor Ogneviuk from Ukraine, interviewed in 2004, talked about the moral aspects of isolating children with disabilities from other children:

> In my mind it is absolutely wrong when, using specialized boarding schools or other institutions, we create reservations for children, preventing them from seeing life in all of its forms, manifestations, and complexities. And this is true not only for children with disabilities. The healthy children have to see that within human society, alongside the healthy ones with able minds, hands, and legs, live children who require their help and compassion. Understanding this problem should become a motivating factor for us.
> (Open Society Institute 2008, 100)

Such segregation deprives children with and without special educational needs of opportunities to learn and live together, and to experience the diversity of human society.

> *There were children in special groups and preschools, with quite separate lives. It was justified by giving them better professional assistance and help.*
> *(Aija Tuna, former program director, International Step by Step Association and Soros Foundation Latvia)*

Rigid curricula, regulations, and the focus on conformity and whole-group activities in traditional preschools and primary schools rendered inclusion of children with special educational needs in mainstream classrooms especially challenging, and parents had concerns.

> *The Hungarian school system is still very traditional, very frontal teaching, content-oriented. No proper, inclusive child-centered methodologies.*
> *(Éva Deák, Partners Hungary Foundation)*

> *Even parents may be against moving a child to a regular preschool environment because they feel that they're losing the help this child needs. There are definitely social benefits for the child, but it can be at a cost.*
> *(Elena Bodrova, Tools of the Mind, US)*

When Step by Step programs started to include children with disabilities, Roma children, and other excluded groups in preschools, it broke new ground in many places.

> *We were the first to promote inclusion in the country before it started being spoken about. We promote education for all, following the specific needs of every single child. That is the philosophy of a child-centered approach.*
>
> *(Cornelia Cincilei, Step by Step Moldova)*

One of the first challenges was to address prejudices and foster acceptance and respect for diversity.

Attitudes toward Children with Disabilities, Roma Children, Ethnic Minorities, Refugees, and Asylum Seekers

Inclusion was a new concept in the countries implementing the Step by Step program. The exposure that the national early childhood experts (country director, master teacher trainer) had to inclusive early childhood programs during Step by Step trainings initially created curiosity.

> *At one of the Step By Step meetings, we saw the video* To Have a Friend *which showed people with disabilities that we all are different, but also all the same. We came back to Ukraine and we thought, "Wow, we didn't realise that these Step by Step principles like child-centered approach, partnership with parents, right of choice and right to education, they're very important for all children." But there are categories of children for whom these approaches are not only good, not only beneficial, but critical. I can tell you that I knew little about inclusion back then. We got big support from parents, especially parents of children with disabilities, or with special needs who wanted to see their children in regular schools.*
>
> *(Natalia Sofiy, Borys Grinchenko Kyiv University, Ukraine)*

Later, the International Renaissance Foundation in Ukraine inspired the Ukrainian Step by Step Foundation to develop initiatives to address the exclusion of Roma children.

> *It was the same with Roma children. The Foundation let us see that there is another category of children who really suffer from this lack of access to education and negative attitudes from teachers and the community, and all of this made us work with them.*
>
> *(Natalia Sofiy, Borys Grinchenko Kyiv University, Ukraine)*

In our interview, which was conducted in 2021, Natalia Sofiy distinguished between the attitudes of teachers toward different groups of excluded children: children with disabilities, Roma children, and internally displaced people (IDP) fleeing the war in the east of the country, which began when Russia invaded Crimea in 2014.

> *Mainly, we worked with the teachers, preschool teachers, and primary school teachers. If we are speaking about children with disabilities, first, they listened to us but didn't believe us because they said, "They have to be in special kindergartens because it's better for them. I have 30 children in my classroom, so it's impossible." Regarding Roma children, it's a different situation. Here, the teachers mainly treated the children OK, but they blamed the Roma families because they thought they didn't care about their children's education. It was very difficult to work with these children because they don't get appropriate family support. With regards to internally displaced people (refugees from the war in the east) teachers were usually tolerant because everybody understood that it was really a tragedy for those families who had to move.*
>
> *(Natalia Sofiy, Borys Grinchenko Kyiv University, Ukraine)*

Changing attitudes often involved, as a first step, raising awareness of parents and teachers about the experience of growing up in poverty and building empathy.

> *We realized that we have a huge group of people, not only in Hungary but all over Europe, who are very, very disadvantaged in many, many ways. Disadvantaged in housing, disadvantaged economically because their education level is low. A lot of them study in segregated schools. Many of them do not attend kindergarten because of their living conditions. I think the program helped teachers to understand poverty. I remember when we created a film about children walking to school and being attacked by dogs on the way and not having breakfast. I think this really gave the teachers a deeper understanding of where these children were coming from. That school after two years in the program started to offer adult education programs for parents. They wanted to learn how to read and write because they had never been successful at school. That was a really deep experience for everyone.*
>
> *(Éva Deák, Partners Hungary Foundation)*

Step by Step programs helped teachers improve their communication with parents of children experiencing exclusion.

> *We organized sessions for Roma parents and teachers together. We also worked with teachers in small group workshops to increase their communication skills both with Roma parents and parents of children with special needs.*
>
> *(Carmen Lica, Centrul Step by Step Romania)*

Open Society sought a more structured approach to addressing teacher and parent biases and to building children's capacity to thrive in diverse contexts. In the early 2000s the Fund for an Open Society in Serbia funded development of the "Neither Black nor White" program, and Open Society funded development of another, "H.E.A.R.T". Zorica Trikić describes what happened next:

> *[H.E.A.R.T.] was a good curriculum but for ex-communist and ex-socialist countries, it seems that it didn't work very well. Then we merged Neither Black nor White with H.E.A.R.T and began this diversity training (Embracing Diversity) that we are now using in ISSA.*
>
> (Zorica Trikić, senior program manager, ISSA)

Embracing Diversity, as it is now known at ISSA, engages adults who work with children, as well as parents and community members, in activities and experiences that support personal transformation through awareness raising about biases and stereotypes, followed by strategies to use to respond and relate differently to one another. The program offers trainings for teachers and a set of activities to use with children to build their awareness and capacities. A linked set of modules supports teachers working with children who come into the classroom speaking a different language at home. The materials became the starting point for Step by Step initiatives focused on the inclusion of children from groups facing exclusion, and they have been used to train police, social workers, and other professionals (Trikić et al. 2017).

> *One of the main initiatives introduced six or ten years ago was Education for Social Justice [later renamed "Embracing Diversity"]. It was introduced in schools, preschools, everywhere where we had teachers working with Step by Step, but not only with them.*
>
> (Hana Zylfiu-Haziri, Kosovo Education Center)

Collectively, ISSA and its members continue to provide a broad set of resources and support to advance inclusion. The next sections explore in more depth how Step by Step approached work with two groups of children: Roma, and those with disabilities.

Reaching Out to Roma Children and Families

Countries with large Roma populations immediately introduced Step by Step in Roma communities during the first year of the program. In Hungary, the entire Step by Step program was built around Roma communities, and programs in Slovakia, the Czech Republic, Bulgaria, and Romania also immediately established pilot sites at preschools in or near Roma communities in the first year of the program.

> The most difficult work was in the eastern part of the country, which had the majority of segregated communities and poor people, the greatest poverty and illiteracy and a lot of animosity towards Roma. There was the toughest work. It was important that [Step by Step Director] Eva Končokova spoke their language. It was also important to support Roma teacher assistants, peer programs, health-related programs, and complex work in the community, not only educational work. There was food, there was everything in those kindergartens, so it was like a fresh breeze coming in.
>
> (Alena Panikova, former executive director, Open Society Foundation—Bratislava)

In line with the experience of Head Start, which focuses on families living in poverty, programs were intentionally comprehensive. Many functioned in multiple languages, involving parents and hiring teacher assistants to ensure programs could embrace Roma culture and language in the everyday life of the classroom. Parent rooms in the preschools became gathering places for parents. In communities that lacked easy access to water, preschools offered showers and made washing machines available. Children were offered health and dental care onsite. Preschools provided families with linkages to relevant benefits and services and in some cases they offered parents literacy programs. Families were visited at home.

> We're serving families who live month-to-month [in the Czech Republic]. We encourage mothers to come to the center while fathers look for jobs or get additional training. We try to create links between people, which can sometimes accomplish more than the program itself.
>
> (Sulavek 1995, 5)

Macedonia, Serbia, Kosovo, Ukraine, Latvia, Croatia, Bosnia, and Slovenia launched Roma initiatives several years after they started implementing Step by Step.

In Serbia, as a result of pressure from President Milošević government on Fund for an Open Society—Serbia, the initial Step by Step pilot preschools distanced themselves from Open Society. In response, the national foundation in Serbia launched programs and built and furnished new kindergartens inside Roma settlements and in camps and communities hosting Serbian refugees fleeing the war in Croatia.

> *In Serbia, the Soros Foundation was always very political, and they had opinions about everything. They were labelled as traitors who wanted to destroy our system and things like that, so it was difficult to enter schools and kindergartens. But we got the opportunity to work in Roma settlements. We understood that sometimes you cannot fight the system, but you have to find a way to play along with it. We had preschool teachers and pediatricians. These kindergartens were facilitated and led by Roma people, very influential people from the neighborhood. We were sometimes accused of some kind of segregation of Roma children. I'm not 100 percent sure. First, because our work was always implemented in cooperation with the official system, with healthcare, with social protection and with education. I compare it with conflict resolution. When you have two sides which cannot communicate, you first do separate work with each side, then bring them together. This is what we were doing. These kindergartens in Roma settlements had a place to wash and iron your stuff. It was a meeting place for mothers. They could have a haircut and learn to read and write. There was a place where fathers could gather and talk about their kids. We had teachers, but also Roma assistants. It was really empowering the whole community.*
>
> *(Zorica Trikić, senior program manager, ISSA)*

Step by Step had a significant impact on the results of Roma children in primary school in both Serbia and Macedonia.

> Data from three years of Step by Step (1997–2000) showed positive outcomes. 100 percent of children who attended Step by Step were proficient in Serbian; only 33 percent of those who didn't attend preschool knew Serbian. During the school year 100 percent attended on a regular basis, versus 47 percent of those who did not [attend preschool]. 100 percent successfully completed first grade, versus 40 percent of those who did not.
>
> (Stojanovic 2000, 22)

> *Our research showed that Roma children who visited kindergartens even for one year had the same results as other children in the country. Before that we had also done some comparative research that showed that children who didn't visit kindergarten had much lower results, and that was just because they couldn't speak the language.*
>
> *(Suzana Kirandžiska, Foundation for Educational and Cultural Initiatives, Step by Step, North Macedonia)*

In Bosnia, where there were few preschools, Step by Step implemented *Getting Ready for School* for parents of young children (Roma and majority population) who would attend the primary school the following year. The program provided weekly workshops for parents and children and loaned toys to families. Anti-bias training was provided to all the teachers and parents involved in the program. It helped establish trust between Roma and majority parents.

> We've been exchanging experiences with other parents. That is important because all those "problem" situations are not problems anymore. We all have similar concerns.
>
> Participating parent
(Center for Educational Initiatives 2008, 35)

When Roma children who participated in the program started first grade the following year, they were welcomed by teachers who knew them from *Getting Ready for School* and they had much less trouble adapting.

Fighting Exclusion through Demonstration Programs, Litigation, and Monitoring Reports

Attempts to dismantle the segregated education of Roma children inspired Open Society to implement creative demonstration projects, including various iterations of Step by Step. One of these was the Roma Special Schools Initiative, which was implemented in Bulgaria, the Czech Republic, Hungary, and Slovakia between 1999 and 2002. It challenged the inordinate number of Roma children assigned to remedial classrooms or special schools for the cognitively impaired. The project placed Roma teacher assistants, who became an important bridge to the Roma community, in special school classrooms and provided educators with intensive teacher training on anti-bias education, child-centered practices, and second language learning.

> *The people who wanted to help us were the teachers in these schools who knew these kids did not belong there but didn't know how to teach them. We wanted to show them that these kids can pass the test for regular first grade or third grade and be integrated at that point into schools.*
>
> (Liz Lorant, former director, Children & Youth Programs, OSF)

After three years, 62 percent of the children had reached grade-level expectations. The results were presented to ministries of education as a challenge to change the status quo of education of Roma children, and they were also used by Open Society as evidence in the litigation of the case *D.H. and Others* in the European

Court of Human Rights, which (following an appeals process) successfully challenged the over-representation of Roma in special schools.

> It's the most important equality case in the European Court of Human Rights. The difficulty has been the implementation. Litigation by itself could not achieve the result that was intended. It had to be accompanied by community activity.
> (Ayreh Neier, president emeritus, Open Society Foundations)

The reintegration of children from special into mainstream schools also proved challenging in many cases.

> Although we prepared that school with the Step by Step program, they were not able to keep the children there. The social gap was much too big. We didn't have the capacity to work with the majority parents there. I think that should have been included in the program, especially knowing how great prejudice in Hungary is.
> (Éva Deák, Partners Hungary Foundation)

A report prepared by the Belgian presidency of the Council of Europe for the Fourth European Roma Platform meeting (2011), which was published around the same time as the *D.H.* decision, underlines both moral and economic imperatives to invest urgently in Roma children.

> There is an urgent need to break the vicious circle of inter-generational transmission of severe social exclusion and poverty, but the current climate makes even more challenging to improve outcomes for all young children in a systemic, integrated way. The situation is a serious blot on Europe's human rights record. In addition, as outlined above, the social and economic implications are extremely negative for the EU as a whole and, in particular, for countries with large Roma minorities. There is a need to act more urgently for Roma children, as childhood is short and the window of opportunity closes quickly.
> (UNICEF and European Social Observatory 2011, 8)

To consolidate evidence to advocate for young Roma children and their families, Open Society partnered with UNICEF and the Roma Education Fund between 2009 and 2020 to produce a series of reports[1], the *Roma Early Childhood Inclusion Reports (RECI)*. They build a detailed picture of early childhood policies and regulatory frameworks that govern early childhood services and frame recommendations in the context of broader evidence-based research and current European policy directions. They describe the barriers Roma face in accessing high-quality programs and highlight successful policies and practices. Governments and Roma communities provided participatory input and feedback throughout the research in each country and reports were launched in each country and at the European Union. The reports had impact, but the immediate results were less than hoped for.

> We had lectures, we had policy briefs, we had roundtable discussions, we had the voices of Roma children, we had communication campaigns, all very, very intensive. I think all the efforts added up to make a tremendous contribution. There weren't any reports like this before. We created a great deal of buzz and advocacy out of them. Even so all the reports and all the advocacy did not fall on fertile ground ... for the ground to be fertile, I think requires a much bigger effort beyond the limits of early childhood development. I think the number one priority for Roma children's inclusion is poverty reduction, poverty alleviation.
> (Deepa Grover, former UNICEF regional advisor for Europe and Central Asia)

Litigation and monitoring reports have not been enough on their own to bring about lasting changes. The next step involved establishing national and regional networks of professionals dedicated to advancing the rights of young Roma children and their families.

Fighting Exclusion through Networking: The Roma Early Years Networks (REYN)

To promote community-led advocacy, Open Society began to offer small grants to networks of early childhood professionals across the region with the dual aim of stimulating and supporting advocacy for young Roma children and, equally importantly, to encourage more Roma and Traveller people to join and become leaders in the early childhood workforce. Modeled on similar networks in the UK, eleven Roma Early Years national networks were established from 2012 onward. Half are hosted by Step by Step early childhood NGOs, and the others by Roma NGOs. The networks give visibility to professionals and paraprofessionals from all sectors (education, health, social protection) who work with Roma children and families.

> We now have 600 members. This is because people working with Roma children feel left behind. They feel their work is not valued. I think during COVID, connections and being connected is so meaningful.
> (Éva Deák, Partners Hungary Foundation)

> *In Slovenia it definitely brought Roma early childhood into focus. Connecting professionals, Roma professionals and paraprofessionals within the country is something that was done for the first time. You know that you are not alone. Back when I was a preschool teacher this helped me.*
>
> *(Aljoša Rudaš, program manager, ISSA)*

The REYN networks foster professionalism, activism, and Roma and Traveller leadership.

> *Many things are being done for the Roma-Ashkali-Egyptian communities without them, because people misuse their positions. Kosovo Roma Ashkali Egyptian Early Years Network (KRAEEYN) is the only organization that is specifically concentrating on early education of these communities. They work on policies that bring Roma activists closer to government policymakers.*
>
> *(Driton Berisha, Kosovo)*

> *In Slovakia we have almost 600 members. The most important thing is that we establish a platform where everyone working with Romani children and their parents can cooperate. It gives us a chance to share experiences and promote good practices. Professional development activities, study visits and connections with the other national REYN and REYN international are crucial. Without that our work wouldn't be so successful.*
>
> *(Miroslav Sklenka, Wide Open School Foundation, Slovakia)*

International REYN, which is based at ISSA, is keen to scale up advocacy.

> *In many countries members of national REYNs are working with ministries, not just on an international-national but at cross-country level. It is an enormous privilege to be sitting here and I won't give up on REYN. That something I can say as long as I'm the person in charge, because I still think that in the European context there is no other organization fighting for the youngest Roma community members. Slowly we are getting there.*
>
> *(Aljoša Rudaš, program manager, ISSA)*

Investing in Roma People

Interviewees noted the importance of investing in individuals, starting with children.

> *Investing in people is what I think is really important. We have to tell the teachers, 'Being equal sometimes is not enough. We count on your deeper dedication.'*

> Sometimes you have a group of children who need a little bit more of your attention in order for this group to catch up with the rest of the generation and be able to go on.
> (Driton Berisha, Kosovo)

And women:

> From the beginning we tried to raise Roma's self-esteem and identity. We could finally see Roma self-representing themselves. I'm happy now that speaking about Roma and education and equality is something normal. We have Roma women now. Many young people who lead NGOs and represent institutions. I'm really glad that nowadays you can see many Roma men and women who work not just in Roma education, but for all children. I think this is the legacy.
> (Alena Panikova, former executive director, Open Society Foundation—Bratislava)

> We have one Roma colleague who was one of the mothers providing activities in her child's kindergarten group. She was so talented, she became an intercultural mediator, because we trained her and now she works for our foundation and is a coordinator of the Roma mediators all around the country. Because of her, more than sixty women from her village started to go for the general certificate of secondary education.
> (Éva Deák, Partners Hungary Foundation)

> We were supporting an amazing group of Roma women leaders [in Serbia]. They are working in kindergartens and are part of the system.
> (Zorica Trikić, senior program manager, ISSA)

Aljoša Rudaš commented on his progression from preschool teacher in Slovenia to program manager leading REYN at ISSA:

> For me personally, what really made the change was the scholarship I received from Open Society to attend the master's degree course in Israel on child development. That changed my life. It is why I'm sitting here. It changed my perspective, my orientation, and views on diversity. I learned about this opportunity through REYN.
> (Aljoša Rudaš, program manager, ISSA)

Supporting Roma leadership is vital, because though there is some progress, there is still so much to do.

> Poverty is everywhere in Roma communities and the situation of those children is even worse than it used to be. What is good is that preschool education is now mandatory for all children and this will help Roma. Without any preparation

for primary school they usually end up in special schools without any chance to succeed. I don't see any significant change in the mutual tolerance between Roma and non-Roma. Although we have the education act that prohibits discrimination and segregation, it still exists almost everywhere. It is systemic and often starts in preschool. Firstly, stereotypes and prejudices that non-Roma parents don't want their children to be with Roma children in classes. Secondly, there are villages where only Roma live, or where only Roma have small children and the rest of the inhabitants are elderly. There is also a higher level of prejudice among educators, pedagogues and teachers. Usually, when we start projects, we have to start with education for social justice.

(Miroslav Sklenka, Wide Open School Foundation, Slovakia)

If you were to compare 2002 and 2021, there is a huge difference. In 2002, if a Roma girl went to high school, there would be questions. The numbers are growing and we are getting well-educated individuals and groups of intellectuals. The least progress is in early childhood development, because Kosovo has not made it compulsory.

(Driton Berisha, Kosovo)

Step by Step faced similar challenges when it began to introduce the inclusion of children with disabilities.

Reaching Out to Children with Disabilities and Their Families

Pam Coughlin, Phyllis Magrab, and many of the American trainers were pioneers in inclusion of children with disabilities in the United States. During trainings in the United States, experts from the region observed and spent time in inclusive preschools, some of them for the first time. In the first few years, Step by Step programs focused on introducing child-centered, developmentally appropriate practices and the involvement of families in classrooms in preschools and then primary schools. The program held off recruiting children who required curricular accommodations and modifications until programs had experience individualizing instruction and working closely with parents.

> *I think the decision at that time by Open Society was a good one. It made a very calculated decision to work on general early childhood programs and not to include children with disabilities initially. What we know about children with disabilities is that developmentally appropriate practices are necessary, but not sufficient. In those settings, there were most likely children with disabilities that were unidentified,*

but children who were in special schools in the region were not initially included in the Step by Step program. You had to shore up and have the base of a good, developmentally appropriate program in order for children with disabilities to be integrated successfully.

(Deborah A. Ziegler, US Step by Step expert team)

In 1997, Open Society supported development of an additional methodology manual and accompanying week-long teacher training to support full inclusion and welcome children with disabilities into Step by Step classrooms that now had several years of experience working with developmentally appropriate practices and with parents. Training and mentoring by US trainers was offered to interested Step by Step programs. The initiative raised awareness and interest in inclusion amongst both educators and parents.

> Children can't be neglected or discriminated against by excluding them from school or by sending them to a special school because they have a physical disorder or learning difficulties. One [Latvian] educator comments, "The social meaning of inclusion is that all children obtain an education, which helps them create a relationship with the surrounding society and prepares them for life."
>
> (Open Society Institute 2008, 90)

There was a high interest in serving children with disabilities in inclusive early childhood programs. I remember, particularly in Russia, as word spread in communities, parents were knocking on the door and asking, "Will you take my child with a disability into this preschool program?" The programs welcomed these families.

(Deborah A. Ziegler, US Step by Step expert team)

It turned out to be as challenging as the initial launch of Step by Step.

> "We strongly believe that inclusive school curriculum can be adapted to the needs of all children by setting the proper individual aims," comments one educator after completing a Step by Step training. "Much depends on teachers' will to change their traditional work, on the positive attitude of society and on the initiative of parents—so what we need is teamwork."
>
> (Open Society Institute 2008, 89–90)

In Ukraine, Step by Step negotiated a formal arrangement with the ministry of education to pilot inclusion in the mainstream education system, as part of a seven-year national experiment.

The legislation was a barrier. We started work with the ministry and contacted and built relationships with the Institute of Special Pedagogy. It was then called the Institute of Defectology in the Academy of Pedagogical Science. We understood that without scientific support we could not make changes. We presented our idea of inclusion, the ministry supports us and we decided to do it together. We called it an experiment, because new ideas or changes could be incorporated under the format of experimental work. We worked a lot with the Institute of Special Pedagogy to try to change their minds and see inclusion differently. It was a long, long, long story! Parent organizations were very strong advocates. And the last president, Poroshenko, and especially his wife, Maryna Poroshenko, did a lot to support inclusive education. She promoted inclusive resource centers and a lot of legislative documents.

(Natalia Sofiy, Borys Grinchenko Kyiv University, Ukraine)

Open Society partnered with the Council for Exceptional Children (CEC) in the United States to develop more advanced training modules and resources to offer to countries and to support a professional learning community within ISSA.

Introducing inclusion into rigid systems of education was a huge feat. By 2004, on the tenth anniversary of Step by Step, when Dina Aidzhanova, executive director of the Community Foundation Step by Step, was interviewed for the ISSA journal, Kazakhstan had integrated seventy children with disabilities into mainstream programs, while Kyrgystan had integrated another forty.

> Several years ago, these children were isolated and they had no model for how to develop themselves because they were in special schools where all of the children were disabled. Our idea was to help these children and to make the first efforts in this direction. It is very painful, and our national tragedy is not to pay attention to these children. It's a small start, but a heroic step, almost a revolution.
>
> (Knox 2004, 14)

In Tajikistan, Step by Step inspired Open Society to support a range of organizations and initiatives working with children with disabilities. This gave visibility to children who had never been seen even in situations where full inclusion was not yet possible.

The idea of inclusive education became part of early childhood education. I'm proud of this. We didn't know that many of these children existed. All of a sudden they appeared, and became visible. They started playing with other children who had never met a child with special needs. This created a whole range of supporting associations for parents of children with disabilities, who became pioneers in moving their children into early education. They started an early intervention program, which created changes and reforms that are still ongoing in the ministry of health.

(Zuhra Halimova, former executive director (Tajikistan) and advisory board member, OSF)

Over several decades, Step by Step introduced inclusion in preschools and schools across the region with deeper work developing in Ukraine, Serbia, Latvia, Russia, Belarus, Kazakhstan, Kyrgyzstan, Mongolia, Moldova, and Azerbaijan.

Changing Attitudes toward Children with Disabilities and Roma

Including children with disabilities into preschools and primary schools opened up opportunities for children and introduced, at least in some measure, examples of a different approach to education and greater empathy for children with disabilities. It offered hope.

> *Children with special needs had been included in our classrooms, but teachers had problems and with the Step by Step approach everything started to be easier. I'm really proud that we managed to involve children with special needs in our classrooms in a more active and participatory way, and parents were so happy with this inclusion. It was very impressive!*
>
> *(Tatjana Vonta, co-author, and former director, Step by Step Slovenia)*

"Before I might have turned my back on a child with special needs," comments one Preschool Education College student from Mongolia. "Now I will open my heart."

(Open Society Institute 2008, 95)

> *Motivation for at least some of the practitioners was when they saw children with disabilities achieving developmental milestones that they never thought would be possible. It was also so motivating that oftentimes children without disabilities did not see children with disabilities as being different.*
>
> *(Deborah A. Ziegler, US Step by Step expert team)*

Some barriers were hard to overcome. Deborah Ziegler, the expert from the Council on Exceptional Children who led the initiative, reflected in our interview on several persistent challenges. First, there was resistance from special educators working in special schools to the idea of moving children into mainstream settings, because they believed their jobs were at stake if special schools were closed. Open Society funded several projects aimed at redeploying special educators within mainstream schools and reorganizing the special schools as hubs of expertise promoting inclusion. Open Society also commissioned case studies in five countries aimed at distilling experiences of countries as they sought to adapt the legal frameworks, governance, and financing needed for inclusive education (Evans 2015). Secondly, many children with disabilities were included in mainstream classrooms, but in many cases their individualized plans remained oriented around modified expectations.

It came down to a question of how far attitudes and expectations had really changed.

> *If I were to step back, perhaps we might have spent a little bit more time on those attitudes and beliefs from a broader perspective, not so much within the early childhood system and special education system, but in the broader society. The right to an education is a human right. I think in many societies, we still haven't acknowledged that to the degree that we need to. The administrators and teachers had high expectations, but because some did not have that vision, they couldn't see that children with disabilities, if given appropriate services, could live independently, have jobs, be self-sufficient and be contributing members of society.*
> *(Deborah A. Ziegler, US Step by Step expert team)*

These experiences raise questions about whether the rights of people with disabilities are less vigorously defended within the rights community.

> *I know I am probably biased in saying this, but I think it is true that individuals with disabilities continue to be the most disenfranchised population in our society. It is this quiet revolution. Some other populations of individuals have not been so quiet. I think the advocacy certainly was there, but not to the degree that it was for other populations. The art of advocacy was foreign to many organizations and individuals in Eastern Europe.*
> *(Deborah A. Ziegler, US Step by Step expert team)*

One interviewee, while expressing gratitude for the investment Open Society made toward promoting the inclusion of children with disabilities in kindergartens and schools, also questioned whether Open Society's leadership consistently advocated as strongly for disability rights as it did for the rights of other groups experiencing marginalization.

> *I read a piece that quoted the president of Open Society. He described Mr. Soros's vision of political philanthropy and equity for all. He listed groups of individuals who have been marginalized—disenfranchised over the decades. It was your typical list, but people with disabilities were not on the list. It raised a red flag for me. It's my vision and my value and I know it is Open Society's value, too, and was probably inadvertently left off the list, but that is why I believe it is a quiet revolution. People with disabilities continue to be the most disenfranchised group out there.*
>
> *(Deborah A. Ziegler, US Step by Step expert team)*

This phenomenon is consistent with other philanthropic organizations advocating for equity for all. Yet, despite this, Open Society has been one of the largest contributors of funding to disability rights initiatives globally.

There are limits to what early childhood education can accomplish on its own—and to the efforts of a single foundation—to counteract the impacts of social exclusion and discrimination on young children and their families. It is painfully obvious that full inclusion of Roma and children with disabilities, two populations that were in great focus within the Step by Step program, is moving too slowly. Meaningful advances have been made, especially in countries where a wide range of partners—governments, World Bank, UNICEF, international funders, the European Union—have come together around these issues. Significantly more Roma children and children with disabilities and other special educational needs are being included in early childhood education than when Step by Step was launched in 1994. But profound gaps remain in early education and these gaps only get bigger as children move through primary education and transition to secondary school. Successful inclusion requires broader actions—litigation, anti-bias education, community mobilization, hard-nosed political will—to overcome legislative and institutional barriers.

Several interviewees, while discussing the challenge of changing attitudes toward Roma, referred to the ongoing challenge in the United States to address racial justice, a testament to the idea that equity and social inclusion are a continuing struggle. It is not something that is accomplished through one program.

> *I have become very disillusioned not with the Roma work, but because of having been stuck here in the States for the last eighteen months with all of the fear around critical race theory going on. How do you get to a point where people see Roma as having value in society?*
>
> *(Dawn Tankersley, US Step by Step expert team)*

> *Social and racial justice in the US has been a continuous issue. The country is finally beginning to address these issues but there is a long way to go. There is a lot of focus on reckoning with that history, on trying to understand everyone's personal journey.*
>
> *(Joan Lombardi, Georgetown University and Stanford University)*

Open Society's focus on Roma and children with disabilities continued throughout the decades of the Step by Step program and beyond, through broader inclusive programming supported by the Early Childhood Program team at Open Society Foundations, jointly with the Education Support Program and the Human Rights Program. Later, the Early Childhood Program also launched an initiative focusing on young refugees and migrants and their families in Europe, the Middle East and North Africa, Asia, and Africa. These investments in people, innovative initiatives, organizations, and networks have helped establish a foundation of expertise and practice that can be built upon as the social justice movement continues to push forwards.

> I think the development of a child with disabilities is the same as the development of a democracy: you must continue to believe, no matter what, and strive every single day to make that reality better.
>
> Mykola Swarnyk, parent, Ukraine
> (Swarnyk 2002, 10)

6

"Don't Think That It Won't Happen": Young Children and Their Families in Times of War

Figure 6.1 Children on the playground of the "Nightingale" Preschool, which uses the Step by Step methodology, working on a paper mâché globe (Sarajevo, 1998).
@Center for Educational Initiatives Step by Step (Bosnia)

A Devastating Conflict That Nobody Expected

In the 1980s ethnic communities seemed to live together peacefully in the Yugoslav Federation. Sarajevo, a multicultural town with mosques, Catholic and Orthodox churches in the same main street, was a symbol of a diverse and tolerant society. This was also how the people from the region experienced it:

> *There were mostly mixed marriages especially in Bosnia. Before the war, I didn't know who is Serb, who is Croat, who is Bosniac. They were all Bosnians for us.*
> *(Suzana Kirandžiska, Foundation for Educational and Cultural Initiatives, Step by Step, North Macedonia)*

But in 1991 a terrible, decade-long conflict started in the Balkans that led to the dissolution of Yugoslavia. It brought with it death, displacement, ethnic conflict, and the rise of nationalist leaders. Slovenia and Croatia declared independence in 1991, and while Slovenia's withdrawal from the Yugoslav Federation was achieved after a ten-day war, in Croatia, which had a sizable Serbian minority population, heavy fighting broke out leading to an extended conflict that resulted in the shelling of the ancient city of Dubrovnik and the siege and destruction of Vukovar (United Nations 2017).

In 1992, the deadliest of all the conflicts in the disintegrating Yugoslav Federation began in Bosnia and Herzegovina. In April 1992, Sarajevo was besieged and in November 1993 the Old Bridge of Mostar, built in the sixteenth century, was destroyed (Kontić and Vučo 2021, 190–1). During the three years of war in Bosnia and Herzegovina around 100,000 people were killed and 2 million people, including many children—more than half the population—were displaced. Thousands of women were raped. In September 1995, following NATO airstrikes on Bosnian Serb positions, the siege of Sarajevo ended, and that same year in November, the United States brokered the Dayton peace agreement ending the war in Bosnia (Kontić and Vučo 2021, 192). However, in 1998, armed conflict between Serbia and Kosovo broke out, leading again to death and displacement. In June 1999, the UN Security Council adopted Resolution 1244 establishing Kosovo as an UN-administered territory, and the war ended with the Kumanovo treaty. As the decade of war ended, millions were living in refugee camps or had emigrated to restart their lives in other countries, and the former Yugoslavia is now divided into seven different countries largely on the basis of ethnic groups (Kontić and Vučo 2021; United Nations 2017).

What Yugoslavia experienced was described at the time as the most devastating conflict in Europe since the Second World War. In Western Europe it was hard to understand how this was possible. Even people from Yugoslavia did not understand what happened:

> *Even we people who lived in ex-Yugoslavia, we didn't understand what was going on and why it's going on like that, so cruel. There are so many things which today we still do not understand.*
> *(Tatjana Vonta, co-author and former director, Step by Step Slovenia)*

In their book *Blood and Honey: Encounters on the Borders of the Balkan*, two Dutch journalists go in search of the meaning of the new borders in the Balkans. They talk with people about the past and what the break-up of the country meant to them. One of them is Jesenko Galijašević, a historian. He puts it as follows:

> Don't think that it won't happen, that there can't be war. The world in which you live, which you take for granted, can be over in one fell swoop. Nobody believed it, nor did we, but it happened anyway.
>
> (Van der Linde and Segers 2021, 207)

We noted this quote in January 2022, though at the time we did not realize how prophetic it was. Less than two months later war expanded across Ukraine, another country where Step by Step was implemented, forcing us to rewrite this chapter. In the summer of 2022, we interviewed members of the ISSA network about their work with children and families who are victims of the war in Ukraine. Again, people did not understand what was happening.

> *I think, the beginning of the war was for everyone, an absolute shock. We didn't believe what happened.*
>
> (Teresa Ogrodzińska, Comenius Foundation for Child Development, Poland)

> *The first day we were in shock, I think the majority of people tried on the second day, on the 25th to leave from the central and from the eastern part of Ukraine to the West. Some of them stayed in western Ukraine in the Transcarpathia region. Many people went further to other countries to Poland, to Hungary, whatever. Our first reaction and the first steps on the third day was to find out where our trainers were, whether they were alive and what happened to them.*
>
> (Natalia Sofiy, Borys Grinchenko Kyiv University, Ukraine)

But let us go back to the years after the conflicts in the Balkans. Everybody who has visited an ISSA meeting or conference has noticed the so-called "Yugoslavian table." Even during those devastating wars, ISSA members from countries of the former Yugoslavia sat at the same table and spoke Serbo-Croat with one another. The atmosphere was, and continues always to be, very warm and open. Radmila Rangelov-Jusović from the Centre for Educational Initiatives Step by Step in Bosnia and Herzegovina had an unforgettable voice, and at meetings she drew colleagues from the region together to sing traditional songs that they all knew. For people from outside of Yugoslavia, it was fascinating to witness these strong human connections, which transcend the war.

Rangelov-Jusović was born and grew up in a multi-ethnic and multi-religious community typical of Bosnia before the conflict. Her father was Bulgarian, her mother Serbian, and her husband Muslim. During the siege of Sarajevo, a bomb killed her father, and her mother was seriously wounded and died a couple of years later. After the war, when many Bosnians left the country, she chose to stay and help to rebuild. Rangelov-Jusović, known to her colleagues as Rada, died in February 2021. The authors of this book were too late to interview her, but her colleagues from the region reflected in their interviews about the important role she played after the war in bringing people together in the country and rebuilding the education system across Bosnia and Herzegovina. She is a symbol of the important function that strong women can play in a reconciliation process through warm and open involvement in the care and education of young children.

> *I remember how the trainers from America were surprised and didn't understand what was going on when we, the ex-Yugo group, started to sing a Bosnian song at the first Step by Step international meeting in Budapest in late fall 1994. At the end of the song, we all started to cry. We were all wounded with everything that the war brought to people in ex-Yugoslavia and especially in Bosnia and Herzegovina.*
> (Tatjana Vonta, co-author and former director, Step by Step Slovenia)

These international connections experienced by Step by Step teams provided a way for professionals to stay connected with one another both during and after the war. It was more difficult to bring together families and educators from the many ethnic communities within each country. Yet many programs did. Step by Step was one of many initiatives supported by Open Society and the many other foundations involved in the difficult process of reconciliation and rebuilding in the region after the conflicts.

What War Does to Children, Parents, and Teachers

> *War is the most horrifying experience a human being can experience. The most unnatural state for a human being. The scale of the disaster in Bosnia and Herzegovina is known, especially to the people who lived here. All those wounds that were left on them. It destroys your personality, it destroys families, it destroys the society, it destroys the economy, it destroys the infrastructure, it destroys aspirations for the future. The result of war are millions of refugees, displaced persons, fear*

of the other and the different, mistrust, post-traumatic stress syndrome, disability, death.

> (Hašima Ćurak, advisor, Ministry of Education and Science, Bosnia and Herzegovina)

In a book chapter written in 2007, Rangelov-Jusović described the effects of armed conflicts on children, families, and communities:

> There was no possibility of movement or travel. People remained hidden in their houses or in shelters. Since the war the country remains covered with land mines. Some areas of the country remain "ethnically clean" … There are limited or no jobs in the devastated environment to return to. Children lived under constant threat of violent death either of themselves or of family members. Thousands of children were confined in basements or other enclosures. If not directly injured or killed, children became witnesses to the killing or rape of family members. Thousands became orphans, living in deep poverty.
>
> (Rangelov-Jusović 2007, 34–5)

To people who never experienced war, descriptions like these are harrowing. The Open Society Fund Bosnia and Herzegovina helped citizens in these terrible periods (Kontić and Vučo 2021, 210–19). During the siege of Sarajevo when there was no electricity and a lack of drinking water, Open Society invested in rebuilding infrastructure.

> The foundation worked to maintain some vestige of normality for people living there—repairing and extending the gas lines, supplying coal, firewood, and charcoal, establishing access to clean water, restoring the bakery, providing seeds for planting and of course, newsprint because access to information assumed an urgency almost as fundamental as food or water. Until the foundation installed a satellite phone system, there was no way the civilian population could have contact with the outside world.
>
> (Soros and Soros 2021, 15)

Over the years Step by Step was active in a number of countries that experienced war, not only those that were once a part of Yugoslavia. Since the collapse of the Soviet Union, there have been armed conflicts in Tajikistan, Kyrgyzstan, Albania, Georgia, Moldova, and in territories contested by Armenia and Azerbaijan. In 2014, Russia annexed the Crimean peninsula, starting a war that escalated in February 2022 with a Russian assault across the whole of Ukraine. Many kindergartens and schools have been bombed, and electricity, heat, and water infrastructure is damaged or destroyed.

Parents and children are shocked, scared. The first need was to find a tool for parents of young children who have to go to the shelters because there were many air attacks, several times per day. People were soon fed up going to the shelters and just ignored the alarm signal which is dangerous. There was no need for complicated activities for parents and children but some simple, breathing exercises that can help them calm down physically and become quieter.
(Natalia Sofiy, Borys Grinchenko Kyiv University, Ukraine)

Rebuilding Infrastructure

In many countries involved in the conflicts in former Yugoslavia early education infrastructure was destroyed. The Open Society Foundation invested in rebuilding kindergartens in Bosnia and Herzegovina and Kosovo. Open Society also invested in infrastructure for refugee children living in settlements in Serbia and provided bilingual classrooms for refugee children and families in Slovenia. This investment in buildings and didactic materials was much appreciated by the teachers and country directors.

The Step by Step program offered me a position in September 1999 as a coordinator. I had to start the next day. I remember when I entered the office, the building was completely empty. There were no chairs to sit on, only some destroyed tables. I started first to buy furniture and then slowly we started to get in contact with kindergartens that were still not yet operating. Many of them were destroyed and were not functional.
(Hana Zylfiu-Haziri, Kosovo Education Center)

Yet in some countries there were negative reactions to the support provided by the Open Society Foundation. Political pressure in Croatia against the national foundation was intense.

Some kindergartens that were equipped with furniture and toys from Open Society had to hide these objects because they were afraid of the ministry of education. I remember a woman from the ministry who terrorised me even when I was director of Step by Step. The ministry was against Soros, not the Step by Step pedagogy. She terrorized kindergartens. She called directors, and said, "You cannot cooperate with Step by Step. You cannot go to their trainings. Otherwise, you will be sanctioned." It was intimidation.
(Nives Milinović, former director, Open Academy Step by Step, Croatia, and former board president, ISSA)

In Serbia the Step by Step program's approach was criticized:

The ministry blamed the Step by Step team for making Serbian kids too soft!
(Zorica Trikić, senior program manager, ISSA)

The Lingering After-Effects of War

The stoking of nationalist sentiments was a major problem in all the post-war countries. The pioneers of the Step by Step program were confronted with the sobering reality of nationalism put into practice. Nives Milinović from Croatia described the situation in a school in a territory that was occupied during the war.

Can you imagine the situation? The town of Ilok, close to Serbian border surrendered and all the Croats were forced to take their bags and leave the town. The school remained open and some teachers continued to teach, receiving salaries from the Croatian ministry of education. After the war, after the peaceful integration, Croats came back to work in the same school with colleagues who were teaching and who had received salaries during the war while they had been refugees.
(Nives Milinović, former director, Open Academy Step by Step, Croatia, and former board president, ISSA)

The interviewees mention many other problems after the war: poverty increased in Serbia and there was a lack of teachers in Bosnia due to migration. Immediately after the war, nobody talked about the post-traumatic stress disorders that many children, parents, and teachers were experiencing. According to Hana Zylfiu from Kosovo, at the beginning of the Step by Step program many teachers were not psychologically ready to teach children and even today some teachers suffer from the psychological impacts of bad experiences during the war. Rangelov-Jusović articulated this:

[Teachers] may have been unable to carry out their duties during the war and may have lost self-confidence along with the trust of the community.
(Rangelov-Jusović 2007, 36)

Not only teachers but children too needed psychosocial support. Organizing creative activities and publishing children's books were two ways the program in Macedonia supported children to express their feelings.

> *Besides the children's creative centers that we've opened in Tetovo and Gostivar for the children from Kosovo, we've offered psychosocial support to the teachers for the schools that took care of the refugee children. Also, with the support of UNICEF, we published 10,000 copies of each of ten picture books. Then we distributed them to the schools in the refugee camps. The Soros Foundation had many other initiatives to respond to the refugee crisis, but these initiatives were related to the Step by Step program. The Soros Foundation also supported theatre performances for refugee children. Some mimes from Germany came to Macedonia and performed for the children.*
>
> *(Suzana Kirandžiska, Foundation for Educational and Cultural Initiatives, Step by Step, North Macedonia)*

The notion that parents also need psychosocial support came later. Parents were afraid to leave their children alone. Young children with traumatic war experiences did not feel safe in kindergartens without their parents. During a visit to a kindergarten in Kosovo right after the war one of the co-authors, Sarah Klaus, remembers the principal was joined by her five-year-old child, who refused to leave her even for one minute.

Step by Step organizations had learned from the experiences of the war in former Yugoslavia, and when the war started in Ukraine, psychosocial support was seen as a priority.

> *Our first priority was psychosocial support for parents who had experienced traumatic situations, through teaching stress management techniques. Secondly, how to communicate with children, how to explain to them what is going on because it was a shock for everybody. When children hear sirens all the time, and after seeing all those terrible things, they are asking questions and parents didn't know how to answer and how to talk to children. This psychological support was our priority.*
>
> *(Natalia Sofiy, Borys Grinchenko Kyiv University, Ukraine)*

Step by Step in Ukraine worked together with psychologists' associations to help children and parents process trauma. But the pressures on psychologists during a war are enormous.

> *In Ukraine, many psychologists and their associations became very active, and they published different recommendations through Facebook and various informational channels, but some of them also became very exhausted. I remember when we organized an international event, and I asked one of the very popular psychologists, who never gave up. But she did not want to come to the conference. She wanted to try to help, but she said, "Natalia, I can't, I just can't."*
>
> *(Natalia Sofiy, Borys Grinchenko Kyiv University, Ukraine)*

Bringing People Back Together

The testimonies about the first meetings in Bosnia that brought together early childhood teachers from the different ethnic groups that had been fighting with one another are very emotional. Rangelov-Jusović describes what she expected from teachers after the war. It was not only the introduction of a new child-centered and democratic pedagogy:

> Teachers need to be models for forgiveness; to transcend their own biases and to reflect a positive outlook for the children in their charge. Educators also needed support in issues such as conflict resolution, problem solving and respecting diversity.
> (Rangelov-Jusović 2007, 36)

To achieve this, a year after the war she and her colleagues tried to bring preschool teachers from different parts of the country and from warring factions together: "I have to admit we took a risk here" (Rangelov-Jusović 2007, 36). She convinced people from Republic of Srpska in Bosnia and Herzegovina to join the training in Bosnia. Rangelov-Jusović managed to build a non-political atmosphere in which all the participants could cooperate within the context of the Step by Step program.

Hašima Ćurak, who started to work at Step by Step just after the war, talked about her first experiences in Step by Step. The staff were full of energy and optimism and the whole floor was full of books.

> *There were didactic materials all around the office, but I was absolutely fascinated by the beautiful books. Somehow, the experience of that space in war-torn Sarajevo and the energy of the staff and the captivating personality of Rada absolutely fascinated me. I felt an incredible desire to participate in all that.*
> *(Hašima Ćurak, advisor, Ministry of Education and Science, Bosnia and Herzegovina)*

The first Step by Step training for colleagues from all over Bosnia and Herzegovina took place in Bihać, in the Sedra hotel in 1996. Hašima Ćurak explained during her interview how much she was looking forward to this first meeting, where teachers from the three ethnic groups from Bosnia would meet. Some were coming from Sarajevo, others from Konjic, Jablanica, Mostar, and Banja Luka, the most important town of the Republika Srpska. They all had to travel through warring territories and cross demarcation borders.

> *It was an incredible experience of fear for us. We haven't seen or passed through these territories in years. We heard about horrible things happening in those places*

> we crossed. The colleagues from Banja Luka came also with a terrible fear. That was the first step, it was Rada's merit to bring them all together despite the fear.
> (Hašima Ćurak, advisor, Ministry of Education and Science, Bosnia and Herzegovina)

And it worked: Hašima, who attended the first meeting, put it this way: "Only the best in us spoke." They all had the same feelings of mistrust toward politicians, who were responsible for the terrible effects of the war, and they were sobered by what nationalistic politics did to inhabitants of former Yugoslavia. Even now, so many years after the war, the interviewees still blame politicians. But Step by Step program meetings helped them start the necessary process of reconciliation.

> The Step by Step program really helped us to overcome the terrible experiences of the war. Even if we spoke about the political situation, we felt free to speak our thoughts, to share them and nobody was judging us. We all hated the governments that started this war and blamed them for the effects of the war.
> (Suzana Kirandžiska, Foundation for Educational and Cultural Initiatives, Step by Step, North Macedonia)

The atmosphere during the trainings was very positive. Thirty years later, some interviewees had tears in their eyes when they recalled the experience. Early childhood education, and more specifically care and love for young children, seems to bring people together.

After the Yugoslav War

It was not easy to organize trainings. Not only was there the crossing of military borders, there was sometimes no electricity. But the interviewees say that despite these problems the atmosphere was fantastic. The trainers were careful to avoid practices that could hurt participants. Hana Zylfiu's mother tongue language is Albanian, but her second language, as it was for all Yugoslavians, is Serbo-Croat. Because Serbo-Croat was the language the Serbian police had used in Kosovo for decades, trainers from Slovenia built trust with participants before using it during trainings.

During and after these wars the Step by Step program had to work in extremely difficult contexts. They were promoting democratic open societies in former socialist countries. The question of whether the Step by Step program is political or not is a contentious one. Rada Rangelov-Jusović (former director, Center for Educational Initiatives Step by Step) and Dženana Trbić (former education coordinator, Open Society Fund Bosnia and Herzegovina) debated this issue.

> *My opinion was that Step by Step was, and still is, very political. Rada would disagree. She said, "No, it's not political. It has nothing to do with politics. It has to do with common sense pedagogy, humanistic pedagogy, and I'm not going to be drawn into political talk at all." She would dismiss it. Step by Step somehow managed to introduce concepts which are still, to my mind, very political, if we think about politics as a certain set of values, of attitudes. But she managed to talk to people about it, to train the teachers, to advocate, without being perceived as political. That was the reason why she was not perceived as a threat at all.*
>
> (Dženana Trbić, former education program coordinator,
> Open Society Fund - Bosnia and Herzegovina)

Rada knew how to talk with people who had lived during the war. She knew how to advocate for democratic early childhood education, without making it seem political.

The Secret of Step by Step: Rebuilding Trust

The many interviews and books published about the region's wars after the fall of the Berlin wall and the collapse of the Soviet Union paint a frightening picture of how extreme nationalism destroyed friendships and family relations, and how people suffered and were traumatized by seeing their relatives murdered or raped by people who had once been neighbors (Nuhanović 2020; Snel 2022). This raises an important question. How did the Step by Step program succeed in rebuilding trust between teachers and parents from different backgrounds? In other words: why were the ISSA network and the Step by Step program so successful in this process of reconciliation?

Listening to the testimonies of the pioneers, it seems to be the result of a combination of factors. First, there is the program itself, described in Chapters 2 and 3, which was inspired by Head Start, a program based on social justice and respect for diversity. Secondly, Step by Step was incorporated into a broader Open Society project that was rebuilding infrastructure and providing teaching materials, books, and toys. Thirdly, early childhood education is a beautiful tool that brings together people who want the best for young children. We see the same engagement in the recent war in Ukraine: ISSA and its members are succeeding in setting up programs for refugee children and their families in countries impacted by the war, or hosting refugees. Finally, the people responsible for Step by Step are strongly motivated. They succeed in uniting people to support young children. They have been real pedagogical heroes. They had been welcomed by the American trainers in a very human way, and they pass on the same warmth to teachers they train. These teachers have the extraordinary ability to communicate as human beings even in the worst circumstances. Tatjana Vonta puts it this way:

> *Even people from the countries who were engaged in war communicated as human beings. It was this feeling that no matter how much the society around us is changing, we are still on the same road and wanted to achieve same goals in our profession. We were not only close as professionals, but we were also friends. Yes, I think that it was a unique atmosphere among us. It was really very, very unique.*
> *(Tatjana Vonta, co-author, and former director Step by Step Slovenia)*

Part Three

Extending and Sustaining Democratic Pedagogy through Civil Society Networks and Expansion to New Regions

7

The "Seed beneath the Snow": The Growth of Early Childhood NGOs and Networks

Figure 7.1 ISSA's Annual Conference 2017, Ghent, Belgium.
@International Step by Step Association

Strengthening Civil Society in the Early Childhood Ecosystem: A New Priority

Earlier chapters have set out the relationship of Step by Step programs with the ministry of education and academia. This chapter explores the role of Step by Step in building and strengthening the third sector of the early childhood ecosystem, civil society, in program countries as well as regionally across Europe and Eurasia.

Beginning in 1998, Open Society refocused education strategies on collaboration with ministries of education, policy initiatives, and time-bound systemic reform activities, de-emphasizing demonstration and pilot projects like Step by Step. Changing the core of the education system was prioritized over Step by Step's approach of introducing alternative methodologies and ideas from the ground up. A strategic decision was taken by Open Society to "spin-off" Step by Step from the Open Society national foundations in each country and to help each program team establish an NGO, a foundation, a network, or an association to carry the program forwards.

The momentum to spin-off programs at Open Society aligned with an overall reduction in the foundation's global budget in 2000. There was interest in avoiding the creation of dependencies, or situations where Open Society was the sole funder. Spin-offs were seen by many within Open Society as a way to encourage programs to diversify income. At the same time the Step by Step leadership team at Open Society believed the spin-off of Step by Step could facilitate the creation of much-needed independent professional networks to promote quality standards, influence policy, provide professional education, support ongoing research, and advocate for equal opportunities for all children. It seemed strategically unwise to turn over a quality-focused initiative fully to ministries of education amid political and economic uncertainties, unstable governments, and a high turnover of ministers. In reality, the decision to spin-off the program created a new plane of activity within the Step by Step program. From 1998/9 onward, Step by Step had two overarching goals: 1) introducing quality, inclusive, democratically oriented, child-centered early education and 2) building, strengthening, and sustaining the burgeoning early childhood civil society in the region.

Spinning Off the National Step by Step Programs

At first, most of the Step by Step program teams were not prepared to move out of the national foundations. To be fair, the teams' expertise was in early childhood, not in NGO management:

> *When they started they were very comfortable inside the Soros Foundation and then in 1998, 1999, they all had to become independent.*
> *(Liz Lorant, former director, Children & Youth Program, OSF)*

> *I think when the NGOs came in, it was a little bit anxiety-provoking for some of the countries because they weren't sure. They were used to getting money from Soros, and so that was stable for them. This was a whole new skill set for them to go out and be NGOs and have to do all of the kinds of business things that involves. My impression was that it worked pretty well.*
>
> *(Kirsten Hansen, US Step by Step expert team)*

Open Society organized intensive trainings and mentoring to support Step by Step country teams as they assessed options for establishing the program independently. Seminars were organized over a two-year period on topics such as facilitative leadership, strategic planning, board issues, financial management, governance, public relations, and proposal writing. Each country was required to develop a three-year strategic plan based on tapered financial support from Open Society. A mentor was sent to each country to support the planning process and plans were approved by the national foundations and Open Society leadership in New York. Over the next few years, Open Society also provided support to some of the NGOs to purchase an apartment or other suitable office space. This provided the NGOs with some stability and gave them a competitive advantage when applying for grants by keeping overheads low. In Romania, the national foundation put together extended technical and financial assistance to support a group of programs that were spinning off, like Step by Step.

> *The new management of the national foundation in Romania came in at the end of 1997, and it was like, "You have three months to put together the Step by Step NGO." The national foundation came up with a funding scheme for five years to help the NGOs develop their sustainability plans. They requested the NGOs come up with some matching funds to receive funds from the national foundation. As far as I remember, it started with Open Society giving 90 percent and the NGO had to come up with 10 percent of the budget in the first year. In the fifth year, Open Society provided 10 percent and the NGO had to come up with 90 percent. I lobbied the national foundation a whole year to become part of that collective process.*
>
> *(Carmen Lica, Centrul Step by Step Romania)*

Countries embarked on spinning-off at different times, based on when they started the program and based on local conditions.

> *It depended a lot on the leadership and the skills of the individuals within those countries, but it was a huge shift. It wasn't just our internal capacity, but it was the receptivity within the country's geography.*
>
> *(Phyllis Magrab, Georgetown University, former board chair,*
> *Early Childhood Program Advisory Board, OSF)*

Two national foundations spun off Step by Step in the early years of the program (Armenia and Slovakia) but the remainder coordinated spin-off to coincide with the fifth year of the program. Open Society tapered financial support continued for at least another three years, sometimes longer, as was the case in Romania. In a number of countries (Kosovo, Azerbaijan) the national foundation supported the establishment of a new entity with a broad education mission and included Step by Step in it. The national foundation and Step by Step teams considered the legal options in their country and debated and decided how to spin off. Most registered as NGOs, others as foundations (Ukraine, Macedonia), several established networks (Belarus, Bosnia, Croatia), and Slovenia created a center at the Research Institute.

> *When Step by Step had to become independent from the national foundation, we decided not to establish an NGO, but to house the program in the Educational Research Institute, which is a public institution. As a research institute we didn't need to ask the Ministry of Education to approve our working plan and all our trainings received accreditation. Of course, our salaries and all financial issues were regulated according to the state level.*
>
> *(Tatjana Vonta, co-author and former director, Step by Step Slovenia)*

The program in Tajikistan was an outlier and Step by Step remained inside the national foundation until the closing of the Early Childhood Program at the end of 2020. In several countries (Bulgaria, Hungary, Slovakia, Kyrgyzstan), the Step by Step program did not survive in the first organization that was established, and the program was later transferred to another nonprofit organization.

> *I'm the director of Partners Hungary Foundation. I didn't want the program to close down in Hungary with the closure of that [first] foundation. This program has its values. It has its network of trainers. It has its schools and kindergartens that implement the program. I persuaded my colleagues and our board to take over, let's say, the ownership and the rights of the Step by Step program.*
>
> *(Éva Deák, Partners Hungary Foundation)*

Building Civil Society in Challenging Political Contexts: "The Seed beneath the Snow"

Step by Step has been implemented in a variety of countries, many with complex political contexts that have challenged the presence of Open Society's national foundations and, frequently, the NGOs associated with it. In the case of Slovakia, the national foundation spun off the Step by Step program during its first year in the mid-1990s to provide the team with a safer haven. The former director of the Open Society Foundation Bratislava reflected:

> Slovakia was special because it was not a very favorable political situation, but the NGO sector was quite strong and cooperating. We simply worked on the basis of what was done at the very beginning, after the Velvet Revolution. People were interested in the continuation of democracy and all the values around it ... [The Step by Step NGO] was detached from the national foundation and could also look for some other resources and cooperation. This freedom was important because the national foundation was at the center of political attention and viewed as an enemy. [Step by Step] remained a part of our strategic plans for a very long time.
> (Alena Panikova, former executive director, Open Society Foundation—Bratislava)

At the time of writing, the context in Slovakia is more favorable. However, in Hungary opportunities for the Step by Step NGO to receive government funding have been curtailed by Fidesz, the current, right-wing party of government.

> Between 2000 and 2010 there were many more opportunities for NGOs. You could apply for EU money which was coming through the Hungarian government. There are a few opportunities, but those NGOs who are, let's say, blacklisted and those who belong politically to the left do not get access to too many resources. We are stigmatized. There is a blacklist and we are on that blacklist. I think by being professional we find a way and work with municipalities, especially those run by the political opposition parties. It would be very, very meaningful if we can have political change. There is a famous Hungarian poet [Andre Ady, 1877-1919], who wrote a poem called The Seed Beneath the Snow. I think the Step by Step program is now a seed under the snow.
> (Éva Deák, Partners Hungary Foundation)

The situation was even more complicated in Central Asia, where NGOs face additional challenges.

> Central Asia, of course, has its own political economy and its own way of thinking. From time to time they deregister NGOs completely. Then they work according to their priorities and sometimes early childhood development is relegated to a "lower level" entity, such as the women's committee. Women's committees are typically weak, with little or no funding.
> (Deepa Grover, former UNICEF regional advisor for Europe and Central Asia)

In the early years of the program, the national foundations in Central Asia had good relations with government and were able to help the Step by Step program, and later the Step by Step NGOs, manage relationships with the government.

> *Central Asia is a much more hostile region to non-governmental organizations than other parts of the Step by Step network. In choosing that format, we were putting them from the beginning in a position where they might not be trusted without the support of the national foundation in Kyrgyzstan or Tajikistan to be able to register organizations and to give the reports to the Ministry of Justice that you have to give with aid projects. There was a level of trust between the foundations and the government that eased some of those paths, but a lot of systems had broken down, especially in Tajikistan in the wake of the civil war.*
>
> *(Kate Lapham, former deputy director, Education Support Program, OSF)*

In a number of countries with authoritarian regimes (Belarus, Russia, Uzbekistan, Azerbaijan), Step by Step NGOs were not able to survive, and closed down as a result of lack of funds or because of political pressure.

> *This idea of the NGO as civil society, in my understanding, has a very natural place in the overall architecture of society in the Western mind, but in our part of the world, NGOs didn't exist. NGOs actually appeared and were created as agents to implement Western projects and ideas, but not as a result of society ... When I see the NGO civil society in Central Asia or Azerbaijan, all the capable people I know either retired or work for academia and the government.*
>
> *(Ulviyya Mikayilova, ADA University, Azerbaijan)*

It is important to distinguish between the success of the Step by Step program and the survival of the Step by Step NGO. In several countries where the NGO implementing Step by Step closed, government agencies and universities continue to use the program resources (methodologies, training manuals, courses) and hire experts and trainers without attribution to the Open Society Foundations or Step by Step. Most importantly, the values and principles at the foundation of the program—child-centered approaches, social inclusion, parent and community engagement—still have some traction in the official early education system.

The Challenge of Sustaining the NGOs

Sustaining the NGOs that were set up with Open Society funding proved to be a challenge, particularly given the relatively low interest in early childhood amongst governments and donors at the time. Moreover, the NGO sector was still emerging in Central Eastern Europe and Eurasia in the decades following the fall of the Berlin wall. Expectations from Open Society and the NGOs may have initially been too high, given the level of development of civil society generally in the region.

> It was certainly part of the vision of the Open Society Foundation that these spin-offs would be independent of OSF, and they would have the ability to apply for grants, raise money, and build organizational capacity. That was noble and it had to be that way, but I think that the countries expected that it was going to happen more quickly than it did. Persistence was key.
> (Deborah A. Ziegler, US Step by Step expert team)

Additionally, the kind of support available (fees to provide training and short-term project-based funding) did not align with the Step by Step aim of reforming the early education system. Rather than training large numbers of private providers, Step by Step teams concentrated on reforming the public system.

> It was extremely challenging for us, for a civil organization to find the ongoing support and the need-based support. Because I think that these changes which we initiate are long-term changes. You cannot do it within two years, within a project.
> (Éva Deák, Partners Hungary Foundation)

Governments also shifted how they offered in-service training, which required Step by Step NGOs to shift how they applied for funding to conduct training.

> The challenge for us now is that we are an NGO relying mostly on projects. It is really tough for teachers to pay for their trainings. For two years, the minister of education was announcing calls for proposals for grants for in-service providers. We were eligible to get those grants. They were symbolic, but they enabled our NGO to become part of the system in general, and to be recognized. Now, people have to use two percent of the salary budget for professional development.
> (Cornelia Cincilei, Step by Step Moldova)

In the case of Moldova, the NGO built long-term partnerships with the World Bank (described in Chapter 3), Liechtenstein Development Services (LED), Charles Stewart Mott Foundation, and UNICEF for work with community-based early childhood centers, rural preschools and primary schools, and institutions of higher education. Step by Step country team members interviewed for this book noted especially, where relevant, their relationships with the World Bank, USAID, the European Union, and UNICEF, highlighting both positive and negative experiences.

UNICEF was very, very helpful after the Open Society stopped financing. We had a lot of grants from UNICEF and from the European Union delegation in Georgia. We had some grants from embassies, but not state funds.
(Eteri Gvineria, Center for Educational Initiatives, Step by Step Georgia)

UNICEF was playing an important role in early childhood education reform projects and they saw us as an important actor. They supported us in playing this important role in the reform.
(Cornelia Cincilei, Step by Step Moldova)

Several were critical of UNICEF and World Bank support to authoritarian governments. Many were frustrated with the lack of bargaining power they now had, sitting within an NGO, instead of inside a large international foundation.

You cannot be a big player like UNICEF, the World Bank or USAID with just know-how. Even the Soros Foundation cannot be a player on the same level, because their funds for education are really very limited.
(Suzana Kirandžiska, Foundation for Educational and Cultural Initiatives, Step by Step, North Macedonia)

In addition to applying for grants and projects and cooperating with government and donor agencies, Step by Step NGOs engaged in income generation to support operational costs. Many sold trainings, manuals, and books, including the Reading Corner books and methodologies described in Chapter 3, directly to teachers, preschools, and schools or to partner and donor organizations. The NGO in Croatia launched magazines for preschool and primary school teachers and parents. In Bosnia, the Step by Step organization was registered as an association and could not charge fees for services. Instead, Step by Step organized and sold different levels of membership, each including a set number of training days and resource manuals. In Slovenia, the Research Institute established a national network of Step by Step preschools to support quality and professional development:

If we had not established that network, I don't know what would have happened. Now, there is a kind of visibility about what we are doing in the country and the kind of influence the program has.
(Tatjana Vonta, co-author and former director, Step by Step Slovenia)

Two NGOs established schools to generate income. The first, Kosovo Education Center, set up a private school that now extends from preschool to high school. The NGO in Romania purchased a building.

We are an inclusive preschool and primary school. We have children with disabilities in each classroom in the preschool and in the primary school and in lower secondary. We have 130 children in preschool and 250 in primary and lower secondary. We use the Step by Step methodology. We bought the building in 2004. That was another adventure to persuade the bank that a non-profit can afford to pay back a loan.

(Carmen Lica, Centrul Step by Step Romania)

The NGO in Romania even managed a furniture factory at one point and funneled profits back into the NGO.

We met one donor who said, "Everybody is giving you money for training sessions and everybody is giving you money for materials, we want to give you money to open something that will hire unemployed people and give you a perspective of sustainability." Classroom furniture in the Step by Step primary classrooms is very different from the furniture that we have in traditional classrooms, so we opened a furniture factory that functioned for eight years. Step by Step classrooms were able to order furniture from our factory. What made us sell it off was the fact that at one point, all the workers in construction and woodworking workers decided to leave the country. It was very, very difficult to find good workers.

(Carmen Lica, Centrul Step by Step Romania)

These connections with businesses in Romania eventually inspired the program to create a second organization, a network modeled on the work of ReadyNation in the United States, aimed at mobilizing business leaders to advocate for better early childhood services. To date the organization has successfully advocated to increase funding for birth to three services and for legislation that makes preschool education progressively compulsory by 2030. They have also established fiscal credit to enable companies to pay for early childhood services for the children of their employees.

Assessing Prospects for NGO Sustainability

Step by Step was one of the first Open Society programs to spin off. As such, Open Society kept a close eye on the new entities, particularly in the early years. Open Society's education sub-board requested an initial assessment of the prospects for sustainability in 1999, while the process of spinning off was still ongoing. In response, independent consultants visited four representative Step by Step countries, using a common framework to develop written case reports, which were consolidated into a brief report. Criteria for NGO sustainability had been developed collaboratively with Step by Step program teams at an international workshop. Their identified prerequisites for sustainability included: capable leadership and organizational capacity; strategy planning for future sustainability; systemic impact; financial competence and guaranteed cashflow; formal recognition and social support for the program; quality assurance for products and services; and, finally, a favorable social, political, and economic context.

The assessment debunked the idea that Step by Step was unaffordable. Instead, reviewers found that the program was worthwhile, relevant and achieving impact, much of it systemic. The program was seen as potentially sustainable if ongoing financing was achievable and if organizational development support was continued. The assessment drew attention to the unrealized potential of Step by Step programs to influence policy and to leverage parents to engage in school governance (Open Society Institute 2000).

Open Society continued to track Step by Step program statistics and NGO financial sustainability, through annual surveys. By the tenth anniversary of Step by Step, Open Society funding made up around one third of the national Step by Step implementation budgets, and this level of support was largely maintained as the program neared its twentieth anniversary. Other major funders included governments, European Union, multilateral and bilateral organizations, and foundations. Earned income was providing around 10–15 percent of NGO budgets. Step by Step NGOs continued to implement a range of programs, dividing resources almost equally between initiatives aimed at general reform of center-based early education (in creches, preschools, and primary schools), and social justice-focused initiatives addressing social inclusion of minority populations and children with disabilities. In the intervening years Open Society tapered off general support to most of the NGOs but continued to offer modest support for translation of new resources, attending international events and conducting audits to help the NGOs maintain their professional status. In addition, Open Society made available funding for innovative grants for new ideas and offered loans or emergency grants and technical assistance to NGOs facing cashflow crises.

In 2013, a global strategy process at Open Society stimulated a second assessment of NGO impact and sustainability. With the help of a consultant, Open Society conducted an internal review, using a survey and interviews to reach out to national foundations, as well as to Step by Step NGOs. The foundations highlighted Step by Step contributions in the areas of teacher training, early childhood policy, and inclusion of children with disabilities, Roma, and other minorities. Step by Step NGOs were perceived as influential and respected contributors to ministry policy by almost all of the national foundations. They reiterated concerns that ongoing funding was crucial for the NGOs and that they can strengthen their management and operations.

In two countries—Belarus and Uzbekistan—rated by USAID as having inhospitable NGO environments, it is understandable that the Step by Step NGOs eventually closed (US Agency for International Development 2012). Interestingly, Step by Step NGOs in some countries with challenging NGO contexts exceeded expectations, and were doing brilliantly, while others seemed to be underachieving, given the favorable NGO context in their countries. This is a reminder that leadership and the ability to adapt and innovate are critical components of sustainability, in addition to political context.

Open Society implemented a final wave of organizational development support, while at the same time winding down ongoing support to Step by Step NGOs by 2018. INTRAC, a UK firm, was hired between 2014 and 2018 to work with nineteen of the Step by Step NGOs to support organizational strengthening and sustainability. Each was paired with one international and one local organizational development consultant, who led them through an organizational assessment and planning process, resulting in a proposal to strengthen the NGO's capacity, which Open Society then financed. At the end of the process, NGOs showed modest improvement in most areas, especially resource mobilization, market analysis, strategy, and structure. Some of the NGOs continued to partner after 2018 with Open Society on new programming focused on Roma, children with disabilities, and refugees.

Creating the International Step by Step Association (ISSA) to Sustain the Movement

The idea to establish a regional association was first proposed at a higher education seminar in 1997. Momentum only grew with the decision by the Open Society Foundations to spin off the national programs.

> I remember when the Soros Foundation decided to spin-off the Step by Step Program, the idea was to keep all these Step by Step programs from all these countries together and this is why ISSA was organized.
> (Suzana Kirandžiska, Foundation for Educational and Cultural Initiatives, Step by Step, North Macedonia)

> There was a huge need to share our experience, to find what is really important for us, to decide where to go, what to do next, what are our needs, because the needs of the countries changed.
>
> *(Tatjana Vonta, co-author and former director, Step by Step Slovenia)*

A regional professional association could play a role in advancing the sustainability of national NGOs. It could secure the mission, vision, and values of the Step by Step program and promote the role of early childhood in building open, democratic societies well after Open Society funding would end.

> [Professional associations] have many reasons to exist and helping their members, whether they be countries or individuals, to scale up and sustain their practice is a key role for those organizations. Without associations, limits are not stretched and as we say the envelope is not pushed to advance the field. Certainly, a major function of a professional membership association is to advance sustainability. Another benefit of a professional association is to nurture communities of professionals. The Open Society Foundation and ISSA created caring communities of professional colleagues. To this day, many of the Step by Step pioneer directors and staff of the foundation and the association continue to support each other professionally. Strong friendships also developed among many, and those friendships continue as we speak. For me, being a part of this incredible program and movement was the highlight of my life both professionally and personally. The memories are precious.
>
> *(Deborah A. Ziegler, US Step by Step expert team)*

> I saw ISSA as a way of sustaining the work and of making Step by Step more than just a project, but something that would have a longevity and sustainability, and that has certainly proven to be true.
>
> *(Phyllis Magrab, Georgetown University, former board chair, Early Childhood Program Advisory Board, OSF)*

The process of establishing ISSA was new for everyone.

> Even the whole concept of NGOs was a very, very new concept for most of the Step by Step directors and forming this legal entity for them to be independent was so important. The vision of the Open Society Foundation at that time was to help them build capacity to do that through the formation of ISSA, which I applaud. It was an aspirational direction for them. There were certainly initial challenges as well as successes in helping to build that capacity.
>
> *(Deborah A. Ziegler, US Step by Step expert team)*

> The ISSA movement was very interdependent and had to be collaborative, and it's messy. It can be hard, but I think they worked through some of the big issues and transitions with that overall goal in mind, like it's just not the folks in the front of the boat that are going to survive, we all have to stick together. The US trainers and folks who felt that we were there in the beginning felt we needed to step back. I felt very proprietary: "Well, who's going to be doing this and this is our baby here?"
>
> *(Kate Burke Walsh, US Step by Step expert team)*

A taskforce was established, and it met several times over the course of a year to develop a mission and vision for the organization. The idea of establishing ISSA in the United States was floated and dismissed in favor of establishing an association in Europe.

> A lot of questions had to be resolved to legally set up this organization, where to have it, where to have its headquarters, and so on. Finally, in 1998, we decided to establish it as an independent international network of founding member organizations. It was badly needed, badly wanted by the Step by Step NGOs. They felt that they had grown together and had benefited so much from cooperation and from learning together. That was the idea of this learning community.
>
> *(Cornelia Cincilei, Step by Step Moldova)*

Open Society scaffolded the establishment of ISSA in the Netherlands, providing legal support.

> I remember [two country directors] telling a story about how the lawyers from the Open Society Foundation marched into an ISSA meeting. (Not marched in, this is the way the directors described it). They marched in with their suits and ties on and their briefcases and the directors were like, holy heck, what did we get ourselves into? Here are the lawyers who are going to tell us what we need to know and do. I remember one of the lawyers saying, I think I'm going to lose my mind [laughs] over how many times they had to go over that same sentence in the by-laws, but that was part of developing an organization and they did it.
>
> *(Deborah A. Ziegler, US Step by Step expert team)*

The first ISSA board put together a three-year strategic business plan linking ISSA's work and open society. Its vision was: "An open society where the entire community works together to help each child to reach his or her full potential" (Strategic Business Plan 2002–5).

The plan argued for Open Society support to secure ISSA as a necessary addition to the early childhood sector in the region. ISSA could represent the interests of early childhood professionals from regions that had been largely voiceless, providing a vital exchange network and a unique approach to early education reform. A second aim was to ensure the long-term survival of the Step by Step program nationally, regionally, and globally.

The first activities included creating standards to define quality early childhood education and structuring continuous professional development to support their implementation.

> *The first pedagogical standards were developed together in a participatory way with the support of internationally recognized experts. Through a participatory approach, we developed a mentoring system and guidebook and two publications about child-centered practices collected from the network that are also used by our practitioners.*
>
> *(Cornelia Cincilei, Step by Step Moldova)*

Open Society led the secretariat between 1999 and 2006, seconding Sarah Klaus (one of the authors of this book) into the role of executive director. ISSA operated initially from the Open Society offices in New York, and later, from 2002, from Budapest, where the first ISSA staff were hired and an office was co-located with the Hungarian Step by Step NGO.

Managing an Expanding Network

In the early years, especially, it was challenging for the NGOs to prioritize their multiple goals: advancing the Step by Step program in their country, establishing and sustaining a new national NGO, and creating and participating in a regional network.

> *I don't think it was 100 percent successful at first. I think it was fraught. I think there was tension between maintaining the program and creating a network. For the individuals who had programs and developed programs, some of them saw this as a bit of an abandonment of them and their work. I think there was some real tension at the outset.*
>
> *(Phyllis Magrab, Georgetown University, former board chair, Early Childhood Program Advisory Board, OSF)*

Expectations exceeded the resources available to the secretariat and the experience of members in the new association.

Everyone came to the table with a different vision and expectation of what ISSA would look like. "I want to have conferences, I want to have journals, I want a learning community, I want an organization who's going to look at quality and equity." Those were the initiatives they knew and were good at. These initial conversations led to a potpourri of initiatives, without building the necessary infrastructure of the association, and that was the difficult hurdle. While there were some painful moments, they were growing moments.

(Deborah A. Ziegler, US Step by Step expert team)

With so many expectations, the organization faced a number of predictable challenges and critical moments. Interviewees drew attention to challenges related to governance, the relationship of ISSA and Open Society Foundations, the expanding membership, and ISSA's evolving mission.

Understanding governance structures was probably the biggest barrier for the formation of ISSA. I remember spending a lot of time on creating scenarios of options for voting and, oh my, wasn't that an opportunity for us to move closer to a democratic society!

(Deborah A. Ziegler, US Step by Step expert team)

The governance structure of ISSA shifted. In the early years all voting members of ISSA were Step by Step organizations and the Step by Step NGOs dominated the ISSA Board, which also included one member appointed by Open Society. As ISSA began to receive more program funding from Open Society, Open Society requested ISSA include external (non-Step by Step NGO) members on the Board to manage potential conflicts of interest. Initially, this created problems.

I remember a big divide between the Board and the membership. Some of the western or professional Board members who weren't network members per se through their organizations had very different visions for where ISSA should go, what it should be and what it could do.

(Kate Lapham, former deputy director, Education Support Program, OSF)

Open Society provided a majority of ISSA's funding and, in the early years, it also provided management and an operational structure.

There was a lot of tension between ISSA and Open Society at the outset. It wasn't clear if ISSA was independent or if it was really an Open Society arm. It couldn't be clear. ISSA didn't have enough organizational maturity to be an independent entity. If you look at ISSA today, it is completely different from when I first engaged with it.

(Phyllis Magrab, Georgetown University, former board chair, Early Childhood Program Advisory Board, OSF)

As ISSA matured, so did the European Union, which began to admit members from Central and Eastern Europe from 2004 onward. The decision to reach out to Western Europeans to expand ISSA's membership base and to move the ISSA office to the Netherlands created some controversy initially and concern that new members might spoil the trust and collective ownership that had grown across the Step by Step teams.

> It was just this sense of a group of people who had really done something together and meant a lot to each other. It was beautiful. I think that played out also a little bit in discussions of whether the network should expand to include members beyond the original Step by Step network. How do we expand to welcome others and still keep that sense of a shared origin?
> (Kate Lapham, former deputy director, Education Support Program, OSF)

> Should ISSA stay as a closed club, Step by Step members only, or it should open up? How should it open up and to what extent? We had very different capacities as organizations and the members were sometimes afraid that they would be lost in a big ISSA. There was still this fear, maybe particularly amongst those from Central Asia, that less attention will be paid to Step by Step members. That was quite natural with the expansion of the organization.
> (Cornelia Cincilei, Step by Step Moldova)

Several interviewees reflected on the importance of Central Asian countries in the network and how to address their interests.

> The East wants to be a co-constructor, not only a consumer. It shouldn't be only a one-way flow. It should be a discussion.
> (Ulviyya Mikayilova, ADA University, Azerbaijan)

> ISSA is so attractive not only because of European countries, but because of the Eastern countries and the Central Asian countries.
> (Tatjana Vonta, co-author and former director, Step by Step Slovenia)

Independently of ISSA, countries in former Yugoslavia organized an informal network and regular sub-regional conferences. The impact of these sub-regional events, organized each year by the Step by Step NGO in Bosnia, has been phenomenal:

> It was incredible networking, incredible energy. We and the other participants were given insight into the practices, theories, and policies of other countries through

workshops and planned meetings. The educators particularly loved to see how their colleagues worked. To see the experiences of working with vulnerable groups, to see how children's portfolios are made, how professional portfolios are made, what the standards are in other countries. It was truly incredible.

(Hašima Ćurak, advisor, Ministry of Education and Science, Bosnia and Herzegovina)

With ISSA's growth in membership, there has also been a growth in activity and a remarkably high level of engagement.

ISSA has enormous capacity to grow and we are trying to use expertise from members for different tasks to work with the ISSA secretariat or to delegate some things to specific members. We organize professional learning, peer learning activities, and Joint Learning Labs. After every conference, you could see this boost of cooperation between members. I think that with new members and with old members going through transformation because some people retired, some new people are coming in, we are becoming richer and richer, and we now have a very strong secretariat.

(Zorica Trikić, senior program manager, ISSA)

Eighty percent [of members] are involved in at least two kinds of network activities. Half of those are actually involved in seven to ten activities. This is a very high level of engagement which shows that what we do and facilitate is really relevant for the members' work.

(Liana Ghent, executive director, ISSA)

The membership is no longer the only driver for ISSA. The organization has positioned itself as a contributor to the field of early childhood.

There were several moments that defined our trajectory. [One of these] was our awareness that we are more than a collection of members, we are also a power that contributes to the field. We became more strategic then, as an association: we do not exist only for the members and through the members. We selected initiatives and projects that in a sense reinforced the membership, and the other way around, the membership could contribute to the new initiatives ... and everything that we did in the initiatives then went back into the membership, either through new resources or visibility or partnerships or simply funding that was sustainable.

(Liana Ghent, executive director, ISSA)

One such mutually beneficial partnership that ISSA has fostered has been with the regional office of UNICEF.

> *ISSA is one solid standard partner that we could trust, we could work with, we could depend on, we could draw on, we could work with their trainers, work with their material, work with their resources. I think through their annual conference, they provided an excellent forum. I think all this also started to help in ISSA's own thinking about early childhood. It brought ISSA into the health sector in a very active way. We worked with ISSA trainers to support health workers. I think they're perceived with a great deal of respect and as being extremely reliable.*
>
> *(Deepa Grover, former UNICEF regional advisor for Europe and Central Asia)*

We also heard pushback from a few members, who sense that NGO needs and problems are not as important to ISSA as they once were. Yet no one can deny that the way that ISSA brought together Europe and Eurasia is extraordinary.

> *ISSA is now the main network in Europe. They are representing the early childhood sector everywhere in the European Commission, in the OECD, UNESCO. The people that worked for ISSA all came from Eastern Europe. That's also something that fascinated me, that the whole Step by Step Program was in a way so inspired by American people and not by Western Europeans. They came first. Suddenly they then came together, the Western Europeans and the Eastern Europeans, and at first it was not always easy, because there were different ways of working.*
>
> *(Jan Peeters, co-author and former board member, ISSA)*

Reflections on Building and Strengthening Early Childhood Civil Society

What could have made the process of "spinning off" Step by Step from Open Society smoother? Several interviewees suggest that a greater focus on human capacity (leadership and expertise) would have been helpful, including providing support to develop more layers of leadership within countries.

> *The problem here is the survival of these NGOs in their own countries. ... New generations of people have come to the NGOs in these countries. Not all of them have had as extensive a training like the first ones. It's not very easy to maintain the same vision about change and promote it systematically.*
>
> *(Cornelia Cincilei, Step by Step Moldova)*

> *If you look at the research data on what is key to successful systems change, it centers around leadership, who is leading with strong knowledge and skills. While we provided professional development and technical assistance to Step by Step, should we have spent more time on developing and nurturing leadership? The Step*

by Step country directors, received the benefit of receiving a lot of resources on leadership development. Hopefully, the knowledge and skills trickled down to the practitioners in their country.

(Deborah A. Ziegler, US Step by Step expert team)

In reality, Step by Step NGO directors did not have either the expertise or time to provide leadership trainings widely in their countries. It wasn't only human capacity at the level of country teams that needed strengthening. Incorporating an NGO development initiative within an early childhood quality-focused initiative required new expertise in the core teams at ISSA and Open Society.

[Open Society] staff were engaged in a lot of technical assistance directly to the NGOs. I think that the question of how you increase the capacity of the regional NGOs to provide that kind of support is a big question.
(Hirokazu Yoshikawa, New York University, former board member, Early Childhood Program Advisory Board, OSF)

I just remember that it didn't feel like we had enough expertise to do what we were doing, to create these spin-offs. I know it took an enormous amount of energy and rejigging of a lot of both ideas and people to make it happen.
(Phyllis Magrab, Georgetown University, former board chair, Early Childhood Program Advisory Board, OSF)

Step by Step NGO directors would have liked to have even more technical support to develop sustainability and organizational capacity.

If we could have focused more on developing the skills necessary to think about sustainability, probably that would have been helpful. We were very focused on delivering high-quality Step by Step programs in all the classrooms. It was challenging when we were faced with fundraising and writing proposals. Probably that was an area that might have been investigated more and supported more.
(Carmen Lica, Centrul Step by Step Romania)

Representatives from ISSA and Open Society concurred.

If we could go back in time, I think I would look with fresh eyes at how to support and challenge all our members to become stronger as organizations, because the result was that four or five were not able to continue, and a few others are in very critical situations. Perhaps we were unrealistic to think that all twenty-nine NGOs would survive – it's just life, it's never 100 percent.
(Liana Ghent, executive director, ISSA)

> I think we would have had a stronger ISSA if we had made a bigger commitment to the member NGOs in the beginning.
> (Kate Lapham, former deputy director, Education Support Program, OSF)

Following their provision of multi-year additional technical support to nineteen of the Step by Step NGOs, an expert from INTRAC made a similar observation:

> While in many cases Step by Step NGOs were seen as leaders in the field of ECD, they had not paid much attention to their own organisational development. [Step by Step NGOs] did not even necessarily see themselves as NGOs, but more as specialist educationalists. This cut them off from the rest of the civil society sector.
> (MacLeod 2017)

Though support to the NGOs could have been greater, the impact of the Step by Step NGOs and ISSA at delivering systems change, which will be discussed in Chapter 9, may be unique in the early childhood field.

> I think it is the only case I can think of regional change in a positive direction for Early Childhood Development systems that was driven through with such a strong civil society role. I think it is an underutilized pathway to scale up.
> (Hirokazu Yoshikawa, New York University, former board member, Early Childhood Program Advisory Board, OSF)

Open Society's Early Childhood Program remained a strong advocate for the power of networks and invested significantly in similar regional professional associations in Asia, Africa, and in Arab countries.

ISSA and the NGOs Today: The Soul of Step by Step

The ISSA members whom we interviewed expressed a lot of pride in the organization:

> When we apply for projects, we emphasize that we are a member of ISSA and that we share knowledge and experience with other ISSA members. Being a member of ISSA gives us some professional recognition.
> (Suzana Kirandžiska, Foundation for Educational and Cultural Initiatives, Step by Step, North Macedonia)

ISSA grew very much. I think it positioned itself very well in the field and has a great deal of recognition from the field and developed very strong partnerships. It offers members a lot of opportunities. I am very proud that I'm part of ISSA. I am very proud that ISSA organized all the conferences and expanded its partnerships.

(Carmen Lica, Centrul Step by Step Romania)

I'm proud of the position on the international arena that ISSA has achieved, of the ISSA relationship with many acclaimed international experts in early childhood education, in new partnerships that bridge across health and education. That ISSA has become the host for the platform for other regional networks and they jointly bring the ECD agenda to the attention of international donors and governments. Its internationally visibility also supports national member NGOs in their dialogue with the ministry of education.

(Cornelia Cincilei, Step by Step Moldova)

And they shared appreciation for the opportunity to be a part of Step by Step and ISSA:

I think I'm most proud of the fact that because of our work, so many changes are visible on a wide scale, in the lives of children, of families, in education laws, in classrooms.

(Liana Ghent, executive director, ISSA)

I think it was a really wonderful opportunity because it was a period of life when so many people from so many countries shared the commitment to early childhood, to the values of democracy. They energized each other and coming back they energized all other people around, because of this, really family. It's like a family of thinkers and people who feel and think in the same way. All of this really caused those changes. I don't know how to say, [chuckles] *it's very beautiful what can happen in your life.*

(Natalia Sofiy, Borys Grinchenko Kyiv University, Ukraine)

With the closure of the Open Society Foundations Early Childhood Program, the role of ISSA in advancing the values of democracy and equity in early childhood is even more acute.

ISSA is very important. It became very important because it did become a network, has become a network. It has found its way to become independent and develop other resources to continue the kind of work that needs to be done. As we look at

the closing down of the Early Childhood Program in Open Society, it becomes even more important that ISSA survives into the future.
(Phyllis Magrab, Georgetown University, former board chair, Early Childhood Program Advisory Board, OSF)

A network is only as strong as its members, and continued investment in ISSA's member NGOs is essential to keep these values alive at the national level.

Liana Ghent, executive director of ISSA, shared her hopes for the future.

We continue relentlessly on our mission, but we do it with a gentleness that is more efficient than just firmness on its own. My dream is that we become stronger at influencing policy systems. If we don't change with the times, we'll soon become irrelevant.

We build on a set of values and principles, and those don't change. They are the fabric of our network, in a way. I think each organization has a soul, maybe in the books it is called organizational culture. This is shaped by history, by its legacy, but also by the people that work in it or its members, its staff, and so forth. Everything we start, we give our best to it and we keep our eyes on what is meaningful. We challenge ourselves constantly to support innovation and knowledge to travel from one country or even one continent to another. We walk the talk and we stayed true to what we believe in.
(Liana Ghent, executive director, ISSA)

8

"Surprised and Thrilled": Rolling Out the Programs

Figure 8.1 An early childhood master-trainer reads a book to kids in the LMA Waterside Early Childhood Center. In Monrovia, Liberia, on March 31, 2014.
© Andrea Bruce/NOOR for The Open Society Foundations

Introduction

Open Society invested in early childhood development in countries outside Europe and Eurasia that were of strategic interest. In many cases, new countries were proposed by George Soros, who remained enthusiastic about the potential of investing in young children to advance open society. Requests to explore early childhood opportunities in a new country sometimes came directly from his office, based on his discussions with political leaders and experts in the country, and they also came from Open Society's affiliated foundations and regional directors.

> It is also soft power. It is a very easy way of entering a country and engaging. I think he also began to see that value, not just the democracy-building value, but its value in getting involved in places that he wanted to be involved in. I think that was another aspect of it.
>
> (Phyllis Magrab, Georgetown University, former board chair, Early Childhood Program Advisory Board, OSF)

Eventually, the work of the Early Childhood Program at Open Society Foundations expanded to include a wide range of interventions and partners. In this book, we focus on those projects that built on the work of the Step by Step program, Open Society's flagship initiative.

The First Steps outside Europe and Eurasia: Haiti, South Africa, and Argentina

Up until this point this book has focused on the experience of implementing Step by Step in Central, Eastern, Southern Europe, and Eurasia. However, in its first decade, Step by Step was also introduced in Haiti, South Africa, and Argentina. These experiences helped shape the larger geographic expansion of Open Society's early childhood work post-2006. Each experience was unique. In Haiti and South Africa, the program was implemented by Open Society's affiliated national foundations, while in Argentina, a national NGO, Fundación Leer, applied to Open Society to start the program.

Tipa Tipa, as Step by Step is known in Creole, aligned beautifully with the efforts of Fondation Connaissance et Liberté/Fondasyon Konesans Ak Libète (FOKAL), the affiliated Open Society national foundation in Haiti, to invest in individuals and communities to promote dignity and a just and durable democratic society. A strong early set of programs at FOKAL focused on expanding and improving vital services such as health and education, which had historically been provided by non-state agencies and organizations. Beginning in 1997, FOKAL built five new model preschool/community center buildings, complete with libraries and health services, in remote areas of Haiti that had dynamic communities and exceptional local leadership. FOKAL also supported renovation and equipping of existing preschools and primary schools. Working with teachers who had little education or teacher training, and in communities experiencing extreme poverty and low literacy, *Tipa Tipa* sought to develop individual and collective activism and responsibility.

> *I visited Step by Step programs in Haiti. They were quite central to the foundation's program in Haiti. I found those to be very good. They built community activity but starting with the schools and starting with the early childhood education. They had a whole series of programs that related to the early childhood education in provincial parts of Haiti, outside of the city of Port-au-Prince.*
>
> (Ayreh Neier, president emeritus, Open Society Foundations)

Promoting parent involvement and children's choices, agency, creativity, and sense of belonging were new in early childhood education in Haiti. Staff who worked at program sites were excited about the potential for Step by Step to contribute to the building of a better society:

> This generation, which has followed that training within the Step by Step program will create a new society, a society with justice and respect for people.
>
> Nurse, Te Kase Community, Haiti
> (Open Society Institute 2008a, 135)

> They work on democracy as a permanent theme: respect for others, self-respect, respect for the environment, and respect for the country. That's the type of education Haiti needs.
>
> Lochner Etiennne, supervisor appointed by the congregation to monitor schools
> (Open Society Institute 2008a, 132–3)

Community ownership was at the heart of the program in Haiti.

In post-apartheid South Africa, between 1997 and 2000, Open Society Foundation for South Africa built new preschools in several rural communities. In Argentina, beginning in 2004, Step by Step was implemented in a small number of sites in the suburbs of Buenos Aires and in the northern province of Misiones. However, the program never extended beyond the initial pilot sites in either country, largely because it did not achieve strong commitment from the government and local communities (Open Society Institute 2000).

In all three countries Step by Step was piloted in communities experiencing great poverty, many located in remote rural areas. The big difference in Haiti, however, was that FOKAL invested in highly motivated communities with inspiring leaders, who were invited to shape the program. Like the Step by

Step programs in Europe and Eurasia, *Tipa Tipa* later became an independent organization. The energy and ambition of the Step by Step team and communities contributed to the beginnings of a movement that eventually brought together the ministry of education, international agencies, and local organizations to expand opportunities for young children. This was abruptly interrupted by the 2010 earthquake, which decimated the ministry and UNICEF buildings and staff, and which shifted attention to addressing urgent, basic humanitarian needs. International agencies took leadership of the sector, and *Tipa Tipa* eventually scaled back the scope of its work. The contrast between the vibrant programs in Haiti and the less sustainable programs in Argentina and South Africa, where less emphasis was placed on community leadership, is a lesson in the immense importance of identifying change agents in communities and investing in them.

Going Global with New University Initiatives

By 2007, the network of the Open Society Foundations was active in sixty countries (Open Society Institute 2008b) and continuing to expand. The Foundations attempted to link education initiatives more directly with the values of open society by fostering programs that combated social exclusion and promoted accountability and diversity. In line with these changes, the Early Childhood Program department leadership moved from New York to London in 2006, staff with expertise in global early childhood were brought onto the team, and the consultant base was expanded. An advisory board made up of leading international experts was established and guided the program until its closure at the end of 2020. The program began to explore opportunities to use Step by Step resources in different contexts.

The first opportunity came in the form of a request from BRAC University's Institute of Education Development (BU-IED) to partner with Open Society to establish a postgraduate certificate, diploma, and master of sciences in Early Childhood Development in Dhaka. It would be the first master's degree-level early childhood program in a country in which the field was expanding and more than 34,000 people were already involved in preschool education management, supervision, and teaching (Institute of Educational Development BRAC University 2010). The core courses for the new degree drew on the eight Step by Step semester-length courses, developed through the higher education initiative.

> The Step by Step materials scaffolded the early childhood development certificate, but they had to be adapted. They had to be tested out, flexed, transformed to fit local context. I think it's always good to start from something tangible and it is pointless in most cases, a waste of resources, to go back to very, very basic principles from the beginning.
> (Tina Hyder, former deputy director, Early Childhood Program, OSF)

The degree program, which launched in 2007 and continues to this day, consists of ten courses co-developed jointly by international experts and faculty from Bangladesh. The first two cohorts were co-taught with international experts and since then cohorts have been taught by faculty from Bangladesh.

> Through the students, the program is contributing to a growing body of thought leaders in Bangladesh who are confident, curious, and contributing at a more conceptual and informed level about the importance of child development.
>
> National faculty researcher and thesis supervisor
> (Institute of Educational Development BRAC University 2010, iv)

Co-creation of a postgraduate program with local and international faculty proved to be an effective approach to introducing reforms in higher education. By intervening at the postgraduate level, rather than at in-service or pre-service levels, the courses sought to strengthen the cadre of early childhood experts responsible for developing, implementing, monitoring, evaluating, and researching effective programs and services. The approach was replicated at institutions in Russia, Myanmar, and Liberia. As a result, new degree courses have been introduced which offer fresh content, innovative teaching and learning, and an emphasis on practical experience and applied research.

Going Global with New Country Initiatives

Between 2007 and 2020, when the Early Childhood Program closed, Step by Step materials and experiences were used to inspire and support the development of new initiatives in a range of countries and contexts. New models drew from the experience of implementing Step by Step but did not seek to replicate it. Not everyone in the global early childhood community understood this initially.

> It was misunderstood sometimes externally that Open Society was trying to pick something up and just take it whole and drop it somewhere without being relevant

> to context. I don't think that actually was the reality of what happened at all, as all our initiatives were led by local partners.
>
> (Tina Hyder, former deputy director, Early Childhood Program, OSF)

In East Timor, Open Society supported the government, UNICEF, and Macquarie University to map early childhood services and needs and develop an integrated early childhood development strategy. In Israel and Palestine Open Society supported NGOs and a university to improve the quality of services for young children from Arab families, by supporting professional development of Arab-speaking experts. In Peru, it supported the ministry of development and social inclusion to improve the quality of *Cuna Mas*, a program which serves children below the age of three and their families, who live in poverty. An adaptation of the ISSA principles was used to scaffold development of the quality system that underpinned the center-based arm of *Cuna Mas*.

Dawn Tankersley, the US trainer and expert who worked with the team in Peru, observed that cultural differences in child-rearing may have contributed to caregivers' interest in and acceptance of the new child-centered approaches and standards that were developed collaboratively with the government:

> *South Americans are a little bit more permissive with kids. It's not as authoritarian. It's just a different dynamic than what was going on in other places I've been. They moved towards child-centered very quickly and just needed ideas of what to do with the kids.*
>
> (Dawn Tankersley, US Step by Step expert team)

The program supplied classroom materials and provided training to caregivers in centers. This had an impact on caregiver interactions there.

> *The kids in the beginning, to me, when we first went into the programs, a lot of them seemed sad. They weren't getting enough stimulation. I think by doing a little bit more training with some other caregivers, you saw them sitting down on the floors. They seemed eager to be able to play with the kids.*
>
> (Dawn Tankersley, US Step by Step expert team)

The former executive director of *Cuna Mas*, Andrea Portugal, emphasized the link between early childhood and wider societal values.

> We strongly believe that democratic values such as dialogue, respect, tolerance, solidarity, listening, citizenship, care for others and the environment are cultivated from the very early years of life ... We seek not only to improve every child's potential, but also to better educate citizens and create a democratic culture in each community we work with.
>
> (Klaus 2013)

The Early Childhood Program partnered with the Open Society Institute for Southern Africa (OSISA), in a multi-year, sub-regional initiative that spanned Lesotho, Malawi, Mozambique, eSwatini,[1] Zimbabwe, and Zambia with the aim of making a significant improvement in the early childhood sector through multi-level interventions. It invested $8 million between 2011 and 2018 to strengthen the capacity of ministries and civil society leaders, to raise public awareness, increase the capacity of professionals, community workers, parents, and research institutes, and to establish national and regional networks. The first phase of the program provided support, technical assistance, and catalytic funding to collaborative initiatives, NGOs, governments, and advocacy organizations engaged in public awareness, service delivery, networking, and capacity building. The second phase emphasized increasing access to early childhood for all children, focusing on children with special educational needs and children with disabilities (Open Society Initiative for Southern Africa 2017, 2020).

In countries like Angola and Zimbabwe, support for early childhood programming counterbalanced the politically controversial work of Open Society in areas such as media and freedom of expression.

> There were journalists who have gone into hiding at various points, because of their engagement with Open Society, but through the early childhood work, we could engage with governments. We were bringing something to the table. It was a very, very good way for Open Society to demonstrate a tangible benefit and a non-controversial value to many governments.
>
> (Tina Hyder, former deputy director, Early Childhood Program, OSF)

Like the Step by Step program, the OSISA initiative strategically supported the strengthening of civil society organizations and actors, through a series of grants and workshops. Step by Step underwent many adaptations, especially in low-resource contexts. The sections below focus on two examples.

Step by Step in Low-Resource Contexts

Step by Step was designed for implementation in a region that shared a set of political values, educational theories, practices, and experiences. It provides children and their parents with opportunities to play and learn in resourced centers. This emphasis on learning environment requires premises and educational materials. As requests came in to extend the program to countries in different regions, leaders asked how flexible the program's play-based, child-centered approach was in countries with different values. Did it have relevance in low-resource contexts and where the workforce had very different skills? This chapter explores this dilemma in two countries, one in Asia and one in Africa.

The Case of Bhutan

Between 2011 and 2013, and again in 2016 and 2017, in Bhutan, Open Society provided technical assistance to introduce training for early grade teachers and to develop a core team of experts to support the expansion of ECE to young children, prior to their entry into school at seven or eight. The initiative was a collaboration between the Royal Education Council, the ministry of education, and the Royal University of Bhutan. Open Society arranged for two Step by Step trainers from Europe, Natalia Sofiy from Ukraine, and Zorica Trikić from Serbia, to provide technical assistance. It was a new and exciting role for both of them. Sofiy first visited Bhutan with Open Society staff and describes the focus of the joint project:

> *The Royal Educational Council and ministry of education wanted us to provide training because there were no kindergartens there, so we decided to provide it for primary school teachers and to explore the possibility of organizing the preschool groups at the schools. Also, they had the opportunity to create community centers for young children, and these primary school teachers could be facilitators there.*
>
> *(Natalia Sofiy, Borys Grinchenko Kyiv University, Ukraine)*

Concerns about the resources available in classrooms and whether it would be possible to set up activity centers, which children can choose to play in and where they can engage in self-directed play, arose almost immediately. It influenced how Sofiy organized the first training.

> *My main fear was how Step by Step could be introduced given the lack of materials. During my first training I was in a mountainous, forested region, and I tried to use things that were already in the forest: leaves, flowers, and seeds. The participants helped me to collect them and we created activity centres. Then I understood that you can implement Step by Step ideas even without fancy materials. When I returned to Bhutan I visited eight of the ten kindergartens. I couldn't reach two of them because the weather conditions were so bad. I was really surprised and thrilled to see how these Bhutanese teachers, very modest,*

> with very limited possibilities and circumstances, managed to arrange everything which was important in Step by Step.
> (Natalia Sofiy, Borys Grinchenko Kyiv University, Ukraine)

A year later, members of the team from Bhutan visited Ukraine, and again, Natalia was relieved when she realized they were able to see beyond the better-equipped classrooms in Ukraine to observe teacher practices.

> They could see the real work of teachers with the children and teachers' experience.
> (Natalia Sofiy, Borys Grinchenko Kyiv University, Ukraine)

Trikić reflected on the flexibility of the Step by Step methodology to the values and curriculum in Bhutan.

> Trainings are like situations where both sides are learning. I think that here, we were learning so much about different cultures and different approaches to learning and modesty. I learned there that the Step by Step methodology and basic principles are universal. They understood it. They knew what we are talking about. They loved the idea. They thought that it fits perfectly in their values when it comes to children, and it fit even more perfectly with this idea of their gross national happiness index because everything is about making people feel well, and accepted, and welcome, and respected, and happy.

> Their enthusiasm, their willingness to learn, their openness to something that is coming from the other part of the world was amazing. They were also very clear that they want to keep some things which are important for them. The morning circle had to start with bells and Buddhist rituals. The Step by Step program created something that is based on universal values, and easy to adapt to local context. You can easily insert parts from your curriculum, insert your values, insert your expectations, and adapt them a little bit.
> (Zorica Trikić, senior program manager, ISSA)

Karma Gayleg, the ministry of education representative responsible for early childhood in Bhutan, summarized the impact of the first round of Step by Step capacity building in Bhutan:

> It helped to ease the academic-ness of about forty or fifty-odd classrooms and made them really child-friendly by removing these traditional desks and benches and then replacing them with comfortable carpets and mats and heating wherever it was cold. It changed our system a bit.
> (Karma Gayleg, specialist, ministry of education, Bhutan)

In 2016, Karma Gayleg met Tina Hyder at a regional event and they arranged for Natalia to return to Bhutan for two weeks to support a more extensive reform of the curriculum.

> *When we made our second effort, we first discussed how we could possibly blend the Step by Step approach into the existing curriculum, so that it becomes more culturally grounded and contextually relevant to what teachers were doing in their classrooms. Natalia and I worked on a contextualized module, and we trained around 40 trainers from across the country. With the help of government funds, we rolled this out in all the districts, and as a result we were able to transform more than 500 first-grade classrooms by building the capacity of first-grade teachers. In fact, my own observation is that this second round of training, which had a more contextualized structure, would have been more effective in terms of making sense to teachers.*

> *We see a lot of Step by Step impact, particularly because the government invested in rolling out the trainings provided by Natalia in the first place. Also, there is a continuing effort to move to child-centered classrooms. We are currently reviewing all the curriculum and referring to the Step by Step approach. We now hope that in the next ten years we will be able to transform the learning environment and classrooms not just for the first years, but up to Grade 3. If we are able to transform all those classes, then we will have succeeded in implementing the Step by Step approach in Bhutan's context.*
> (Karma Gayleg, specialist, ministry of education, Bhutan)

The second round of technical support, which came in response to a request from the ministry of education, amplified the impact of the earlier collaboration by deepening the contextualization of the program.

Not everyone believed Step by Step could be effective in all contexts, even when adapted. Tina Hyder, formerly the deputy director of the Early Childhood Program, reflected during the interview:

> *I think it goes back to something else in the beginning. The difference is between early childhood education (ECE) and early childhood development (ECD), and I always saw Step by Step as having a stronger focus on ECE and therefore having a better fit within education systems, including preschool educational systems. Bhutan was a space where we did perhaps much less than we've done in other places, but there was huge response. It is a small country, very specific, but ready to improve its pre-school teacher training, and therefore, we were able to offer the experience of both policy and practice, what ministries need to do, how they run our training, the ongoing support the practitioners might need. It was a very, very*

good fit at the right time, and a good meeting of the need and response as there was already a system in place with informed policy makers and practitioners to work with and take what Step by Step had to offer and adapt to context. But in Liberia, there was a different starting point.

(Tina Hyder, former deputy director, Early Childhood Program, OSF)

It is to Liberia that we now turn.

The Case of Liberia

The context in Liberia was different from that of anywhere else the Early Childhood Program had worked. Following fourteen years of civil war, very little remained of Liberia's relatively limited services for young children and families, and young children faced obstacles to their survival and development. Pregnancy and birth risks remain high in Liberia. Even today, 40 percent of women give birth at home without the help of trained midwives. As a result, it has some of the highest rates of maternal mortality globally. A tenth of children do not live to their fifth birthday, and the majority who die do so from preventable causes such as malnutrition, malaria, pneumonia, diarrhea, HIV, and measles. Widespread food poverty has dire consequences, resulting in a third of children experiencing stunting, which is associated with poorer overall development (UNICEF 2022).

Yukhiko Amnon, formerly from the ministry of education in Liberia, and Tina Hyder, formerly deputy director of the Early Childhood Program at Open Society, have written about the multi-generational impacts of the war on young children.

> The conflict left a profound legacy in the lives of young children and their families. Although not substantiated, it is anecdotally apparent that during and immediately after the conflict, teenagers, warlords, lone women, and rape victims formed significant numbers of Liberia's new parents. This has left many children with little or no care at all, in highly vulnerable situations. Acute cases of malnutrition, dysfunctional family care, poor health, and limited development outcomes were and remain common. What is striking is that many of today's parents were in fact children during the war and, consequently, probably did not receive the consistent care and nurturing, supported by effective public services, that enable children to thrive, grow, and acquire the necessary skills to parent their own children.
>
> (Amnon and Hyder 2015, 201)

Responding to a request in 2007 from the minister of education to support early childhood education, Open Society's Early Childhood Program together with colleagues from the Open Society Initiative for West Africa (OSIWA) initiated a mapping exercise to identify strengths to build on.

> *We listened to what the ministry of education was trying to do in terms of expanding the early childhood services. We were then able to find the right people, the right consultants, and to create good relationships with our OSF officers in Liberia. We needed good engagement with our local offices, because again, we were sitting in London. It's difficult to really understand context, the nuances of political engagement, and how OSF itself is perceived by other actors from such a distance. That understanding is essential if interventions are to succeed.*
> (Tina Hyder, former deputy director, Early Childhood Program, OSF)

The first joint activities focused on creating an enabling policy and financing environment to support the emerging early childhood sector in Liberia. Open Society collaborated with the World Bank to hire local researchers, supported by international consultants, to map the early childhood context and develop a cross-sectoral early childhood policy with defined roles for each ministry, which was then approved by Parliament. Although not initially an area of interest for many international agencies working in the country, early childhood education made it into the country's ten-year Education Sector Plan and ultimately into international development aid to rebuild the education system.

> My first Liberia consultant visit for Open Society was in partnership with the World Bank team. In collaboration with the Ministry of Education we assembled every group involved in early childhood and mapped where they were working. The twelve groups attending were operating in two of the fifteen counties. That was a definite indication that we must garner the support of local, national, and international partners, government, faith-based education secretariats, civil society and even find new partners to design and develop the early childhood eco-system and its human capital.
> (Kamara Ferguson 2020)

Over more than ten years (2008–21), Open Society funded pilot projects and capacity building efforts to support the embedding of early childhood education and development across sectors. This included piloting early childhood classrooms at women's markets, in primary schools and in rural communities; developing early education curriculum and teacher training; introducing family literacy and home visiting programs; and launching community-based group programs for pregnant women and fathers-to-be. To complement these policy and program-focused initiatives, Open Society funded a robust agenda of capacity building to build up a workforce and a cadre of early childhood professionals. This included regular trainings, workshops, and a national conference for staff from the many institutions working with young children; study visits to South Africa and the United States; scholarships for seventeen Liberians to gain postgraduate certificates and/or master's degrees at the University of Haifa and the Early Childhood Development Virtual University; establishment of a four-tiered system of training to address the different needs of parents, community workers, teachers, and experts; and the introduction of early childhood development courses at higher education institutions across the country.

All of this was supported by local staff and long-term consultants hired by Open Society, most notably Sia Barbara Kamara Ferguson, a prominent former director of the US Head Start program, and a Peace Corps volunteer in Liberia in the 1960s.

> Our theory of change involved multi-level awareness, knowledge building based on early childhood science, development of pilot sites and a community of learners to better educate those most intimately involved in early childhood including mentoring and coaching for the team at the Ministry. Several critical factors have contributed to achieving these results. They include the Early Childhood Program's longevity in terms of leverage funding, partnerships and a consultant team committed to supporting the co-development of a Liberian early childhood eco-system.
>
> (Kamara Ferguson 2020)

From the start, the focus in Liberia was on early childhood development rather than on early education. In such a war-torn country, the mandate was broader. Like Step by Step, however, the initiative sought out and supported change agents and people committed to young children, equity, and inclusion.

> *Understanding [the devastation after the war], we didn't start with teacher training, we started instead with community, with parenting materials, and then over time built a systematic ladder of qualifications for people working with children. This slow investment led to a dedicated group of people and organisations in Liberia, that were committed to a shared vision and committed over time to build a system ... It's a very difficult, under-resourced environment to work in, hugely politically volatile, but over time, by working with a consistent core group of people, they effected a substantive change to the early childhood system there, which the World Bank and UNICEF built on.*
>
> (Tina Hyder, former deputy director, Early Childhood Program, OSF)

This layering of initiatives and opportunities was possible because OSIWA had an engaged office and staff, working closely with the actors on the ground. An internal Open Society Foundations review captured this learning:

> It was noted that the Early Childhood Program's work in the Liberian context can be seen as a test bed for the systemic approach. Despite funding being relatively thinly spread and much need, the strategy used in this portfolio has made an important contribution. In an environment where the education and health systems have been so broken down, a narrow focus may be less successful. It indicates that we should not always avoid a systemic approach based on the assumption that it is too broad. The investments made in this portfolio have been small but are proving to be catalytic.
>
> (Open Society Foundations 2018)

The project in Liberia invested in people and organizations—government, NGOs, INGOs, academia—over a period of a decade to contribute substantially to rebuilding systems that support young children.

Lessons Learned from Working in Low-Resource Contexts

Several distinctions between the work in Bhutan and Liberia are notable. First, the initiative in Bhutan was initially time-bound (two years) and focused on teacher training, drawing heavily on Step by Step. However, Open Society was responsive to a request for additional support from the ministry of education several years later, which resulted in revisions to the curriculum. While the first joint activities focused on methodology, introducing child-centered approaches, the second collaboration went further to elaborate and contextualize the national curriculum. In contrast, the program in Liberia spanned more than a decade and engaged across sectors with a broader focus on early childhood development. In both countries, the ministry of education was a primary partner; however, in Liberia, where the ministry led implementation of the cross-sectoral early childhood development policy, Open Society also participated in strategy retreats, renovated and equipped the ministry offices where the early childhood team worked, and provided salaries for additional staff. The Monrovia office of OSIWA collaborated with government, NGOs, academic organizations, and INGOs and not only supported advocates, but also advocated directly for early childhood as a government priority. In Liberia, the initiative brought together staff from three teacher training institutions and eighteen colleges to develop courses to train an early childhood workforce. Open Society provided full scholarships, study visits, and trainings and contributed to a national conference to build the professional capacity in the country.

Seed-funding a variety of initiatives across the wider early childhood ecosystem (see Chapter 9) was essential in post-war Liberia. A similar cross-sectoral approach also featured in Haiti, which embedded adult literacy and health programs in the communities implementing Step by Step.

New Countries Provide an Anchor for Regional and Global Work

The experience of working in such a variety of contexts grounded Open Society's subsequent investments in regional and global initiatives. A key aspect of open societies is the principle that people have both the right and responsibility to shape, through advocacy, input, debate, and elections, the decisions that impact their lives. Strong civil society organizations and networks are essential for this purpose. Open Society supported professional regional networks in Europe, Eurasia, Asia, Africa, and in the Arab region, as well as global networks and early childhood networks focused on themes like early intervention, Roma, and refugees. These networks endure and serve as hubs of information sharing, advocacy, and learning, and they elevate the authentic voices and perspectives of national experts in regional and global forums.

> *I think we helped others to advocate for the services that mattered to them in contexts that they knew better than we did, and I think that's the right way to do things. OSF invested in the global early childhood ecosystem nationally, regionally, internationally, to reflect represent and consolidate voices, convey information to and from members, and as a conduit for best practice, for understanding, and interpreting, whether about the Sustainable Development Goals or issues such as migration or support for parenting.*
>
> (Tina Hyder, former deputy director, Early Childhood Program, OSF)

Like the work in Step by Step countries, the global portfolio kept grassroots interests at the forefront.

> *There's a whole movement about localization right now. In some ways, you were ahead of that. I think that's the point here. Foundations need to focus on community, it seems to me, and listening to community and responding to community and having that bottom-up thinking. That means giving up some power.*
>
> (Hirokazu Yoshikawa, New York University, former board member, Early Childhood Program Advisory Board, OSF)

> *I think we got the balance right. The investment in civil society was right in building the leaders, the practitioners, the grassroots services, those people who are actually on the frontline with children or families or providing training or development. Other, larger agencies can seem so removed sometimes from what's really happening on the ground, although I think we were good peers and colleagues. Our contribution was often our emphasis on equity, on marginalized groups, and civil society.*
>
> *(Tina Hyder, former deputy director, Early Childhood Program, OSF)*

Open Society also supported development of global child assessment and financing tools, childcare initiatives, and advocacy and collaborated with other donors to encourage global institutions and agencies to prioritize early childhood. It joined international partners pushing to include early childhood development in the Sustainable Development Goals (SDGs).

> *At least in the years that I was on the advisory board, the global policy work felt like it was coming at a point where it could make a difference around the SDGs and immediately after the SDGs, when there was this opportunity for much greater global coordination and advocacy around ECD. That took advantage of that moment to really make a difference.*
>
> *(Hirokazu Yoshikawa, New York University, former board member, Early Childhood Program Advisory Board, OSF)*

This global work, like the work in Liberia, used an early childhood development rather than an early childhood education framework, and it coalesced around the familiar themes of equity and social inclusion.

> *We weren't a big funder, but we were often a catalyst and a glue, and we represented a particular philosophy of inclusion and equity that was not necessarily championed by any of the other foundations. We became a key component of all the various groups that began to organize, to solidify the work of early childhood. When the World Bank and others brought people together, we were always included, because we had changed things in that region. As we became interested in more than the region, we became interested in the deeper issues that were embedded in the philosophy of Step by Step, and those deeper issues really relate to equity and inclusion.*
>
> *(Phyllis Magrab, Georgetown University, former board chair, Early Childhood Program Advisory Board, OSF)*

Over time, though, more donors entered the field, wielding more funding and eventually greater influence on global early childhood priorities.

> *What was interesting was watching other philanthropic foundations come in with much bigger budgets and I think we still exerted influence beyond the budget that we had because of our longevity and our past history. Over time, we did get swamped by bigger actors in terms of leverage.*
>
> *(Tina Hyder, former deputy director, Early Childhood Program, OSF)*

Open Society was unique in investing over long periods of time in people and organizations that function as agents of change and that can bring forward the movement toward democracy and equity. This contrasts with the many donors focusing on achieving quantitative outcomes through rapid, government-led scale-up projects.

> *We'll miss the principles and the values that come from the rights, advocacy, inclusion, and perspective that's just at the very core of the Open Society Foundations. That perspective in early childhood can get lost if you're simply focusing on scale.*
>
> *(Hirokazu Yoshikawa, New York University, former board member, Early Childhood Program Advisory Board, OSF)*

> *I think I'm quite proud that we stayed with things. Some other donors now, just two years they're gone, three years they're gone.*
>
> *(Tina Hyder, former deputy director, Early Childhood Program, OSF)*

Part Four

Transforming Early Childhood Education Systems

9

"This Is Yours": Successful Transformations of Early Education Systems

> *In the Open Society Foundations, we've always wanted to see systemic change because you can have good practices and good schools, but they are just for the lucky few. We want to see quality education for all children, that's our goal.*
> (Dženana Trbić, former education program coordinator, Open Society Fund - Bosnia and Herzegovina)

Figure 9.1 Professionals from Slovenia and Italy participating in a week-long training on quality-informed, non-formal early childhood education and care at the International Step by Step Association, Leiden, NL 2022.

Strategies toward Sustainable Change

Most programs that seek to implement a new pedagogical approach aim to reach as many teachers and schools as possible. At the start, Open Society's Step by Step program sought to reach as many preschools as possible. Later, the program also tried to realize systemic and sustainable improvements in the early years of primary school too. Silova (2008) describes several phases in Open Society's strategic approach to education reform. In its early years Open Society focused on implementing pilot projects, such as Step by Step, that focused on training teachers and trainers. The underlying assumption was that pilot projects would be replicated by governments and/or by international donors. However, eventually the foundation realized that the link between demonstration projects and sustainable systems change was often weak (Silova and Steiner-Khamsi 2008). A representative of a national Soros foundation described it as follows: "We were strong on the mission but weak on strategic thinking" (Silova and Steiner-Khamsi 2008, 55).

At a workshop in 1998 in Matrahaza, Hungary, a strategic reorientation was put forward to education program directors and board members of the Open Society Foundations. This was the start of a second strategic phase, which focused on the sustainability and systemic impact of Open Society-funded pilot education initiatives. It entailed influencing and supporting changes at higher levels in the education system, as well as encouraging system-wide replication of Open Society's pilot projects by governments. It also inspired the "spinning off" of education projects that were operated by the national foundations, and the establishment of new networks of civil society organizations that could advance the open society values and mission independently and indefinitely. In the third phase, Open Society concentrated on national education policymaking and advocacy to influence reforms, linking these with pilot projects wherever possible (Silova and Steiner-Khamsi 2008).

Translated to the Step by Step program, this more strategic approach to sustainability had important consequences. The survival of the program could no longer depend solely on the quality of the project's implementation and the professional education capacity of the program staff. With guidance and support from the Open Society Foundations, Step by Step programs would become independent of the national foundations. Sustainability now depended on the ability of the country teams working inside the national foundations to take on "the challenge of establishing and directing new non-governmental organizations in countries that have previously had no history of permitting a strong third sector" (Klaus 2004, 7). By 2004, twenty-seven of the thirty Step by Step programs were operated by independent early childhood organizations, including NGOs and membership associations. These newly established NGOs formed partnerships and secured independent funding to maintain program growth and retain quality (Silova and Steiner-Khamsi 2008).

The resulting development model for a Step by Step country evolved from a two-year pilot project in preschools into an eight-year trajectory embracing changes in preschools, primary schools, higher education institutions, and in ministry policies, as summarized in Figure 9.2.

As the model illustrates, the Step by Step program launched in each country with the introduction of training and demonstration classrooms in preschools and continued with the training and creation of demonstration classrooms in primary schools. Ongoing professional development and training in project sites by the core Step by Step country team continued for at least five years to

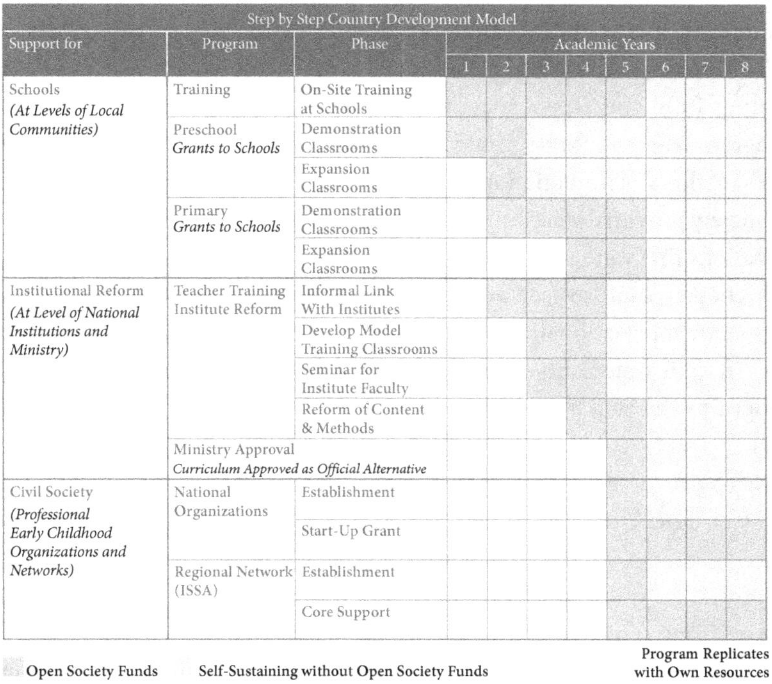

Step by Step Country Development Model									
Support for	Program	Phase	Academic Years						
			1	2	3	4	5	6	7	8
Schools (At Levels of Local Communities)	Training	On-Site Training at Schools								
	Preschool Grants to Schools	Demonstration Classrooms								
		Expansion Classrooms								
	Primary Grants to Schools	Demonstration Classrooms								
		Expansion Classrooms								
Institutional Reform (At Level of National Institutions and Ministry)	Teacher Training Institute Reform	Informal Link With Institutes								
		Develop Model Training Classrooms								
		Seminar for Institute Faculty								
		Reform of Content & Methods								
	Ministry Approval Curriculum Approved as Official Alternative									
Civil Society (Professional Early Childhood Organizations and Networks)	National Organizations	Establishment								
		Start-Up Grant								
	Regional Network (ISSA)	Establishment								
		Core Support								

Open Society Funds   Self-Sustaining without Open Society Funds   Program Replicates with Own Resources

Figure 9.2 Step by Step Country Development Model.
@International Step by Step Association

support the establishment of high-quality demonstration sites across the country. Beginning in the second year, if not before, linkages were made with faculty at teacher training institutes (pre-service and in-service) and faculty were invited to participate in higher education seminars. Promising preschools were selected to serve as model training sites, and these sites were provided with materials and furniture to enable them to host visitors and trainings. Agreements between the national Open Society Foundations and the ministries were signed at the start of the program in each country. By the fifth year, it was expected that preschool and primary methodologies would receive official approval from ministries as alternatives that could be introduced in any interested preschool or primary school.

According to the model, to secure the longevity of the Step by Step movement in each country and across the region, national civil society organizations were established in each country in the fifth year of the program, and the Step by Step team was "spun off" from the national Open Society Foundation into an independent entity. In 1998 the International Step by Step Association, a regional network, was established by Step by Step teams to advance the values of democratic, inclusive, child-centered early childhood.

Collectively, the country development model outlined at least eight years of funding from the Open Society Foundations. During the first five years, the program team would be funded and would operate from within the Open Society's national foundation in the country. From the fifth year onwards, Open Society provided start-up and follow-on grant(s) to the non-governmental organizations that were now leading the program.

This chapter captures the reflections of Step by Step NGO directors, US trainers, and international experts about their efforts to introduce systemic changes in ECE systems to ensure the sustainability of the democratic reforms introduced by the Step by Step program.

The Competent System as a Framework for Understanding Step by Step

We know from research that to realize sustainable change, a program must intervene at every level of the educational system. The CoRe study commissioned by the European Commission explored conceptualizations of *competence* and professionalism in early childhood, and identified systemic conditions for developing competence at all levels of the early childhood system in order to improve quality in a sustainable way (Urban et al. 2011; Vandenbroeck, Urban, and Peeters 2016). This chapter uses the framework of the CoRe study to analyze how Step by Step impacted early childhood systems.

Figure 9.3 describes the different levels of a competent system that are important to realize sustainable change: the teacher, preschool/school, civil society organizations, local governments and training centers, the ministry of education, and international organizations and donors. This competent system is surrounded by a triangle consisting of research and training, policymaking, and practice, and successful programs are active in making the efforts of research, policy, and practice visible and comprehensible to one another (Peeters and Peleman 2017). The competent system presents a positive view of change and a notion that real reform can happen when there is a shared goal (in this case the democratic approach and the child-centeredness of the Step by Step program) that connects the areas in this triangle. The CoRe framework can be applied to Step by Step's aim of achieving universally available and accessible high-quality inclusive ECE services for all children and their families.

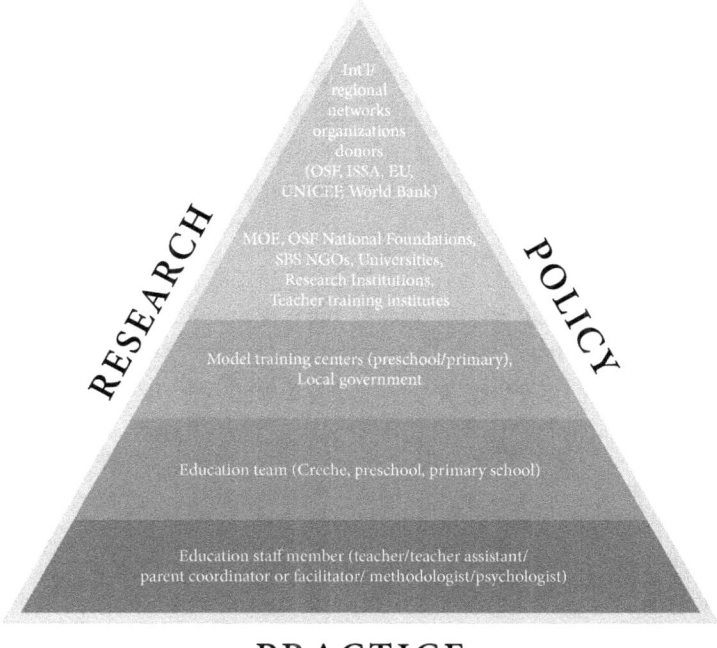

Figure 9.3 The CoRe framework and research/policy/practice triangle applied to the Step by Step program.

@International Step by Step Association

The Step by Step Approach as a Shared Goal to Change the Education System

An Open and Flexible Program

Not everyone agrees with the choice of the Open Society Foundations to use an American program to introduce democratic reforms into European education systems. Henriette Heimgartner, who worked for the Bernard van Leer Foundation after the fall of the Berlin wall, opted to construct a new pedagogical approach for their new program in Poland by linking Polish practitioners and researchers with German experts.

> *I don't want, as a first step, some Westerners walking into here and telling these Polish people what to do. After back and forth, I said to Teresa, who ran the program in Poland: "Okay, Teresa, you are going to find some innovative people. I cannot imagine in a population of 47 million people, you don't have a couple of innovative psychologists to do training on ECE. Just find them."*
>
> (Henriette Heimgaertner, board chair, ISSA, formerly Bernard van Leer Foundation)

However, those with more familiarity with the US Head Start program note similarities in how both Step by Step and Head Start need to be adaptable to multiple cultural and policy contexts. More specifically, Head Start was designed for the United States, where decisions about early education and childcare are decentralized to states and localized for communities, so flexibility is built into the program design.

> *Head Start has a focus on interrogating the idea of cultural relevance in early childhood programming and the notion of community-initiated models and the integration of culturally specific models of socialization in early childhood development.*
>
> (Hirokazu Yoshikawa, New York University, former board member, Early Childhood Program Advisory Board, OSF)

Head Start's evidence-based program is successfully implemented in US states with different contexts, and the program has developed tools and a system of coaching and professional development for practitioners. According to several interviewees, this openness and flexibility and the availability of didactical materials and tools made Head Start particularly suitable for introducing a democratic and child-centered pedagogy in the region.

> *I think the flexibility in the approach of the program is perhaps one of its most important strengths because it allows organisations in various countries to follow their national curriculum, and to approach the curriculum using the Step by Step methodology. It was a tool to promote principles and values, principles that support quality in early education for every child. In that respect, the program helped the NGOs make a shift from teacher-centred to child-centred principles and to support this shift with a whole comprehensive resource package that had not just the tools, but mechanisms for training, coaching, or piloting projects.*
> (Liana Ghent, executive director, ISSA)

Step by Step programs have capitalized on this flexibility to develop unique national approaches to early childhood. Step by Step-inspired methodologies, trainings, and curriculums in each country have been shaped by the national NGOs and local experts and respond to national education laws and strategies, local languages and cultures, and the historical trajectory and current ecosystem of early childhood in the country. They are not copies of Head Start, but Head Start inspired them to embrace parent involvement, child-centered, developmentally appropriate approaches, and democratic values of equity and social inclusion.

Reflecting on Practice and Creating New Pedagogical Practices

The openness and flexibility of Step by Step allowed practitioners and trainers to "make mistakes," to reflect on daily practice, and to construct new pedagogical practices adapted to diverse social and cultural contexts. From this perspective, the approach is quite similar to contemporary western European pedagogies like the north Italian approach (Malaguzzi et al. 1998).

> *You can always do things differently, but you never know whether it will work. This pilot programme showed us how to continue even when the way forward wasn't obvious. We had such freedom to try different methods. We had the chance to make mistakes and start again.*
> (Alena Panikova, former executive director, Open Society Foundation—Bratislava)

But there were differences between the countries involved. Several interviewees commented that teachers in Central Asian countries had less freedom and flexibility in their classrooms to work according to the Step by Step pedagogy, and perhaps more time was needed to support changes in practice in classrooms and, more broadly, educational reforms in general.

> *As you moved further and further east, I think the concepts of Step by Step were much more foreign. It wasn't part of the cultural context and so it was much harder to motivate the teachers, the Step by Step directors, the ministry people.*
> (Dawn Tankersley, US Step by Step expert team)

While Step by Step offered opportunities for practitioners to reflect on their personal and collective pedagogic practices, more time may be needed to support changes in different cultural contexts to achieve sustainable results.

Investment in Continuous Professional Development Based on Trust, Warm Relationships, and Ownership of the Change Process

Building Trust through Participation

> *In communist times, people had very, very limited contact with other people. They only trusted their family members and outside their families there was not much trust because the party was always behind them. Now, for the people involved in our Bernard Van Leer project in Poland for the first time, they have an idea that they can also trust other people outside their families, and they have similar ideas, and they can create something together.*
> (Henriette Heimgaertner, board chair, ISSA, formerly Bernard van Leer Foundation)

Some interviewees took issue with the idea that there was broad mistrust within society because of the era of communist-led governments, and some referred instead to mistrust of an American-led program. Yet it was important that innovative projects in ECE invested in the development of a comprehensive system of participation based on trust and warm relationships, which lead to ownership of the change process through the responsibility given to the actors. Again, we see the link with the north Italian approach:

> Participation nurtures professionalism. The staff member should be the first to nurture the pleasure of participation, draw meaning from meetings, and find the opportunity to qualify and enrich his/her professionalism through participation.
> (Rinaldi 2005, 54)

Step by Step also gives a lot of autonomy to practitioners, and most teachers that followed the training or the mentoring sessions became actors of the change process. After a while they felt an ownership of the values and the principles of the program. Participation also has an impact on the children: they became actors in their own learning process. But again, there were differences between and within countries.

> We were not dogmatic. We tried really hard to say: "This is something we're giving to you. Let's see how it works. You don't have to do this exactly the same way. This is yours. There are certain things that are foundational, but this is yours."
> (Roxane Kaufmann, US Step by Step expert team)

> It is not freedom from restraints. It's freedom for responsibility. That responsibility goes down to the kids. They can take responsibility for their classrooms. Obviously, they have to take responsibility for their own learning and be guided into that maturation process. When I was in the classroom, I wanted the classroom to run by itself.
> (Kate Burke Walsh, US Step by Step expert team)

For Alena Panikova from Slovakia, trust was an important condition for success in working with teachers in a participatory way, and trainers were selected from the teacher community. They knew the problems in the sector and one of the most important criteria for their selection for the job as a mentor or trainer was their ability to motivate and support teachers. The transition from a teacher- to a child-centered approach is for many teachers not obvious. It requires a change in their professional identity, so they need to trust that it will work in practice (Peeters and Vandenbroeck 2011).

> It often comes down to those intangible things, like trust. Can you, as a teacher, relinquish control in your classroom and trust the kids without feeling that your role is diminished? I think it was also an indicator, over time, that we were building trust with the people in the countries, the directors, and the curriculum folks who were really managing some of the schools and that they trusted us to be able to ask those vulnerable questions.
> (Kate Burke Walsh, US Step by Step expert team)

A Participative Approach Created Committed Mentors

What emerges in nearly all the interviews is the warmth between trainers, mentors, and practitioners. We see the same in the ISSA network. Liana Ghent calls it "trying to be decent human beings in everything we do." Chapter 3 includes testimonies about the warm atmosphere during the first training in the United States. This approach to starting a new program with intensive training and a mentoring system that builds ownership through participation and a warm climate of trust has proven to be effective in other projects seeking to create a more democratic and child-centered approach (Peeters and Vandenbroeck 2011).

> *It was really a special program because of so many women being involved. For me, it was like a big group of friends. My impression was that the people there were really devoted to it, excited about it.*
> *(Alena Panikova, former executive director, Open Society Foundation—Bratislava)*

But alongside the warm, participative approach, the US training was also an efficient transmission of the necessary knowledge and competencies needed to convince teachers of the value of the Step by Step approach. This significant investment in training all the country directors and master teacher trainers in the United States ended up being cost-effective, because members of these early cohorts remained with the program for years, even decades, and they have trained thousands of teachers in their own countries. Another important condition for success, noted in a scale-up study of the Macedonia program, was that the Step by Step team selected competent teachers and directors of preschools who were able and willing to take part in the program (Misik and Velkovski 2011).

The program provided not only intensive participatory training, but also high-quality resources that could be used in all forms of continuous professional development: mentoring, courses, professional learning communities, peer learning groups, and so on. The Step by Step methodologies, training manuals, brochures, and videos played an important role in convincing policymakers from ministries of education to support the child-centered approach of Step by Step, and they inspired development of new curricula in many countries. Crucially, tools were translated into all the languages of the different countries and adapted to each context by the Step by Step team in that country. This, of course, was a huge investment on the part of the Open Society Foundations (Ionescu et al. 2018).

> *The most important thing is that we have the tools, the ISSA resource pack, and we have videos that we produced, which are the basis for critical analysis and for building up a shared understanding of child-centred education, and for thinking critically about our own practices.*
> *(Tatjana Vonta, co-author and former director, Step by Step Slovenia)*

ISSA continues to support collaborative professional development, including through professional learning communities (Brajković 2014) and joint projects, which bring together Step by Step practitioners with practitioners and experts from across Europe and Eurasia.

Working inside the Triangle of Research, Policy, and Practice: Not Always an Easy Task

The CoRe Study (Urban et al. 2011) introduces the components of a competent early childhood system that develops through mutual relations between individuals, teams, preschools, research and training centers, and the broader social and political context, and that operates on local, national, and international levels. Competent systems flourish best inside the triangle of policy, research, and practice. The implication is that innovative projects should engage in dialogue with universities, training centers, and policymakers and this is what the Step by Step program did.

Higher Education Institutes and Universities as Partners

The initial two-year plan for Step by Step involved linking the pilot sites with local universities and higher education institutes that would provide pre-service training for ECE practitioners. Professors were included in the very first training in countries in 1994. From 1996 onward Step by Step implemented an extensive "Higher Education Initiative" which was as big as the preschool and primary programs and focused on university professors (see Chapter 3). By 2003, Open Society Foundation had trained nearly 2,000 university professors from across the region in multiple training programs, and also developed eight semester-length university courses (each with a solid syllabus with activities) and a guide on how to organize Step by Step classrooms.

> It was enormous! But our mistake was that we were influencing individual professors, not the higher educational system.
>
> (Sarah Klaus, co-author and former director, Early Childhood Program, OSF)

Many professors were invited to training but initially there was no structured set of plans for the reform of pre-service teacher training programs.

> I knew what a child-centred approach is, but only when I started to become familiar with Step by Step was I aware of everything that the child-centered approach represents.
>
> Teacher, Faculty for Education, Armenia
> (Ionescu et al. 2018, 63)

According to ISSA (Ionescu et al. 2018) and several interviewees, universities in most of the countries where Step by Step was implemented were very traditional and teacher-centered. The initial university training for early education teachers focused on theoretical knowledge with little relevance to pedagogical work in the classroom. There were some didactical courses on art, music, dance, drama, physical education, nature, language, and mathematics, but the link between theory and practice through internship was weak.

Step by Step was not the only organization that found it difficult to work with universities to introduce sustainable change in early education. Henriette Heimgartner, who worked for the Bernard van Leer Foundation in Poland, and Deepa Grover, who worked across the region for UNICEF, had similar experiences.

> *I have later on often reflected on the fact that I didn't involve the university because it was so difficult to find people that understood what we were talking about.*
>
> (Henriette Heimgaertner, board chair, ISSA, formerly Bernard van Leer Foundation)

> *We (UNICEF) tried at that time to do some work with pre-service training. To get schools of higher education and universities to change their curricula and their methodology takes seven or ten years, and that's whole generations of young children. It was more pragmatic to work with in-service training, but ultimately, systems at the university level, higher education institutions, need to be changed because the kind of things students are taught over there are not necessarily practical. They're not up to date with the science of early childhood, with contemporary pedagogy, which is now much more child-centered. They're given a lot of theory, a lot of things that students have to memorize. It's very complicated to break into higher education because that's a whole different kind of sector to work with. You come into conflict with university professors who've been around forever and who've lived through and been trained during the old times ... it needs a generational change. It's just too difficult to break through existing barriers.*
>
> *(Deepa Grover, former UNICEF regional advisor for Europe and Central Asia)*

Although all Step by Step programs were able to establish strong connections with at least one higher education institution, and most established connections with multiple institutions, doing so across a region or country has been even more difficult. The program's connections with higher institutions are generally about relationships with individual professors, for example, who serve as representatives on the boards of the Step by Step NGOs, or teachers or professors of higher education that become Step by Step trainers (Ionescu et al. 2018). In Moldova, a funder identified work with higher education institutions as a way to better sustain the changes that the ISSA Quality Resource Pack proposes. The higher education institutions that were included in the project showed a much more limited understanding of child-centered approaches than the staff of the Step by Step organization did, creating conflict about how change should happen. But in some countries, like Armenia, we see positive developments.

> At this moment, the faculty of education is in the process of modernising its teaching process and the content of programs for future teachers. The goals of this process are very much in line with the goals pursued through the Step by Step approach. The process influenced the staff. They are aware that the programs are changing and that they will need new content, tools and materials to prepare future teachers for their profession. Another important change regards the conceptualization and organisation of the practicum. There have been changes in the way that the faculty establishes partnerships and cooperation with other organizations. They can invite organisations and individuals from outside to provide some activities for the faculty and students. All these changes supported their idea to introduce the Quality Resource Pack of Step by Step and connected the faculty with the Step by Step Benevolent Foundation.
>
> Head of Department, Faculty of Education, Armenia
> (Ionescu et al. 2018, 68)

Can Civil Society Organizations Change the ECE System?

Chapter 3 describes how the initial strategy of the Open Society Foundations focused on piloting Step by Step in preschools and schools to inspire interest in the program and gain ministry approval for the program as an official alternative approach. In these early years, the program operated out of the well-established national foundations affiliated with the Open Society Foundations. After 1998, Open Society focused on developing civil society organizations as the leading actors of change. NGOs were set up to continue to develop and expand the Step by Step program, and their role included embedding it into the education system. Continuous professional development was organized not only by the NGOs, but also by in-service training institutions. In some countries (Albania and Macedonia), the ministry hired master trainers at model sites and these new staff (funded by the ministry) provided training and mentoring. In most countries, this seemed to be a good strategy. The number of teachers who received continuous professional development from Step by Step organizations and model sites together with in-service training institutions, usually with ministry support, was impressive.

> *The strategy that was adopted by the Open Society Foundations and by the trainers who were hired to promote child-centered education was to create model classrooms with this furniture that would break down the tradition of having children sit one behind the other at tables. The aim was to organise the environment differently and to train teachers from these classrooms so that they become role models. There were at least two people per institution that were trained, and two classrooms per institution that were promoting this change, because a teacher could not do it alone. That was a really good strategy from the very beginning, and it worked. We saw our role as an NGO that implemented changes through in-service teacher training. We're on the list of training centres of the Ministry of Education. Last year, we even got accredited by the national authority on quality and education.*
> *(Cornelia Cincilei, Step by Step Moldova)*

But in some countries, NGOs were not able to change the early education teacher training system, particularly if universities or higher education institutes were not involved in the process of change or were not convinced of the importance of this democratic and child-centered approach and resisted the Step by Step approach.

> *We had this imbalance between excellent early childhood centres, with teachers who believed in Step by Step ideas, and on the other side, we had the pre-service teacher training, which lacked ownership of the Step by Step pedagogy. Two different worlds. If you empower one teacher, the system will not change in our region. You have to influence policymakers and initial training centres.*
> *(Ulviyya Mikayilova, ADA University, Azerbaijan)*

The Step by Step program's Higher Education Initiative engaged universities and pre-service training institutions from 1996 onward (see Chapter 3), because they realized how important universities are in achieving sustainable systemic reforms. There are examples of long-term projects that have been set up in which the NGOs and the universities or higher education institutions work together.

> *One of the priorities became reaching out to the faculty of the pre-service teacher training institutions because unless the initial training changed, we would have to continue to retrain teachers. That was a very good strategic decision. There was, as you know, great resistance in those higher education institutions and I would say that we are now in the final stage, just one month left of this long-term project implementation of more than 10 years.*
>
> (Cornelia Cincilei, Step by Step Moldova)

In a limited number of cases, the collaboration between higher education institutions and the Step by Step NGOs had some negative side effects. For instance, some used Step by Step resources without acknowledging their source. In other cases, professors failed to understand the Step by Step approach, due to their insufficient understanding of child-centered pedagogy and how to put it into practice.

> *University professors who were involved in those reforms took our materials, and they embedded them in national documents but with no mention of the source. The problem is not that we didn't get any credit, but it is a pity that we were not more involved in clarifying the approach, not only to teachers but also to the governmental people, and people from the Education and Teacher Training Agency. There still is a big gap between what's written in policy papers, and what's going on in practice.*
>
> (Nives Milinović, former director, Open Academy Step by Step, Croatia, and former board president, ISSA)

Studies commissioned by UNICEF show that the gap between theory and practice and the lack of interdisciplinary collaboration between lecturers is still a problem in Montenegro, Bosnia, Kosovo, Albania, Serbia, Ukraine, and Georgia. But in Serbia and Georgia there have been some interesting reforms of the initial training programs (Peeters 2016; Peeters 2018; Peeters 2021; Peeters and Miskeljin 2018). An analysis of proposals for a new bachelor program for preschool teachers in Georgia, for instance, indicates that there is a need for more internship (practice) and also for more clusters of courses in which several lecturers work together with coaches who are responsible for the supervision of the students during internship (Peeters 2021).

> *I think that it's now time for interdisciplinary work, and they will push this idea when they find out that they cannot develop their knowledge and their science*

without an interdisciplinary approach. Then they will have to change themselves, because it will be hard to survive.
(Tatjana Vonta, co-author and former director, Step by Step Slovenia)

Collaboration with the Ministry of Education (MoE)

According to the CoRe study, another important condition for achieving sustainable change in the education system is strong collaboration with the ministry of education (MoE). The national foundations in each country launched Step by Step with two-year agreements with the MoE. The agreements gave the foundation permission to introduce Step by Step in the education system and stipulated that after two years of implementing and evaluating Step by Step in pilot kindergartens, the ministry would, if the initiative was successful, grant approval for any interested kindergarten to take up the program. Like the collaboration with the universities and pre-service training organizations, this was not always possible to realize. In some cases, this collaboration was smooth. In others, particularly where there were authoritarian governments, it was challenging. Yet some countries had success in working with the ministry despite the fact that ministry staff changed with each new government.

For more than two decades the CIP-Center for Interactive Pedagogy (CIP Center), the Step by Step organisation in Serbia, has been recognized for its expertise and contributions towards improving the quality and inclusiveness of education. Throughout political changes and educational reforms the CIP Center has managed to find a way to cooperate with the ministry of education and donors to support the reform processes through capacity building of teachers and developing models for improving specific aspects of the education system. The ministry of education has always pursued its own pathway to reform, and as a result the Step by Step methodology was never adopted fully as a mainstream approach. However, within the framework of cooperation with the ministry and through projects, key elements of the Step by Step program have been disseminated through our trainings and mentoring support to preschool institutions, primary and secondary schools.
(Milena Mihajlović, CIP-Center for Interactive Pedagogy, Serbia)

ISSA's study on quality improvement (Ionescu et al. 2018) describes how in Albania, Bosnia and Herzegovina, Kosovo, Kyrgyzstan, and Slovakia the ministry of education and other government entities (such as municipal governments in Slovakia) have been major allies in the implementation of the Step by Step Quality Resource Pack.

Until 2010, there had been differences between ISSA's definition of quality and the requirements in national policy documents, but now on paper the approaches are almost the same. The problem is with the implementation, as we are working with a huge number of schools and teachers. I am working directly with fifty-one schools. We provide training and monitoring, but mentoring is missing.

Head of primary education department,
National Institute for Education, Armenia
(Ionescu et al. 2018, 68)

In Serbia, as in other countries involved in the Step by Step program, the Step by Step organization CIP is seen as a key player in the ECE sector. CIP has had a lot of impact on official documents and on the development of pedagogical principles and standards. A concrete example is the new Serbian preschool curriculum framework, "Years of Ascent," published in 2018. It is a child-centered and holistic curriculum, one of the best in Europe (Peeters and Miskeljin 2018). The name Step by Step is not mentioned in these official texts, but according to Zorica Trikić this is not important: "*It is about creating a positive change, not about ownership!*" When the political situation is difficult, Zorica Trikić advises "*not to fight the system, but to find a way to play along with the system.*" In periods when the government was not favorable toward a democratic and child-centered approach, it was important to open up the dialogue with the MoE.

> *I don't say that there were not people who created challenges. Some people would say: "Soviet education was not bad, everything was good. We just have to return to Soviet education." In this case, we had to maintain a dialogue.*
>
> *We talked to the minister of education and we cited Vygotsky. This is very important because he knew Vygotsky from his training in pedagogy. When you mentioned Vygotsky to people of the MoE, they felt more comfortable and said, "Yes, yes, yes, of course, we know Vygotsky," and they would be more interested.*
>
> (Zuhra Halimova, former executive director (Tajikistan) and advisory board member, OSF)

Changing the National Early Education System Is Not a Linear Process

Politics Matter

What we learned from the interviews is that reforming systems is not a linear process. There were periods when ministers were supporting change and in those periods Step by Step got a lot of support and was able to influence the development of new curricula, official texts, and policies. This was the case in the 1990s in Moldova.

> *In the two years that I spent at the ministry of education, I was part of a team of reformers, and the vice-minister was the promoter of many reforms. It was a very good time for those changes. The challenge was that people were not ready for that and many things were apparently pushed top-down. There was quite a lot of resistance.*
> *(Cornelia Cincilei, Step by Step Moldova)*

But in many instances, a change in government can block the process of reform of the ECE system for years. Sometimes governments seek to return to the former education system; in other cases, nationalist authoritarian parties have come into power that were hostile toward the Open Society Foundations. In those periods of resistance Step by Step organizations often refocused on in-service training, rather than policy reform. This required a flexible team.

> *The Step by Step program became the official curriculum for preschools for many years. The main features also became part of the official national curriculum in primary schools. After the elections, the new government saw the Soros Foundation as an enemy and we were not allowed to enter the kindergartens. But many components of the program were already put into the national curriculum both for preschools and primary schools and the Step by Step association, through other projects, continued to organize trainings about the learning environment, parent involvement, and active teaching strategies.*
> *(Suzana Kirandžiska, Foundation for Educational and Cultural Initiatives, Step by Step, North Macedonia)*

> *We have developed three training modules which we delivered to all the teachers in the country through a cascade process. That was a time of opportunity, when the ministry promoted change. Unfortunately, now the situation is different. After several years of communist party governance again, many changes have been reversed. As an NGO we managed to become an in-service teacher training centre that is officially accredited, and people come to us to learn how theory can be translated into practice.*
> *(Cornelia Cincilei, Step by Step Moldova)*

System Changes Sometimes Happen Years Later

Most donors invest in projects of two or three years, and they expect concrete results even if the project is time limited. The Step by Step program was running for a very long period and illustrates how important improvements in the ECE system sometimes appear years later.

> *In 2017, the new concept of the New Ukrainian School was launched, up to 90 percent inspired by the Step by Step program in primary schools. And now the new standards for preschool education are being developed, again inspired by Step by Step. We can conclude that after twenty-five years the principles are now a part of the education policy of the ministry of education.*
>
> *(Natalia Sofiy, Borys Grinchenko Kyiv University, Ukraine)*

In many countries, the introduction of a child-centered approach in pre-service training provided by higher education institutes and universities took at least ten years. As noted above, this is the case for Ukraine, Montenegro, and recently in Georgia (Peeters 2021).

Strategic Thinking in a Complex Political Context

Managers of innovative education projects, who mostly have an academic background, tend to focus on pedagogic issues and often find it difficult to enter into dialogue with policymakers (Milotay 2016; Peeters and Peleman 2017). At the beginning of the Step by Step program the focus was on pedagogy. Through intensive trainings and mentoring, teachers gained competencies to work in a more child-centered way. There was less focus on working with policymakers to change laws or with universities and higher educational institutes to reform pre-service education programs. George Soros described this first approach "as chaotic, appropriate to the confusion of the revolutionary process in Eastern Europe" (Silova and Steiner-Khamsi 2008, 46). As noted earlier, the Open Society Foundations put more focus on sustaining changes in the ECE and primary school system as its work in education evolved. Some national programs were much more successful than others at achieving permanent changes in the education system by strategically convincing policy makers about the importance of such reforms.

> *The reason for our success is that we started the program in partnership with the ministry of education. We built strong partnerships at all decision-making levels. The strategy was to first have the partnership with the ministry, then to inform all the counties, and we signed a partnership with each county school inspectorate. It was part of our strategy that it had to be in the interest of the county to be part of the program. We decided that we would start in the capital of each county in the first year. We met with all the county school inspectorates and the preschool principals to explain what the program was about …*

> *In 1997, we put together a working group of Step by Step teachers and primary school inspectors and our team. Together we developed a methodology and a ministerial order stipulating that the ministry would pay for two teachers in each Step by Step primary classroom. That ministerial order was issued in March 1998. Nobody, since then, stopped it or cancelled it. No matter which party came into the office, they kept it as part of the alternative methodology. Yes, I went, and I literally met with everybody at the ministry who came into office.*
>
> (Carmen Lica, Centrul Step by Step Romania)

Opportunities to embed democratic values and approaches into national education policies also arose naturally, through government-initiated education planning process and policy initiatives. Many Step by Step Directors used these opportunities to introduce new approaches into education systems.

But of course the success of the Step by Step program in reforming the early education system is not solely the responsibility of the Step by Step director.

> *It depended on how a particular country reacted to the political confusion. Not all countries were prepared for changing their ECE system or were not at the same level of reorganising themselves. And sometimes Step by Step went too fast. We were working on Roma inclusion and someone came to me and said: "You are like a rooster singing too early in the morning and making everybody nervous." Many times, we were singing too early and people had problems following us, or the conditions were not yet right. It was hard to find out at what point we should start singing.*
>
> (Tatjana Vonta, co-author and former director, Step by Step Slovenia)

How Effective Was the Open Society Foundations at Introducing Child-Centered, Democratic Reforms into Early Childhood Education Systems?

Was the Step by Step program effective in achieving impacts at each level of the early education system, as defined in the Competent System (Urban et al. 2011)? On the individual level and the level of the institution (preschool and the primary school) the program succeeded in introducing competencies that are essential to the implementation of a more democratic and child-centered approach. The interviewees are positive about the openness and flexibility of the Step by Step approach. Starting from this common vision, training and mentoring sessions were set up in which teachers had the opportunity to acquire important competencies that are crucial for working in ECE. This included reflecting on their own practice and those of their colleagues and introducing new pedagogical practices in their work with children and parents. Step by Step also helped to create an atmosphere of trust among teachers through its participatory approach to training and mentoring.

On the third level, Step by Step's model training centers provided a source of inspiration for thousands of teachers, and the in-service training that they organized was well received by practitioners. However, collaboration with universities and pre-service training institutions was less consistently productive. Although many professors participated in specialized Step by Step trainings for faculty of higher education institutions, in most countries these did not lead to reform of the pre-service training programs to make them more practice-oriented and child-centered.

On the fourth level, the national one, the strategy of working through civil society organizations was in many instances successful. In most countries Step by Step organizations developed their in-service training services and many even survived when authoritarian governments were in power. However, building collaboration with ministries was not possible everywhere. It depended a great deal on the type of parties in power: if they were more authoritarian, it was very hard to influence education policy. And influencing government policy was not a linear process. Sometimes elements of the Step by Step approach were taken up by government officials years later, without mentioning Step by Step.

The effect on the international level is a success story, and is described further in Chapter 7, which explores networking. The International Step by Step Association (ISSA) is recognized by regional and international organizations as a partner, giving it many opportunities to disseminate the vision and democratic, inclusive values that underpinned the Step by Step program.

10

Systems Change When People Change: Lessons from Long-Term Investment in Early Childhood Education

Figure 10.1 Two children in a Step by Step primary program discuss the November class calendar (Chisinau, Moldova 2008).

@Step by Step Educational Program Moldova

Democratic Transitions Create Opportunities to Reform Early Childhood Education Systems

The velvet revolutions that rolled across Central, Eastern, and Southern Europe and Eurasia in the beginning of the 1990s were dramatic events that created high expectations across society about a life with more freedoms and opportunities for the next generation. They created momentum for parents and educators to explore democratic approaches to raising and educating young children, to prepare them to thrive in a different kind of society. Open Society's investment in innovative early childhood, inspired by a democratic pedagogy, came at an opportune time, linking education with the new political and social environment. Interviewees commented on this "magic moment" as a time when changes were possible.

The start of the Step by Step program was a great adventure. George Soros's surprising decision to invest over $100 million in early childhood after meeting Dr. Fraser Mustard was all the more extraordinary given both that the Open Society Foundations did not have experience with the early years and that so few international donors were interested in early childhood at the time. Yet, while it was undoubtedly risky and ambitious, Step by Step was also a profoundly hopeful initiative. The fall of the Berlin wall and the dissolution of the USSR, Czechoslovakia, and Yugoslavia had created a crisis in the early education sector in this region. Many kindergartens closed and were converted for other uses. Despite this, Open Society saw great opportunities and risked investing to encourage teachers and parents to work in a more democratic way and to give the next generation of young children opportunities to experiment with democratic values and relationships.

> *Honestly, I think if Open Society hadn't been there early childhood development would have received very limited attention in Eastern Europe. At that stage, I think that the commitment, vision and support with which the Step by Step approach was introduced really rescued young children.*
>
> *There would have been a model nursery school or kindergarten here or there but the systematic effort, shining the light on young children, sustained advocacy, I don't think these would have happened without the Open Society's Early Childhood Program. There simply was no one else. The importance in early education of quality, of diversity, of equity, all these wonderful, valuable concepts, I think were really established and promoted because of their efforts. UNICEF took a lot of inspiration from Step by Step. Seriously.*
>
> *(Deepa Grover, former UNICEF regional advisor for Europe and Central Asia)*

On reflection, the dramatic period after the fall of the Berlin wall created an ideal moment to introduce new pedagogical approaches. It offered an opportunity to introduce a paradigm shift in the sector, reinstating parents as the first educators of their children; opening classrooms up to parents, children with special needs, Roma children, and other excluded groups; promoting diversity, individualization, responsibility, critical thinking, creativity, and individuality in early education systems; introducing new service modalities such as community-based early learning and parenting programs; and creating and empowering networks of professionals and civil society organizations committed to advocating for young children and families and uniting for professional excellence.

Yet not all crises inspire change and hope for the future like the political shifts of the 1990s. As this book is being written, the pandemic, the war in Ukraine, the refugee crisis, and climate change have created real, existential threats for young children and their families, challenging the early childhood sector to respond effectively. The pandemic in particular stripped the blindfolds from society. It revealed the deep social and economic effects of long-term under-investment in early childhood and parents worldwide, the disproportionate responsibility for childcare that is placed on women, and the real cost of not valuing the early childhood workforce. Globally, the struggle is on to recruit and retain early childhood staff. More often than not, frontline early childhood jobs are low status, inadequately compensated (below or barely achieving a living wage) and offer few opportunities for ongoing professional development and advancement. As inflation rises, staff leave for better-paying jobs and the costs of keeping the services that remain open spiral out of control. The three co-authors of this book are split, with one author fearing political shifts to the right will bring back a trend toward authoritarian, traditional approaches in early childhood, while the other two are more hopeful that the pressure created by the need for more and better early childhood services will reinvigorate the sector.

The expansion of Step by Step illustrates how the political transition to democracy creates momentum to introduce a more democratic approach in early education, catalyzing an opportunity to push things in a positive direction. But tipping points can work both ways, and not every political crisis creates possibilities for the introduction of a child-centered, democratic pedagogy in early childhood education.

What Motivates Educators to Change Their Practice to a More Democratic Approach?

One strength of Step by Step was that from the start it invested heavily in people: country directors, master teacher trainers, and educators in kindergartens. The Open Society Foundations, and specifically, Open Society's affiliated national foundations across the region, identified and attracted highly motived experts—change agents interested in contributing to the transition to more democratic societies—to join the Foundation and launch Step by Step. Later, these same individuals became leaders of the NGOs that spun off from the Open Society Foundations to become independent professional early childhood organizations. The commitment of the original Step by Step teams to the program is demonstrated by the fact that so many from these first cadres remain active in the NGOs established through Step by Step.

What matters is not only that Open Society invested so much in building capacity and empowering those first cohorts of country directors, trainers, and teachers, but also how Step by Step did it. High expectations were set by the leaders of the program, Liz Lorant and Pam Coughlin. At the same time the US teams and trainers respected participants' knowledge and were responsive to their needs. The American training teams, like the country teams, were hand-picked and represented some of the best trainers and mentors from across Head Start's national technical assistance network. Their expertise was applied: it came from decades of experience supporting programs serving young children and families across the United States. According to interviewees, it made a difference that the American trainers took such care of the teams from Eastern Europe and Eurasia, creating a safe environment for learning and getting to know one another. The US trainers created a warm climate and culture of participation. New country directors and master teacher trainers felt that they belonged to an important project that aimed not only at reforming the early education system, but also at creating more democratic societies. They became a network of real change agents, who played a crucial role in Step by Step and who continue to play an important role in early childhood education in Europe and Eurasia today.

The resources developed for the program contributed to its success. Rather than purchasing a copyrighted, rigid program, Open Society invested in the development of new resources—methodologies and training modules—which, while designed around best practice, allowed country teams to adapt to national cultures, languages, and curricula. Years later, when ISSA developed teacher standards and principles, these evolved to be inclusive of variations in program content, focusing on broad teacher competencies relevant to quality child-centered programs. Likewise, during their time in the United States, trainees spent significant time visiting a range of high-quality, inclusive, child-centered programs, observing practices. The aim was to show them that the core principles of the program could be reflected in a variety of settings designed around the diverse needs and interests of individual children, their families, and communities.

The first cohorts who visited the United States brought back home a vision of what they were trying to achieve. They shared this across all levels of the education system: with ministries, academicians, local authorities, kindergarten directors and staff, and with parents and communities. The initial trainings in-country sought to create the same warm atmosphere experienced by those who had visited the United States. Intensive, individualized mentoring was provided by US trainers to country teams and by country teams to kindergartens. Step by Step is a relationship-based, responsive program that works with educators over many years to support their acquisition of new practices. Mentoring responded to the observed needs and interests of teachers. Trainers and mentors were given new skills to enable them to create empowering professional learning environments. Model sites in-country, like those the early cohorts had visited in the United States, demonstrated the advantages of child-centered approaches not only for children and parents, but also for teachers interested in the program, who were inspired by what they saw. The quality and variety of the resources, the trainers, the trainings, and the model sites, were visible to communities and fueled their interest in co-funding the extension of the program to more classrooms and sites. In this way Step by Step became accountable not only to ministries, but also to parents and communities, as well as educators.

In almost all participating countries the adoption of new practices on a wide scale reinforced the formal agreements that Open Society had with the ministries of education, and it fueled the approval of the program as an official alternative and the certification of Step by Step-informed teacher training courses. Expertise has been built and layered into the education system over an extended period of time. The materials and resources generated by the program, together with the cohorts of experts it has trained, continue to bring democratic values and practices to policy reform tables across the region. This approach differs dramatically from the rapid, reflexive, cascade training process that is utilized in so many reform efforts, many of which do not have enduring results. In contrast, evaluations of the Step by Step Program, which followed up initial trainings with substantial mentoring, peer support, professional development, and professional networks, consistently demonstrate the impact of continuous professional development on teachers' competencies and on their adoption of child-centered approaches. This can be seen from the earliest evaluations conducted by local evaluators, through to studies of ISSA's quality improvement work, which developed on the foundation of the Step by Step program (Ionescu et al. 2018).

The American trainers succeeded in building trust among the country representatives and at the same time participants felt ownership of the change process that was going on. As the program got going, interesting experiences were shared among teachers, trainers, and country representatives during numerous continuous professional development activities. Building trust and encouraging active participation of teachers, parents, and children in countries were essential to the success of the program.

The success of the emphasis on building trust provides an important lesson for future early education reform projects. A warm approach and responsiveness, combined with high levels of professionalism and experience, can play an important role in facilitating the rebuilding of bridges and the reconciliation between ethnic groups after a conflict within a country, and it can also support the building of trust with groups experiencing exclusion. Investing in the future of young children can motivate people to come together to change systems.

Crossing Boundaries: How Does the Exchange of Educational Theories, Practices, and Experiences across Borders Contribute to Building Democratic Education Systems?

The transfer of knowledge and ideas inspires innovation. In the field of early education this phenomenon has not been unidirectional, from West to East or East to West, as illustrated by the worldwide appeal of the ideas of the American Dewey, the Italian Malaguzzi, and the Belarussian Vygotsky. Rather, at its best it is a fluid process. We chose to explore this theme of "crossing boundaries" for two reasons. Firstly, we wanted to understand how good a fit Head Start was with early education systems in Europe and Eurasia and to discuss whether selecting a European, democratically oriented pedagogy could have had advantages, as any number of excellent, geographically convenient programs exist, as we explain below. Secondly, the authors wish to draw attention to ISSA's extraordinary achievement: the creation of a collaborative professional network that transcends national boundaries as well as the very different political histories that were present in different regions of Europe and Eurasia.

What inspired Open Society to opt for American rather than European expertise to guide its early childhood work? From one perspective, the choice was incidental: Open Society staff reached out to leading experts in the United States, where the foundation's international offices were based, and found the expertise and leadership they needed. We identified three reasons that this choice was particularly effective. First, Head Start, as noted earlier, has a democratic focus, providing a broad framework, rather than a prescribed program. It is a national program in a federal environment. States receive block grants from the federal government and follow national quality framework standards, but decisions about program methodologies and content are created from the ground up by the Head Start programs and the communities they serve. Parents are at the center of Head Start and have roles in governance as well as in delivering services. Head Start has always understood that early childhood is at minimum a two-generation program, and its comprehensive approach provides parents with linkages to welfare, health, and social services, continuing education, and employment opportunities. The idea that early childhood programs should be user-focused, multi-sectoral, and community-led distinguishes Head Start from many European counterparts. For Step by Step, Head Start was a good choice: it is a very broad pedagogical framework that emphasizes parents and families, and which can be adapted to the different contexts in the different countries.

Returning to the question of whether it would have been advantageous to use a European model requires exploring the pedagogical models operating in Europe in the early 1990s, when Open Society launched into early education. On one level, there were ample examples of European early childhood programs built around democratic pedagogy with a focus on child, educator, and parent participation and a number of these were being shared through the European Commission's Childcare Network (1986-96), coordinated by Peter Moss. Changing early education from a top-down, teacher-centered approach toward a child-centered approach with parent participation was also the driving force in Denmark and the north-Italian approach as well as in several projects funded by the Bernard van Leer Foundation in France, Berlin, and Ghent, as outlined below.

Danish early education pedagogy from the 1980s onward focuses on ensuring children are socialized to become active participants in decisions that have to do with the community in the classroom, promoting solidarity, democracy, and humanism (BUPL—The Danish National Federation of Early Childhood Teachers and Youth Educators 2006). In Italy, there was a similar evolution toward more democracy in the 1970s, not only toward children, but also parents and educators. In cities like Pistoia, Reggio Emilia, Modena, San Miniato, and Bologna, a democratic pedagogy was put into practice called *Gestione Sociale*, in which parents together with educators develop the policy of municipal early childhood centers (Galardini et al. 2022). In Berlin, childcare and kindergarten centers use a pedagogy known as *Situations Ansatz*, or the Contextual Approach, in which the participation of children in the life of the childcare center, and their experiences, actively shapes learning. The program encourages children's self-motivation, curiosity, and exploration, as well as collective activities with other children and childcare workers: "Participation can only succeed if democracy prevails and equality comes first. For everyday work, this means that, for example, when voting during a children's conference, the teacher's vote counts as much as that of a child" (Erzieherin-ausbildung.de 2023). In France, *crèches parentales* (parent run crèches), originating from the activism in 1968, were deeply connected to values like openness, liberation, and communication, bringing parents and professional educators together into a common pedagogical project. Parents work half a day with the professional educator every two weeks (Peeters 2008). In the 1980s in the city of Ghent a local team, led by one of the authors of this book, introduced a more democratic structure, team meetings, and common trainings between directors and child care workers. Centers collaborated to introduce initiatives that involved parents, such as visits to libraries and museums, and walks in nature (Peeters 2008). New kindergartens across the city adopted the *Freinet* pedagogy, a child-centered approach, and in those new schools child parliaments were set up so children could actively participate in decisions in which they were concerned (Departement Onderwijs en Opvoeding—Stad Gent 2010).

Yet while democratic approaches in early childhood were common across Western Europe, as noted above in the examples from Denmark, Belgium, France, Germany, and Italy, they were not easy to access for a foundation like Open Society, and they could not necessarily be rolled out on the large scale demanded by the Step by Step program. This brings us to the second reason Head Start was likely a better fit for Open Society's new early childhood initiative than European counterparts: it had the capacity to respond at the level and scale required by Step by Step. In the first year, the program matched fifteen pairs of American trainers with as many countries, and additional countries joined it every year. These trainers returned to countries multiple times each year over several years and they were soon joined by pairs of primary educators and educators specializing in the inclusion of children in disabilities. We cannot think of a European program at the start of the 1990s that could support such a rapid rollout.

The third reason Head Start was an effective choice revolves around civil rights and inclusion. The civil rights aspect of Head Start aligned particularly well with the vision of the Open Society around the urgency of including Roma and children with disabilities and special needs, two flagrant examples of structural exclusion that were prevalent across the countries implementing Step by Step. In an inhospitable region, Head Start offered an inspiring framework to set up an inclusive pedagogy for migrants, minorities, and children with disabilities.

Although in Western Europe the *crèches parentales* in France and childcare centers in Berlin implemented some interesting initiatives with migrant parents, there was no exchange of this experience. The emphasis on cultural diversity in early childhood education in Western Europe came later than it did in the United States, a number of years after Step by Step launched in Eastern Europe and Eurasia. It was only at the end of the 1990s that the Diversity in Early Childhood Education and Training (DECET) network was set up with support from the Bernard van Leer Foundation, inspired by experiences from the United States, principally the work of Louise Derman-Sparks (Derman-Sparks 1989). At the time in Western Europe the ethnic diversity aspect received limited attention in early education. In northern Italy, where Reggio Emilia was created, for instance, there was limited immigration in the early 1990s, and working with children from different ethnic backgrounds was not a central concern.

The theme "crossing boundaries" also resonates with what the program accomplished across Europe and Eurasia. In addition to linking Eastern European and Eurasian early childhood experts with their counterparts in the United States, the program created avenues for collaboration across countries participating in the Step by Step program and with Western Europe. When Step by Step was launched in the early 1990s, many experts in Eastern Europe and Eurasia did not have much contact with developments in Western Europe and beyond. The establishment of ISSA as a network for NGOs implementing Step by Step across the region promoted sharing and joint programming, initially within a network of twenty-five country programs. As ISSA evolved over the next ten to fifteen years into a pan-European and Eurasian issue-driven network, with open membership that has embraced inclusion of new members from across Western Europe and beyond, it created a continental forum for professional sharing, exchange, and advocacy. It has become the go-to network for practitioners and other professionals from Europe and Eurasia and is respected for its expertise and contributions to the field. ISSA is one of only eight non-governmental organizations in the European Commission Working Group on Early Childhood Education and Care, and is recognized by UNICEF, WHO, OECD, and other global networks and partners, which rely on ISSA to represent civil society and expertise from this region. It is an unusual example in which the reconnecting of Eastern and Western European experts and representation of the European region are led by partners from Eastern Europe. This is an extraordinary accomplishment, and perhaps not particularly obvious, since ISSA is registered in the Netherlands and now has offices there. Yet despite these accomplishments, all three authors are left with the perception that there remain many in Western Europe who are not ready to accept Eastern Europeans as professional equals and leaders. Many people continue to be surprised by the innovative practices, research, and resources emanating from Eastern Europe. This is something we believe must and will change as professionals from across Europe have more opportunities to share experiences and work together.

We end this section by relating a remarkable example of the circular journey of one Step by Step initiative, *Getting Ready for School,* which crossed many boundaries, from the United States to Eastern Europe/Eurasia and back again. Developed initially for Step by Step in the region by Cassie Landers, *Getting Ready for School* is a set of resources to support parents in their role as educators (see Chapter 3). Over a nine-month period, the program holds workshops with parents to introduce learning activities that parents can do at home with their children. It is a structured, manualized program focusing on pre-literacy and pre-numeracy and designed initially to support children who did not yet have access to preschool in Step by Step countries. It has been used widely by Step by Step NGOs in a variety of programs, including those serving Roma and refugee families. Through an interesting set of connections, the resources were selected by the Head Start Family Literacy Center to share with ninety-six Head Start programs participating in a family literacy initiative. By 2012, the materials and training had been requested by more than 600 Head Start programs. The program content has been further enhanced and piloted to reinforce self-regulation and it has been evaluated by researchers from Columbia University (Marti et al. 2018; Noble et al. 2012). Step by Step has thereby contributed new resources to the US Head Start program: what goes around, comes around.

One lesson for future projects is the importance of embedding flexibility in reform processes. For Step by Step this meant selecting a democratic program with a broad framework, rather than a prescribed one. It is important that curricula and content are created from the ground up and that they focus on the communities they serve, starting from a vision that emphasizes the role of parents and families and which can be adapted to the different contexts in different countries. The interviews illustrate how important it is that donors and foundations invest in networks in which pedagogical experiences can be shared and improved.

Reform Takes Time: Long-Term, Flexible Investments Offer Clear Advantages

The scale of the support of Open Society differed from that of most other foundations. While most foundations invest in a limited number of countries over a restricted period, Open Society implemented Step by Step in a large number of countries over an extended period of time. It started as a two-year initiative for preschool and ended up lasting more than two decades.

> *Open Society was engaged for more than twenty-five years with early childhood in these countries. That's another lesson I think you can bring out for other foundations. Step by Step was not short term because to really make change, you need long term investments that fit the changing needs of countries and communities.*
>
> *(Joan Lombardi, Georgetown University, and Stanford University)*

During the early years of the program, the Open Society Foundations, Georgetown University, and national experts developed the competence to adapt the program to national contexts and to respond to challenges. Four months into its implementation, the program invested in additional trainings and a companion guide to the core methodology, focused on democratic practices that needed reinforcing. This was a response to observations that long-held, authoritarian practices in some countries had not shifted. But the longevity of the program also paved the way for deeper uptake. For example, in some countries opportunities to participate in national early education policy reform processes arrived a decade or more after the start of the project. The longevity of the program also made it possible to take on new initiatives and to extend it across all levels of the early education system. Over the first decade what started as a preschool program for children between three and five years of age extended downwards to serve infants and toddlers and upwards to engage with primary schools, including supporting the transition to middle school. Trainings for select university faculty were provided to all countries and important tools like the ISSA Quality Resource Pack and pedagogical resources to support inclusion and diversity were developed for practitioners and adapted and translated for use in participating countries. Likewise, participating country teams were able to negotiate funding for trainings and initiatives that were responsive to their specific needs.

We cannot think of any other example of a funder that invested in a single early childhood education program in so many countries over such a long period of time. This long-term investment strategy proved successful and offers lessons for future donors and foundations. Long-term, flexible investments enable changes to evolve over time in relation to the unique social, political, and economic context in each country.

The Secret of the Success of the Step by Step Approach

Step by Step Introduced Democratic Pedagogy at Multiple Levels

As noted earlier, ideas and theories about democracy in early childhood education, from Dewey and Vygotsky to Malaguzzi and Freinet, were flowing East and West well before the internet made it easy. Step by Step and the European projects referenced above share a common belief that introducing democracy in preschools and in schools is key to building a democratic society. In this way early childhood education has a political function in society.

> *I think early childhood is deeply political. Early childhood spaces, policies, and services, the attitude of the state to the family, the rights of the child are deeply political issues. I think the way that services are funded, articulated, conceptualized for children is highly, highly political, whether that's about the status of women, the status of the family, the role of the states, even the contents.*
>
> *(Tina Hyder, former deputy director, Early Childhood Program, OSF)*

This is the perspective that Open Society took, and it inspired the investment in the Step by Step program. Years later, George Soros observed:

> We introduced Step by Step, a variation of Head Start, in every country where we had a foundation in the former Soviet Empire, through a [multi-year] program. We spent over $100 million to implement child-oriented education for disadvantaged children, because education for disadvantaged children has a considerable effect. Step by Step primary school children think for themselves, are more active, self-confident and this affects their later development. There are

class distinctions. Those left behind can be brought into the mainstream ... The key is families – to help them become more engaged with their children. One of the effects of our program was on parents. The primary responsibility is the family. It is the basis of our civilization. But where there are disadvantages, the most effective point of intervention is early childhood development

George Soros, founder, Open Society Foundations
(Soros 2007)

Parents and children have a voice in early years and schools and can decide together with teachers how and what children learn. The Step by Step approach, like the Malaguzzi, Vygotsky, Dewey, and Freinet pedagogies, pursues a democratic culture that increases hope and self-confidence at multiple levels in early education systems. In Step by Step, though, the layering in of democratic practices extended beyond children, parents, and teachers. It also included the establishment of national non-governmental professional organizations that advocate for democratic values in society at large. This is consistent with Bronfenbrenner's ecological model of development, which emphasizes the layers of influence that surround and impact a child's development (Bronfenbrenner 1979; Bronfenbrenner and Morris 1998). Step by Step promoted democracy:

- **Toward children** by supporting their agency, their personality, creativity, and wellbeing and by investing in them as future citizens in an open society. Step by Step cultivated competences in children that are crucial for democracy, such as critical thinking, responsibility, teamwork, appreciation of diversity, inclusion, and conflict resolution, and gave them opportunities to experience democracy in classrooms.
- **Toward parents** as the primary educators of their children, who have the right to know how their children are being educated, to participate in the process, and to hold preschools and schools accountable by being involved in governance.
- **Toward teachers and the teaching team** by employing facilitated leadership practices in preschools and schools to enable teachers to become more autonomous, giving them ownership over planning, in communicating with parents, and in shaping their ongoing professional development.
- By setting up **national early childhood civil society organizations and institutions** to ensure democratic values have a place in the early childhood ecosystem in each country. National Step by Step NGOs have become part of the democratic dialogue with ministries and, like ISSA, are recognized for their expertise.

Hašima Ćurak expressed the depth of the commitment to democracy in her interview:

> *In all segments of its work, in all meetings, in all plans, in all policies, in all conferences, Step simply pushed people to learn the democratic principles, to learn to cooperate and actively participate in building a better society for our children and a better education for all our children and all members of our society. I think they worked on that implicitly, and I'm very grateful for it. Especially in the years when that was what our society needed the most. They created a strong bond between people regardless of their nationality, education level, race, or gender. They always took us back to how important children are in the big picture of our professional habitus. They always brought out that primal kindness in us. When we talk about primal kindness, we're talking about democracy, consideration, support, and so on.*
> (Hašima Ćurak, advisor to the Ministry of Education and Science, Bosnia and Herzegovina)

Step by Step reinforces the importance of ensuring that a program embeds values of democracy and open society in early education in multiple ways, and at different levels of the early education system. Equally important is that this democratic approach remains alive through teachers' and educators' ongoing reflection and professional development and through active parent engagement. Step by Step did this formally by gaining approval as an alternative methodology for preschools (in virtually all countries) and for primary schools (in a good number of them). Democratic methodologies were implemented by teachers in large numbers of preschools and primary schools in participating countries, including in model demonstration sites, many of which are still used for trainings. At the beginning of the project, reform of pedagogic institutions, universities, and institutions of higher education was less successful. But in some countries Step by Step later introduced new approaches to faculty in higher education institutions. ISSA's principles have also influenced new national standards. According to several interviewees, Step by Step introduced a foundation of democratic early childhood education that national governments and international partner organizations, like the World Bank, UNICEF, and the European Commission, have been able to build upon.

How Women Led the Transformation

Early childhood education is a female-dominated field of work. The care and education of young children has always been considered "women's work." The proportion of male workers is low in most European countries, between

1 and 3 percent, and only the Scandinavian countries and Germany do slightly better (between 5 and 10 percent) (Jensen 2017; Peeters, Rohrmann, and Emilsen 2015). In all the countries in the region, including those involved in Step by Step, the result is a so-called gender regime, specific "configurations of practice": gendered arrangements of work, social, and emotional relations within institutions (Connell 2009, 72). The negative aspects of this female gender regime—low status and pay—are often what get emphasized, and these features are present in the care economy and early education. Although there are differences among countries and institutions, the gender regime in early childhood centers can be characterized by a dominance of women, rather flat hierarchies, and a strong need for harmony (Peeters, Rohrmann, and Emilsen 2015). What emerges from listening to interviews with the main actors in Step by Step is that the largely female Head Start trainers introduced, from the beginning, a culture of working together that took advantage of the positive aspects of this feminine gender regime in early education. The democratic approach and the focus on trust and on warm relationships were very much appreciated by the national representatives, the majority of whom were women, too.

Reading the transcripts of the interviews gives rise to a sense that the success of Step by Step was in part due to the extraordinary leadership and commitment of the women who were engaged at different levels of the early education system (teachers, trainers, directors, policymakers), and who successfully introduced changes in the culture of early education and in its policies and practices. The leaders of the Step by Step program were astute experts, advocates, strategists, diplomats, learners, risk takers, and entrepreneurs. Part of the success of Step by Step was its mobilization of strong women, including impressive examples in countries that had experienced armed conflicts, where they brought people from ethnic groups that were in conflict with one another back together. But in other countries involved in Step by Step, too, the authors and reviewers observed that this project rested on the shoulders of strong women.

Future early education reform projects can take inspiration from the idea that the female gender regime, which is so typical in early childhood settings, can also be used to leverage changes that reinforce democratic early education systems, characterized by a flat hierarchy, and based on a warm approach and strong, harmonious relationships with children and parents from diverse backgrounds.

Open Society Foundations: A Special Kind of Funder

From the beginning, the Open Society Foundations was a different kind of funder. As a foundation it focuses on broad issues of social change—justice, freedom of expression, and equity—and situates human development initiatives within a strong rights framework. This framework is uncompromising, and Step by Step had traction within Open Society not only because it promoted democratic principles and human development generally, but also because it was, with equal weight, advancing human rights, counteracting discrimination, and introducing an agenda of equity and dignity.

> I'm most pleased with our work with Roma in Eastern Europe, an excluded community. Preparation for school supports their participation in regular education. It is developing a new generation of educated Roma, who break the stereotype that prevails. This is probably the most effective way to solve social exclusion
>
> George Soros, founder, Open Society Foundations
> (Soros 2007).

In countries experiencing war it helped that the mission of Open Society was broad and that the foundation had a big profile, engaging directly with governments and international agencies at the highest levels. Support in these circumstances was also comprehensive. The foundation helped preschools and schools rebuild infrastructure and provided educational materials and furniture. Interviewees expressed how important this material support was in those extremely difficult days.

To support those social change projects Open Society relied on national foundations that had a lot of autonomy. At the beginning of the Step by Step program this large footprint of Open Society was an important advantage. The foundations played a critical role in establishing and maintaining relationships with the ministry of education, government, and pedagogic institutes; they identified early childhood experts interested in new pedagogies and put together a team of change agents to implement the program.

> *The people who have been chosen to lead various programs with the national foundations in the Balkans were chosen because of who they were, because of their democratic, anti-nationalistic political orientation and dedication to opening new ideas in the field of education. The majority of them were very young and not widely known at the time—but all of them shared proper values, combined with high enthusiasm, which was the key to the success of the program.*
>
> (Beka Vučo, former regional director for the Western Balkans, OSF)

Then the foundations supported this team with extensive logistical, operational, and legal structures to enable them to gain approval for the program and adapt it to the national context; to select, renovate, and furnish classrooms; and to provide participants in the program with ongoing training and mentoring. After five years the foundations facilitated spin-off of the program in each country into a new NGO or into an existing organization, and then continued to monitor and support these independent entities.

Step by Step took advantage of what Open Society had learned from implementing other programs. As a result of learning from the experience implementing a multi-country health education program for teenagers, Open Society insisted that Georgetown develop a written manual that ministries could approve and put emphasis on pedagogical approaches (methodology). Likewise, the foundation made use of an economy of scale, investing heavily in imported classroom furniture and materials at the beginning of the project, and ten times less in the expansion phase, relying on parents and communities to source classroom furniture locally.

Open Society invested in more than the implementation of an early education demonstration program. One of the distinguishing features across all the work of the Open Society Foundations is a commitment to build a strong civil society to drive change. Often against all odds, the foundation invested in and nurtured a new network of civil society organizations devoted to child-centered, democratic early childhood. Open Society also advocated for greater international investment in early childhood.

> *It's monumental. The investment in building the civil society that works in the early years, and in this paradigm shift from teacher-centered to child-centered, bringing in the Step by Step program but also investing in supporting the development of civil society that can take it forward. This constant support not just at the country level but at regional level, too, the network, empowering civil society, later bringing in other foundations, advocating inside the Open Society Foundations for the early years but also advocating among other philanthropic stakeholders to support the early years.*
>
> (Liana Ghent, executive director, ISSA)

These efforts elicited many partnerships. Multiple donors partnered to bring the Step by Step program to life. Even in its first year, when Open Society footed most of the costs, the program counted on in-kind support from national governments that, for instance, paid for substitutes when teachers and assistants attended trainings. From the second year, the program garnered substantial in-kind and co-funding from communities, local governments, national governments, and other donors, many of which funded teacher assistants and co-funded renovation and equipping of new classrooms and sites. The large expansions noted in Chapter 3 involved initiatives funded by the World Bank and USAID. After the NGOs were established as independent organizations, this process of partnership building accelerated and new partnerships formed with the European Commission and UNICEF and other foundations. Ultimately, Open Society's investment in Step by Step helped catalyze the investments of others.

The experience of the Step by Step suggests that early education projects have a greater chance of success if they are built on a broad foundation. Our research reinforces the value of grounding education reforms in political, social, and human rights frameworks and ecosystems. Unusually, Step by Step's vision embraced human rights, democracy, and inclusion. The program took on both democratization of the early childhood education system in its broadest sense, introducing democratic, child-centered practices in early education systems, while prioritizing equity and social inclusion, by enroling previously excluded children and families. Roma and minorities were prioritized immediately and the inclusion of children with moderate disabilities was introduced at scale once high-quality Step by Step, child-centered programs were available to welcome them.

The human rights and equity field operates through civil society networks and this served as a model for Step by Step's sustainability, though this turned out to be problematic in more authoritarian countries. Reform was not limited to the formal education system, but included the establishment of a strong early childhood civil society eco-system: national professional organizations linked through a regional network. The early childhood field needed a "first mover," a big donor like Open Society willing to take the risk of prioritizing investments in early childhood early in the political reform process that was unfolding across the region. Today, the early childhood development and education field has more traction and it is more common to see larger investments in early education and early childhood development. But in the early 1990s the focus on early childhood education and the scale of the Open Society commitment ($100 million at the outset) were extraordinary. It is a risk few organizations would have dared to make. As Step by Step demonstrated success and gained momentum, it also gained additional supporters and enthusiastic co-funders: local and national government, communities, international agencies and organizations, and bilateral organizations. Having a confident donor, which was comfortable with risk-taking, flexible and responsive programming, sustained investment and willing to take on the difficult process of building civil society, ultimately made the project stronger and more sustainable.

Limits of the Step by Step Program

Not everything Open Society attempted worked out as intended. In many countries where it was implemented, democratically oriented early education has not taken hold across systems in practice, and has survived only in policy documents or in some sliver of practice. Here we draw attention to several limitations.

Step by Step struggled to make meaningful changes to the pre-service education system. While Step by Step had immediate, visible impacts in preschools and primary schools, the impacts at the higher education level were diffuse and, in almost all cases, were not visible at the institutional level. Although many individual professors participated in courses set up by Open Society and were exposed to new approaches in early education, in most countries Step by Step did not succeed in significantly reforming pre-service teacher training. Rather, in most countries where it was active, pre-service education programs continue to transmit a teacher-centered approach. Theory continues to dominate, and the link with practice remains weak.

Making changes in the higher education system is not an easy task and it is a big commitment. In the intervening years, significant progress has been made in pre-service training in a number of countries, often as a result of UNICEF, World Bank, or European-funded projects and linkages. Open Society had more success in Russia, Myanmar, and Bangladesh, where it worked diligently over several years with specific institutions to establish postgraduate degree programs. These efforts have also proven to be more sustainable, illustrating what is possible with more targeted, sustained efforts that reform an existing program or introduce a new one in a single higher education institution.

In a number of countries, challenging political contexts led to strained relationships with the ministry of education, which affected the program's systemic impact. Collaboration with the ministry varied from country to country, influenced heavily by national political contexts. In countries striving to become open and democratic the program did quite well, while in those where a more authoritarian or nationalistic government took hold it was much more difficult to retain the support of the government. In some cases, the ministry of education was hostile toward Step by Step. Where the political situation changed over time, collaboration with the ministry often did too, with the result that Step by Step's influence on early education was not linear.

Open Society's strategy to sustain the program through investments in civil society was both bold and naïve. Not all the newly established non-governmental organizations have been able to survive in unfavorable ecosystems. Investing in civil society was successful in some countries, but challenging in countries where the government was not open toward civil society organizations, and it was absolutely impossible to keep Step by Step organizations open in environments that were legally and politically hostile toward NGOs. Furthermore, establishing and running an NGO requires different competences from operating an early education program, and several interviewees highlight the need for continuous professional organizational development to support their survival. Futhermore, even where the NGOs have been very effective advocates for democratic values in early education, small- and mid-sized NGOs have limits. They cannot compete with large players like the ministry, the World Bank, UNICEF, and other organizations. In some of the interviews, we hear the disappointment of Step by Step pioneers, who did not achieve the same results as their colleagues in countries with more favorable contexts. Even very motivated teams cannot sustain and grow the program in very challenging political environments. Yet it is also possible to differentiate the sustainability of the Step by Step program from the sustainability of the NGO. In several countries with challenging political contexts, the program survived in the education system, though the NGO stopped operating. And in some cases, even where the NGO and program are no longer active, a cadre of committed early educators interested in child-centered approaches and equity and social inclusion remains.

The Deep Roots of Exclusion

Over the course of Step by Step, thousands of excluded children were welcomed into parenting programs, creches, preschools, and primary schools. In the tenth year of the program (2004), this amounted to approximately 15,000 Roma children, 30,000 children from other ethnic minority groups, and 15,000 children with disabilities. Yet in many countries discrimination has been exacerbated by nationalist political movements and by COVID.

> The narratives of this government have strengthened prejudices in Hungary. This is in the core of their political narrative to find enemies and then distract society. The last ten years were even worse. Inclusion is not on the political agenda.
>
> (Éva Deák, Partners Hungary Foundation)

> What creates inequity is related to policies that are in place and to what extent inequity and discrimination actually are embedded in systems and the way services are or aren't available to certain groups. I think we have made some progress in the global community in previous years. In terms of COVID, the most affected groups are those that had already been disadvantaged before. We have to re-intensify our efforts.
>
> (Liana Ghent, executive director, ISSA)

Even though the challenges are growing, there are few funders focusing on equity and inclusion in early childhood.

> I think few donors have advocated for Roma children, children with disabilities or early childhood intervention. The lens of equity, social justice and support for the most disadvantaged groups is really something that Open Society deserves a lot of credit for because there are so few other donors. In fact, I worry that we will not have a strong partner in these areas now that Open Society has left the early years field.
>
> (Liana Ghent, executive director, ISSA)

> The focus on Roma gave Open Society a boutique space in the world of inclusion and exclusion and it allowed it to make a programmatic and policy difference. I feel disappointed that there weren't other foundations that partnered in a very serious way around the issues of equity and inclusion for young children.
>
> (Phyllis Magrab, Georgetown University, former board chair, Early Childhood Program Advisory Board, OSF)

The problem may also be embedded in the field of early childhood.

> I think the field doesn't do a great job of focusing on equity issues, and that's, I think, what Open Society did with the program. It was to really put a central emphasis on issues of equity and inclusion, and that's continuing to be a challenge in many systems where it kind of gets ignored whether you think about language diversity, or indigenous populations, or populations with disabilities, or issues of race and caste, and discrimination. The field still has a long way to go to address those kinds

of issues as core to what workforces are trained in and how programs and policies are conceptualized and implemented.

(Hirokazu Yoshikawa, New York University, former board member, Early Childhood Program Advisory Board, OSF)

Addressing exclusion requires making radical changes in society that go way beyond the field of early childhood and education.

It goes beyond the kind of policy framework for children and families, doesn't it? It's about economic models, it's about political models. I think capitalism thrives on having an underdog, basically cheap labor and cheap labor comes in many forms and one of the forms are some migrants, for instance, you keep wages low because people are in fear of their status, they need the money, and they'll work for less.

I think there are huge political changes that would underpin a real recognition and acknowledgment of equity broadly across society of social inclusion that applies for all, and I don't think we've seen that anywhere. We get glimpses every now and then, of countries where even income inequality is much less. We're seeing the opposite, though. We're seeing trends that exacerbate inequality. When we see stressors like climate change, COVID even, migration. You see a polarization, and the rich get richer, people who have less are even further pushed. There's an economic model that needs to change, which is not only about redistribution of wealth. It is about voice and access and accountability and ensuring adequate representation of people who are systematically discriminated against.

(Tina Hyder, former deputy director, Early Childhood Program, OSF)

Looking Ahead: Democratic Early Education in Europe, Eurasia, and Beyond

This book uses as an example the changes in Central, Eastern, and Southern Europe and the former Soviet Union after the fall of the Berlin wall to explore the impacts in early education that follow a radical, largely unanticipated political and social transition. Through narrative accounts it elaborates how educators and communities responded to the opportunity the Step by Step program offered to build democratic, open societies through reform of early education systems.

Where does this leave early education in Europe, Eurasia, and beyond? On the one hand, early childhood education, as a field, has garnered attention in international development, including in humanitarian contexts. There is momentum to universalize pre-primary education, to reinforce broader early childhood development and parenting in the early years, to identify, support, and include children with disabilities and developmental delays. Yet the space for early education that has a democratic and inclusive focus is not as clear cut. There is war in Europe, and in a number of European and Eurasian countries there is a frightening and pronounced shift toward authoritarianism. Inclusion of minorities and refugees is a persistent challenge and prejudices and stereotypes abound. Democracies are at risk worldwide.

> *Step by Step grew in the context of its time. We are facing different issues now. We are coming out of COVID. Poverty is worse. Climate is having much more impact.*
> *(Joan Lombardi, Georgetown University, and Stanford University)*

In her interview, Phyllis Magrab, one of the pioneers of the Step by Step program, spoke about the tipping point in early education, recognizing that it is now seen as a good investment opportunity. But she was not sure that a democratic focus will continue to get the same level of engagement that it has had in recent years:

> *I am watching what is happening in the world around us as it becomes more authoritarian, much less interested in human development and what happens to people, and I wonder if that is a force that is going to become a counterforce that is going to say, "This isn't what we care about. What we care about is people following the rules." It is hard to figure that out. I have no crystal ball. The field has certainly matured. There is a lot of evidence-based science to support where the field is going and is intending to go.*
> *(Phyllis Magrab, Georgetown University, former board chair, Early Childhood Program Advisory Board, OSF)*

Beka Vučo, former regional director at Open Society, leads us to a final question: who will carry democratic early childhood into the future?

> *It is obvious that after thirty years, with the existence of the Open Society Foundations and its programs, the difference can be felt throughout Central and Eastern Europe. These new generations that went through the various educational systems, from Step by Step kindergartens all the way to the Central European University, are now slowly making an impact. It may be invisible, but it exists. They're still fighting and the battle is not over yet.*
> *(Beka Vučo, former regional director for the Western Balkans, OSF)*

Their persistence and dedication are even more important now that the Open Society Foundations has wound down the Early Childhood Program and much of its work in basic education.

The Early Childhood program of Open Society ended in December 2020. Fourteen months later in February 2022 the war in Ukraine began. ISSA took immediate action, seeing it as their duty to prioritize and make visible to the humanitarian community the need to support young children and their families impacted by the war. ISSA and its member organizations had experience working in times of war and afterward, and of working with refugees in countries implementing Step by Step, as well as in Germany and Greece. ISSA mobilized its network of member organizations to help families with young children who were still in war zones and the refugees who were fleeing to countries across Europe.

> *I think our main approach was to try to figure out early on where is it that we can help the most. Our first effort was to reach out to colleagues in Ukraine, to colleagues in neighboring countries, but also to various partners, existing partners, possible future partners. Because we are a network, we put in a lot of effort in trying to understand what is happening, but also trying to understand who else is doing something to help, where could we be the connector or a channel. As a membership association, we looked at strengthening our members, supporting our members, strengthening readiness in the countries. Again, because we focus on early childhood, we looked at support for early learning and care.*
> (Liana Ghent, executive director, ISSA)

ISSA drew on existing resources and knowledge in the secretariat and among the members of the network and translated resources into Ukrainian and the languages of countries hosting refugees. Leveraging its expertise, network mechanisms, and partnerships, ISSA served as a channel to distribute useful didactical materials to help refugees, built capacity at country level to work with trauma-informed approaches, linked its members to relevant partners and donors, and actively engaged in fundraising to channel or facilitate funding for the members working on the ground in Ukraine and in other countries. Significant in-kind donations were also raised: 195,000 story books published by ISSA in Ukrainian were distributed in partnership with Amazon and Save the Children. ISSA members also received donations of 13,400 new laptops and software to support refugee centers, kindergartens, teachers, and families in host countries. From the first day of the war, ISSA was an active advocate for making early learning and early care a priority in emergency responses of large agencies and of funders.

> *We understood early on that every country had different kinds of challenges. Some countries, like Moldova, were primarily transit countries, although refugee families do stay there longer than they anticipate. Other countries, like Poland, received huge numbers of refugees that tried to settle.*
> (Liana Ghent, executive director, ISSA)

In some countries like Poland, playgroups or family hubs were set up for young children and mothers.

> We decided that we would focus on activities that proved successful in the past. In March, we were invited by UNICEF to discuss what we could do. Our proposal was to set up playgroups and pre-school groups for young children and mothers in the places where there are a lot of refugees. UNICEF gave us money and we could create thirty such groups in different parts of Poland. We started to talk with local governments of several towns in Warsaw because we decided that it would be best to start from local governments, thinking about potential spaces and for continuation and financing, but also, we were open to non-governmental organizations, if they were interested. We signed agreements with Gdynia, Gdańsk, Sopot, Lublin, Rzeszów, Dębica, Łomianki, and Warsaw.
> (Teresa Ogrodzińska, Comenius Foundation for Child Development, Poland)

ISSA's Polish member organization, the Comenius Foundation, launched trainings for Ukraine women to become animators in the playgroups. At the time of writing, they have trained more than 100 Ukrainian animators.

Not every country where Step by Step was introduced has sustained the program. After every revolution comes setbacks, but even in the most difficult places, the "seed beneath the snow" which was planted by Step by Step awaits the moment when it can grow. The democratic approach it embodies has persisted and continues to evolve—in the form of ISSA and its member organizations responding to the war in Ukraine, in the way its approach and teaching materials have been embraced by educators and absorbed into ECE practice and systems in many countries across the world, and most of all in the adults, still in their twenties and thirties, who experienced Step by Step classrooms.

In an ever more complex world, early education that is responsive to diverse families and communities; that celebrates children's agency and teachers' ingenuity; and that embraces equity, inclusion, and participation is even more relevant. Our research reinforces the value of long-term investments in reform programs that address all levels of early education systems. It draws attention to the importance of building trust with program participants, nurturing a strong civil society, and understanding that lasting change is cultivated within and by individuals: children, parents, teachers. Cross-country collaborations and exchanges of ideas of experiences—like those cultivated through Step by Step—enrich and inform the field of early childhood education and offer an unparalleled opportunity to release the potential of the next generation.

Appendix 1: Biographies of Interviewees and Focus Group Participants

Figure 11.1 Children visiting the Museum of Mining and Metallurgy in Bor, Serbia, on September 15, 2018.

© Sanja Knezevic for the Open Society Foundations

Driton Berisha is currently one of the team leaders of the Opre Roma Kosovo movement. Previously he managed the Roma Early Years Network and initiatives focused on inclusion of Roma, Ashkali, and Egyptian children in preschool education at the Kosova Education Center. He is a member of the Steering Committee of the Kosovo Roma Ashkali Egyptian Early Years Network.

Elena Bodrova is co-founder and knowledge advisor at Tools of the Mind. Dr. Bodrova's work applies Lev Vygotsky's theory to education beginning in Russia where she worked in the Institute for Preschool Education and continuing in the United States where she co-developed the *Tools of the Mind* early childhood program.

Appendix 1: Biographies of Interviewees and Focus Group Participants   227

Cornelia Cincilei is the country director of Step by Step Moldova since 1994 and is currently director of the Step by Step NGO in Moldova (Programul Educațional Pas cu Pas). She was a member of the first two ISSA-elected Boards (1998–2004), a member of ISSA's Program Committee, and she has contributed to several of ISSA's conceptual documents. In 2018 she was re-elected to the ISSA Board and is currently serving as board treasurer.

Hašima Ćurak is a pre-primary advisor in the Agency for Pre-Primary, Primary, and Secondary Education in Bosnia and Herzegovina. She has been a preschool educator since 1987, and she remained in Sarajevo throughout the war working with children and refugees. She was one of the first participants in the Step by Step program, when it was launched in Bosnia and Herzegovina in 1996, and became a mentor of teachers and other mentors.

Éva Deák is the executive director of the Partners Hungary Foundation, which hosts the Step by Step program. She has been connected with Step by Step since 2000.

Sia Barbara Ferguson Kamara was the lead international early childhood consultant (2010–20) in Liberia for the Open Society Foundations Early Childhood Program and ministry of education. For twenty-one years, she was an administrator of the District of Columbia's Department of Human Services, and prior to that she served as associate commissioner in the US Department of Health and Human Services with responsibility for the National Head Start Program. Between 1963 and 1965 she was a Peace Corps volunteer in Liberia.

Karma Gayleg is Early Childhood Care and Development (ECCD) specialist at the ministry of education in Bhutan. Since 2007, he has contributed significantly to the development of early childhood in the country, including coordinating the government's collaboration with the Open Society Foundations Step by Step program to introduce child-centered practices in first-grade classrooms and early years groups in primary schools. He has extensive experience in program and curriculum development, parenting education, and training practitioners and has been associated with international and regional early childhood networks.

Liana Ghent is the executive director of ISSA since 2006. Under her leadership ISSA grew as a network, broadening its programmatic focus to include all aspects of early childhood development and expanding the membership to include diverse organizations from across all of Europe and Eurasia. Previously, she was co-president of the Civic Education Project, a higher education organization co-funded by the Open Society Foundations in Eastern Europe and the former Soviet Union.

Deepa Grover is a senior advisor in the Office of the Director General, Early Childhood Authority, Government of Abu Dhabi. She was a UNICEF regional advisor until 2019 and in this role supported early childhood development policies and programs in twenty-two countries in Europe and Central Asia.

Eteri Gvineria is both associate professor at the Institute of Pedagogy, Tbilisi State University, Georgia, and executive director of the Center for Educational Initiatives Georgia, established in 2002. She has directed the Step by Step program since it was launched in Georgia in 1998.

Zuhra Halimova served as the executive director of the Open Society Institute Assistance between 1996 and 2016. She also served as a member of the Open Society Foundations Global Education Support Program Advisory Board, and member of the Open Society Foundation Youth Program and International Harm Reduction Program sub-boards. She is a consultant, advisor, and expert on post-conflict transitions, democratic institutions, human rights, freedom of expression, women's rights, governance, and empowering civil society.

Kirsten Hansen was a member of the original design and development team for Step by Step and one of the lead authors of the original Step by Step preschool methodology, core documents, and training modules. She brought into the project more than thirty years of experience with early childhood programs, including Head Start, and served on the faculty of the Georgetown University Center for Child and Human Development. She traveled extensively in the region representing the program, conducting workshops, and providing coaching to Step by Step teams.

Henriette Heimgaertner is president of the ISSA Board and previously served on the board in the role of secretary. She has more than thirty years of experience in developing sustainable early years program in various European countries. At the time that Step by Step was established she was a program manager at the Bernard van Leer Foundation, responsible for the foundation's work in Central Eastern Europe.

Appendix 1: Biographies of Interviewees and Focus Group Participants 229

Tina Hyder was executive director of Amna (previously, the Refugee Trauma Initiative) between 2021 and 2022. Before this, Tina was a member of the Open Society Foundations' Early Childhood Program, from 2009 to the end of 2020, serving in the role of deputy director. Prior to joining Open Society, Tina worked with Save the Children UK as a global advisor, following roles as a university lecturer and community worker.

Roxane Kaufmann was a member of the original design and development team and one of the lead authors of the original Step by Step preschool methodology, core documents, and training modules. She brought into the project more than thirty years of experience with early childhood programs, including Head Start, and served on the faculty of the Georgetown University Center for Child and Human Development. She traveled extensively in the region representing the program, conducting workshops and providing coaching to Step by Step teams.

Suzana Kirandžiska is the executive director of the Foundation for Education and Cultural Initiatives Step by Step in North Macedonia. She has been with the Step by Step program since its launch in 1994, and also teaches acting at the Faculty of Dramatic Arts at the Ss. Cyril and Methodius University in Skopje.

Kate Lapham is the chief of party for USAID's All Children Succeeding activity in Uzbekistan. She is an adjunct faculty member at the University of Dayton and has served as the lead for USAID's Education in Crisis and Conflict Network. For eighteen years she worked in various education-related positions at the Open Society Foundations, most recently as deputy director of the Education Support Program. In her first years with Open Society she lived in Central Asia, managing the USAID-funded PEAKS project, which supported the expansion of Step by Step there.

Carmen Lică is the executive director of the Centrul Step by Step pentru Educați și Dezvoltare Profesională România, the NGO established for the Step by Step program. She has been the director of the program since it launched in Romania in 1994.

Joan Lombardi is a senior scholar at the Center for Child and Human Development and senior fellow with the Collaborative on Global Children's Issues at Georgetown University. In addition, she is a visiting scholar at the Stanford Center on Early Childhood, Graduate School of Education, Stanford University. Over the past fifty years, Joan has made significant contributions in the areas of child and family policy as an innovative leader and policy advisor to national and international organizations and foundations and as a public servant.

Liz Lorant joined the Open Society Foundations in 1984, as its first employee, representing the Soros Foundation Hungary in New York. She served as director of the Children & Youth Program, implementing innovative regional programs, including not only Step by Step, but also Reading and Writing for Critical Thinking (a teacher training program), the International Debate Education Association, and initiatives addressing health education, child abuse prevention, community education, and career education. Liz Lorant led development of the Step by Step program and was a member of the board of the International Step by Step Association, following its establishment in 1999.

Phyllis Magrab is professor of pediatrics in the School of Medicine, Georgetown University, USA, where she serves in many roles, including as director of the Center for Child and Human Development, which collaborated with Open Society to launch the Step by Step program in 1994. She was a member of the advisory board of Open Society's Early Childhood Program between 2011 and 2021 and served as its chair from 2016 to 2021. She has also served as a board member of the International Step by Step Association. Dr. Magrab is also a UNESCO Commissioner and UNESCO chair and vice-chair of the US-Afghan Women's Council.

Ulviyya Mikayilova is a dean in the School of Education and assistant professor at ADA University in Azerbaijan and serves in a number of advisory and board positions. She is a member of ISSA's Program Committee and has served as a regional advisor for Central Asia. Between 1998 and 2014 she led the Step by Step program in Azerbaijan.

Milena Mihajlović was executive director of the CIP-Center for Interactive Pedagogy, the NGO established by the Step by Step program, until October 2023. She has also served as a board member of the International Step by Step Association.

Nives Milinović was the director of the Open Academy Step by Step in Croatia between 2003 and 2018, and previously managed the education portfolio at the Open Society Institute Croatia. She has served on the board of the International Step by Step Association, including as president.

Appendix 1: Biographies of Interviewees and Focus Group Participants

Aryeh Neier, president emeritus of Open Society Foundations, is an American human rights activist who co-founded Human Rights Watch and directed the American Civil Liberties Union. He was the president of Open Society Foundations between 1993 and 2012.

Michelle Neuman is lecturer in educational practice at the University of Pennsylvania, USA, and senior fellow at Results for Development. Her applied research focuses on strengthening early childhood development and education in low- and middle-income countries. Earlier in her career, she served as senior program officer for Open Society's Early Childhood Program. In her previous roles at the World Bank, UNESCO, and OECD, she led analytical work and provided technical guidance to government officials to inform their early childhood policies and programs. She was recently awarded the Playful Learning and Innovation Impact Fellowship from the Federation of American Scientists.

Teresa Ogrodińska is founder and vice-president of the Board of the ISSA member organization, Comenius Foundation for Child Development, established in Poland in 2003. The Comenius Foundation is partnering with ISSA, as well as many other organizations, to provide services to refugees from the war in Ukraine.

Alena Panikova was the executive director of the Open Society Foundation – Bratislava between 1995 and 2013. Between 1993 and 1995 she led education programs in the foundation. She continues to serve on the board of Škola Dokorán (Wide Open School), the organization established by the Step by Step program in Slovakia.

Aljoša Rudaš is program manager at ISSA, leading the Roma Early Years Network. Before joining ISSA he was an early childhood educator and counsellor at a Step by Step preschool in Slovenia. In 2016, he was awarded a scholarship from the Open Society Foundations to attend the University of Haifa in Israel, where he obtained an MA in child development.

Miroslav Sklenka is the executive director of Škola Dokorán (Wide Open School), the organization established by the Step by Step program, and which hosts the Roma Early Years Network in Slovakia. Škola Dokorán works with socially disadvantaged young children and their parents.

Natalia Sofiy is associate professor, Department of Special and Inclusive Education, Borys Grinchenko Kyiv University, Ukraine. She began working with Step by Step as country director at the International Renaissance Foundation in 1994, and between 1999 and 2019 she was director of the Ukrainian Step by Step Foundation, the Step by Step NGO in Ukraine.

Gerda Sula is lecturer at the University of Tirana, Albania, and executive director of the Step by Step Center, the Step by Step NGO in Albania. She has been working with the program since 1996, first as a master teacher trainer and later as country director.

Dawn Tankersley is an early childhood educator with special expertise in bilingual education, diversity, and inclusion. She first traveled to Eastern Europe to conduct preschool training in 1998 and later moved to Budapest and traveled throughout Europe and Eurasia, working for Open Society and the International Step by Step Association as the lead program expert on a variety of projects. She co-authored a number of ISSA core publications and played a central role in Step by Step's work with Roma communities. She also served as Open Society's lead Step by Step expert and trainer in Argentina, Dominican Republic, and Peru.

Dženana Trbić was the education program coordinator at the Open Society Fund – Bosnia and Herzegovina between 1994 and 2022.

Zorica Trikić is senior program manager at ISSA, where she has worked since 2014. Prior to that, she was program director at the CIP-Centre for Interactive Pedagogy, the NGO established by the Step by Step program in Serbia. She is a co-author of a number of ISSA core methodologies and publications and has played a central role in Step by Step's work with Roma and refugee communities promoting quality and equity in early childhood education and care.

Aija Tuna leads the National Culture and Arts Education programme for children and youth at the National Center of Culture at the ministry of culture in Latvia and is a board member at the Knowledge Creation Lab. Between 2006 and 2009 she was program director of the International Step by Step Association, and prior to that she directed education programs at the Soros Foundation Latvia, during the early years of the Step by Step program.

Tatjana Vonta, a co-author of this book, was associate professor at the University of Primorska, Slovenia, and senior research fellow at the Educational Research

Institute in Slovenia. She led the Step by Step program in Slovenia from 1994 to 2014 and has served on the ISSA board, including as President. She played a leading role in ISSA's work on quality and has served on many task forces. She has also been a consultant to Open Society Foundations Early Childhood Program.

Beka Vučo held the position of the regional director for the Western Balkans for thirty years. She helped establish the Open Society Foundations national foundations in the region and supported their collaboration with various thematic programs and initiatives, including Step by Step. She is founder and president of *My Balkans*, a charitable organization based in New York and the Balkans that supports organizations and individuals through arts, culture, and education who are fighting for freedom of expression, social openness, artistic excellence, educational advancement, and societies that promote justice and equality.

Kate Burke Walsh contributed to the original Step by Step preschool methodology and led development and implementation of the Step by Step Primary Education Initiative, including designing and serving as lead author of three program methodologies and the accompanying teacher training modules. She was a core member of the US technical assistance team that coordinated support to Step by Step countries and traveled extensively in the region representing the program, conducting workshops, and providing coaching to Step by Step teams.

Martin Woodhead is emeritus professor of childhood studies at The Open University, UK. His international work includes projects with Save the Children, Council of Europe, OECD, Bernard van Leer Foundation, UNICEF, and UNESCO. He was special advisor to the UN Committee on the Rights of the Child in the preparation of *General Comment 7: Implementing Child Rights in Early Childhood* and associate research director of Young Lives, a longitudinal study of child poverty in Ethiopia, India, Peru, and Vietnam, based at University of Oxford. Between 2008 and 2015 he chaired the advisory board of Open Society's Early Childhood Program.

Hirokazu Yoshikawa is the Courtney Sale Ross professor of globalization and education at NYU Steinhardt and a university professor at NYU, and co-director of the Global TIES for Children Center at NYU, USA. His work studies the effects of public policies and programs related to immigration, early childhood, and poverty reduction. Of particular interest to this book are his experiences with the Head Start Program, refugee programs, and global issues of equity and inclusion. He served on the Open Society Foundations Early Childhood Program advisory board between 2015 and 2021.

Elena Yudina is the head of the Department of Preschool Education, Moscow School of Social and Economic Sciences, and a consultant expert for the World Bank.

Deborah A. Ziegler, a national policy advocate and international expert on children with disabilities and their families, was one of the first Step by Step trainers and later led implementation of Step by Step's initiative for children with disabilities, including developing training resources, international workshops, and coordinating teams of trainers to support national programs. For two decades she traveled extensively in the region representing the program, conducting workshops, and providing coaching to Step by Step teams. She also served on the board of the International Step by Step Association.

Hana Zylfiu-Haziri is a Program Manager at the Kosovo Education Center, where she leads the work of the Step by Step program. She has been working with Step by Step since its launch in Kosovo in 1999.

Appendix 2:
Methodology: Oral History Interviews and Desk Review of Evaluations, Reports, and Documents

It was not the aim of the authors of this book to describe the implementation of the Step by Step program in detail in each country or globally. Instead, we tell the story of the pioneers that engaged in this large-scale project at different levels. This book draws mainly on oral histories of people (Sommer and Quinlan 2018) who played an important role in the Step by Step program. Oral history interviews provide an opportunity to hear the voices and narrative accounts of the main actors. Through interviews and focus groups lasting between one and two hours we were introduced to the experiences, successes, and failures of a number of key actors, and we learned about the social and political contexts in which they worked. The interviews and focus groups followed methodological protocols. Using as a guide *Early Childhood and Open Society*, a publication consolidating Open Society Foundation's work in early childhood over two decades (Klaus 2020), and the experiences of the authors with early education reform initiatives, a core set of open-ended interview questions were formulated. Questions were then further adapted and personalized to each of the interviews and focus groups.

Interview participants were selected from across the main stakeholder groups and from a range of leadership roles. They reflect the geographic and thematic scope of Open Society's Step by Step-related early childhood work. This includes participants from the early years of the Step by Step program as well as participants, who became involved in initiatives in later years. Several interviewees were identified from the global early childhood community to provide an external perspective. Interviews and focus groups were conducted throughout 2021. Additionally, a focus group with representatives from organizations responding to the war in Ukraine was organized in summer 2022 and several follow-up interviews were conducted in 2022 and one in early 2023. In total, forty-three people located in different parts of the world participated in taped video interviews: thirty-three in individual interviews and ten in four focus groups. Focus groups provided insight from several perspectives on a specific topic, for instance, early childhood in times of war, inclusion of Roma children, etc. Brief biographies are provided in Appendix 1.

A number of participants have served in several roles over the past two decades. For instance, one interviewee started as a master trainer in a national Step by Step team and later became a senior program manager in the International Step by Step Association. The cross-section of those interviewed for this book served in the following roles, with some serving in several positions over the course of the program. We counted among the interviewees and focus group participants:

- Five American early childhood experts who developed elements of the Step by Step program
- Eight Open Society Foundation staff, including the former president, the department director who launched the Step by Step program, and two advisory board members of the Early Childhood Program. Five of the eight interviewed Open Society staff were affiliated with national foundations.
- Three staff members and two board members of the International Step by Step Association
- Fifteen country directors or master trainers from national Step by Step programs
- Three Step by Step leaders of Roma origin
- Ten international experts, including seven academics from Europe/Eurasia and three from the United States
- One former regional early childhood lead for UNICEF
- Two ministry advisors (Bosnia and Herzegovina, Bhutan)
- One interpreter and translator

Interviews were transcribed and coded using the key themes, identified by the authors, as a guide. These emerge in several chapters across the book. Authors added notes and highlighting to coded interviews, identifying strong and interesting points to include in developing the written chapters. Coding of interviews took place in parallel with review of relevant evaluations, reports, and documents described below. Once interviews were coded two of the authors met for four days to define the content of each chapter and to assign each to a lead author. Then the writing of the chapters could start. Chapters were then reviewed, discussed, and added to by co-authors, through an iterative process and emerging themes were identified, emphasized, and reinforced in the final chapters. Throughout the process, chapters were shared with colleagues for feedback, as the book came together.

Evaluations, Reports, and Documents

In addition to the interview content, the authors draw on the many reports and publications that have been published about the early childhood and education work of the Open Society Foundations and the Step by Step program over the past thirty years. These include evaluations and reports commissioned from and published by the Open Society Foundations, as well as those commissioned and published by independent organizations and individuals. An overview of evaluations of the Step by Step program commissioned by Open Society Foundations or other international agencies is provided below.

- ***National Expert Evaluations (1996)*** Thirteen of the initial Open Society National Foundations each hired an independent local evaluator to conduct an assessment of the Step by Step preschool program at the end of the second year of implementation, through a coordinated process. The primary purpose was to gain insights into the national responses to the program and to inform its further strategic development. The methodology for this multi-country evaluation was created with the help of an independent evaluator (METIS Associates) in the United States. National evaluators used a common set of instruments to conduct interviews with Step by Step team members and a representative of the ministry of education. They also visited three randomly selected pilot preschools to observe and interview kindergarten directors, family coordinators, teachers, and parents. Each evaluator produced a written report and these vary in length and depth. The unpublished individual country reports and a short summary report are retained in the Open Society archives.
- ***Evaluation of the Step by Step Program (1998)*** USAID funded a quasi-experimental child outcome study in four countries—Romania, Bulgaria, Kyrgyzstan, and Ukraine—to gain a better understanding of the use of child-centered learning approaches in promoting democratic behaviors. The evaluation, which was implemented by the Education Development Center, Inc, through USAID's "Improving Educational Quality Project II," assessed developmental progress of children in Step by Step and traditional classrooms. It investigated impacts on teachers, families, and administrators and asked questions about democratic behaviors in classrooms and about program sustainability (Brady et al. 1999).
- ***Sustainability Review of the Step by Step Program (2000)*** This internal Open Society review investigated sustainability of Step by Step NGOs in

four countries: Bosnia, Kazakhstan, Latvia, and Slovakia. The findings are drawn from reports prepared by independent international experts, each of whom traveled to visit the program in one country, and from an overview of the strategic business plans developed by Step by Step teams preparing to spin-off from national foundations (Open Society Institute 2000).

- ***Building Open Societies through Quality Early Childhood Care and Education: Case Studies of the Step by Step Program (conducted in 2004, published in 2008)*** As Step by Step approached its tenth anniversary, Open Society Foundations launched the Case Study project to chronicle a decade of efforts to reform early childhood education systems in Europe, Eurasia, and the Americas. An international steering committee advised the project and provided workshops and mentoring to more than 100 researchers from twenty-eight countries implementing Step by Step. The resulting publication consists of twenty-four qualitative case studies, organized around six themes: quality, creating child-centered learning environments, teacher professional development, inclusion of children with disabilities, reaching children outside of preschools, and family and community engagement. These "thick" narrative studies capture a diverse range of perspectives and experiences and proved to be a rich resource for this book (Open Society Institute 2008). The case studies produced by the teams in Romania, Slovakia, and Ukraine were also included in a longer form a book edited by Robert Stake and published by Guilford Press (Stake 2006).

- ***The Step by Step Early Childhood Program: Assessment of Reach and Sustainability (2008)*** Between 2005 and 2008, RAND Education was contracted by the Open Society Foundations to conduct an independent survey-based study of Step by Step program directors in thirty countries to assess program capacity, reach, perceived effects on teachers, and sustainability (Stasz et al. 2008).

- ***Evaluations of the Getting Ready for School Initiative (2012)*** Between 2008 and 2011, Open Society contracted the American Institutes for Research to conduct a quasi-experimental child outcome study to assess the impact of the *Getting Ready for School* Initiative in Armenia, Bosnia, Kazakhstan, and Tajikistan. The initiative provided regular workshops to parents, or parents and children together, for children, who did not have access to preschool (American Institutes for Research 2012a, b, c, d).

- ***Roma Special Schools Initiative (1999–2004)*** Between 1999 and 2004, Open Society contracted Proactive Information Services and independent national researchers in four countries to evaluate the Roma Special Schools Initiative, which was implemented in Bulgaria, Czech Republic, Hungary, and Slovakia. For decades Roma children have been grossly over-represented in special schools as a result of discriminatory education systems and testing regimes. Through provision of child-centered and individualized teaching and learning and enriched language support, coupled with anti-bias training for teachers and communities, the initiative demonstrated that the majority of the Roma children assigned to special schools could achieve expected national standards and re-integrate into mainstream schools. Evaluation of the initiative, including child outcome data, is captured in annual reports (Proactive Information Services 2004; Rona and Lee 2001)

- *Scaling Up Studies in Macedonia (2011) and Romania* (2012) In 2009, the Wolfensohn Center for Early Childhood Development at the Brookings Institute commissioned eight studies highlighting strategies for scaling up effective early childhood programs. With funding from Open Society Foundations and the Bernard van Leer Foundations, the initiative provided workshops and supported researchers to develop national case studies. Researchers from two Step by Step countries (Macedonia and Romania) participated and produced reports analysing the process of national scale up of Step by Step in their countries (Misik and Velkovski 2011; Ulrich 2012).
- *Survey of National Foundations' Perspectives on the Impact, Sustainability, Organizational Capacity, and Professional Credibility of the Step by Step NGOs and the Step by Step Program (2013)* In 2013, Open Society staff conducted a survey of staff from seventeen national foundations that had launched and implemented the Step by Step program in order to capture their perspectives on the professional contribution and potential of the program. This unpublished report is retained in the Open Society archives.
- *Step by Step Sustainability Strengthening Program* (2018) Between 2013 and 2018 Open Society contracted the UK consulting firm INTRAC to provide technical assistance to improve capacity and sustainability of Step by Step NGOs and the International Step by Step Association. A set of individual and collective organizational reports provides lessons learned and an assessment of the impact of the NGO strengthening initiative (Hayman and Lewis 2018).
- **Evaluation of the *Program for Children and Families Strong from the Start – Dam Len Phaka (Let's Give Them Wings).*** Open Society supported

the piloting, scale up, and an impact evaluation of a multi-session and multi-modal parenting initiative implemented in Roma communities in Serbia. The evaluation, which compares 450 families (parent and child) participating in the parenting program with a control group, was conducted by an evaluation team drawn from Results for Development, Deep Dive and the University of Belgrade (Results for Development 2019). This study is discussed in Chapter 5.
- The International Step by Step Association has commissioned several studies to document the impact of their quality improvement work, which has been supported through the Open Society Step by Step program (Howard et al. 2010; Ionescu et al. 2018).

In addition to the internationally commissioned evaluations described above, experts in countries participating in Step by Step have conducted a range of national studies. Some of these were initiated to provide evidence to secure ministry approval to replicate the program in-country, and others have been commissioned by Open Society national foundations, by ministries, by other agencies, or by the academics themselves. In 2004, Professor Martin Woodhead was hired by Open Society to collect information about existing national studies that compare Step by Step and traditional classrooms. A survey of Step by Step teams uncovered twenty-six national studies, including a group of quasi-experimental child outcome studies, which, from his perspective, could inform development of a research review for publication. Though a summary publication was never produced, several of these studies have been published in summary form in the journal *Educating Children for Democracy*, which was published between 2000 and 2006 by the International Step by Step Association.

The later chapters of this book trace the use of resources developed as part of the Step by Step program in other contexts and countries, including Argentina, Myanmar, Bangladesh, and Liberia, and relevant publications are cited and discussed there.

Finally, the authors had access to Step by Step program documents—reports, strategy papers, budgets, statistics, memoranda, photographs, presentations—which provide a foundation for the interviewee narratives. In connection with the publication of this book, the International Step by Step Association created a website (https://www.issa.nl/Step_by_Step_Program) about the Step by Step program history with links to key resources and reports, enabling interested readers to consult primary sources.

Notes

Chapter 1

1 For brevity this book uses the term "Eastern Bloc" to encompass the countries of the post-Second World War Warsaw Pact, Albania and Yugoslavia. Collectively, this includes Albania, Bulgaria, Czechoslovakia, East Germany, Hungary, Poland, Romania, the Soviet Union, and Yugoslavia.
2 Macedonia (formally, Former Yugoslave Republic of Macedonia or FYROM) was renamed Republic of North Macedonia (or North Macedonia) in 2019. In this book, we use Macedonia when refering to time periods prior to 2019, and North Macedonia to refer to time periods from 2019 onwards.

Chapter 2

1 The exceptions are the program in Slovenia, which embedded in the Research Institute, and the program in Tajikistan, which remained within the National Foundation. Chapter 7 will explore the different kinds of spin-off organizations that were established.

Chapter 3

1 *Creating Child-Centred Classrooms (3–5 years old)* was drafted rapidly, for immediate use in 1994, and later refined to incorporate feedback and published in 1997. A complementary manual, designed to fill in gaps in the first manual, *Education and the Culture of Democracy: Early Childhood Practice,* was published in 2003. The original manual was extended, re-written, and re-issued in 2019 under a new title: *Child-Centered, Democratic Preschool Classrooms: The Step by Step Approach.*
2 One exception was Albania, where the buildings were in such poor condition that the program selected smaller kindergartens and refurbished and implemented the program in all classrooms from the beginning.

3. Notably, the average cost per classroom across the initial countries was driven up dramatically by major renovation costs in Albania and Romania.
4. In 2000, Step by Step in South Africa opted not to expand the program beyond the initial model sites.
5. The exceptions include several countries that had recently joined the program (Tajikistan, Uzbekistan), and several countries where the process or politics were particularly challenging.
6. The full list of countries implementing the core Step by Step Program includes Albania, Armenia, Azerbaijan, Belarus, Bosnia & Herzegovina, Bulgaria, Croatia, Czech Republic, Estonia, Georgia, Haiti, Hungary, Kazakhstan, Kyrgyzstan, Kosovo, Latvia, Lithuania, Macedonia, Moldova, Mongolia, Montenegro, Romania, Russia, Serbia, Slovakia, Slovenia, Tajikistan, Ukraine, Uzbekistan. Argentina, and South Africa introduced pilot programs, though not on a national scale.

Chapter 4

1. This section on teachers is based on the testimonies of program participants who were interviewed in 2021 and 2022, as well as from Open Society Foundation internal reports (Open Society Foundations 1995) and Step by Step Case Studies produced by national research teams in 1996 and 2005 and for the tenth anniversary of the program (Open Society Foundations 1996; Open Society Institute 2008).

Chapter 5

1. Published reports are available for North Macedonia, Croatia, Czech Republic, Slovakia, Bulgaria, and Serbia. An overview report covering four countries was produced in 2012. Reports for Hungary and Romania were produced, but not published.

Chapter 8

1. Until 2018, this country was known as Swaziland.

References

American Institutes for Research. 2012a. *Evaluation of the Open Society Foundation getting ready for school initiative in Armenia*. Washington, DC.

American Institutes for Research. 2012b. *Evaluation of the Open Society Foundation getting ready for school initiative in Bosnia*. Washington, DC.

American Institutes for Research. 2012c. *Evaluation of the Open Society Foundation getting ready for school initiative in Kazakhstan*. Washington, DC.

American Institutes for Research. 2012d. *Evaluation of the Open Society Foundation getting ready for school initiative in Tajikistan*. Washington, DC.

Amnon, Yukhiko, and Tina Hyder. 2015. "Chapter 11: Building the foundations: Early childhood development in Liberia." In *Partnership paradox: The post-conflict reconstruction of Liberia's education system*, edited by Christopher Talbot and Aleesha Taylor, 199–210. New York: Open Society Foundations.

Asmolov, Aleksander G. 1994. "Strategy for the development of alternate education in Russia." In *Preschool education in Russia: Handbook of normative-legal documents and scientific-methodological materials*, edited by Rina B. Sterkina, 34–44. Moscow: ACT.

Barnett, Steven W. 1985. "Benefit-cost analysis of the Perry Preschool Program and its policy implications." *Educational Evaluation and Policy Analysis* 7 (4):333–42. doi: 10.3102/01623737007004333.

Barnett, W. Steven, and Colette M. Escobar. 1987. "The economics of early educational intervention: A review." *Review of Educational Research* 57 (4):387–414. doi: 10.2307/1170429.

Bodrova, Elena and Elena Yudina. 2018. "Early childhood education in the Russian Federation." In *Handbook of international perspectives on early childhood education*, edited by Jaipaul L. Roopnarine, James E. Johnson, Suzanne Flannery Quinn, and Michael M. Patte, 59–69. New York: Routledge.

Brady, Joanne P., David K. Dickinson, Julie A. Hirschler, Theodore Cross, and Laurette C. Green. 1999. *Evaluation of the Step by Step Program*. Newton, MA: Education Development Center.

Brajković, Sanja 2014. *Professional learning communities*. Leiden: International Step by Step Association.

Bronfenbrenner, Urie. 1971. *Two worlds of childhood: U.S. and U.S.S.R.* London: George Allen & Unwin Ltd. Original edition. New York: Russell Sage Foundation, 1970.

Bronfenbrenner, Urie. 1979. *The ecology of human development: Experiments by nature and design*. Cambridge, MA: Harvard University Press.

Bronfenbrenner, Urie, and Pamela A. Morris. 1998. "The ecology of developmental processes." In *Handbook of child psychology*, edited by William Damon and Richard M. Lerner, 993–1028. New York: John Wiley & Sons.

BUPL—The Danish National Federation of Early Childhood Teachers and Youth Educators. 2006. *The work of the pedagogue: Roles and tasks*. Copenhagen: BUPL.

Center for Educational Initiatives. June 2008. "Promoting equal access to education: Supporting success for Roma children through a parent-school partnership project." *Early Childhood Matters* 110:31–4.

Cole, Michael, and Irving Maltzman. 1969. "Editors' preface." In *A handbook of contemporary Soviet psychology*, edited by Michael Cole and Irving Maltzman, ix–xiii. New York: Basic Books, Inc.

Commander, Simon, Une J. Lee, and Andrew Tolstopiatenko. 1996. "Social benefits and the Russian industrial firm." In *Enterprise restructuring and economic policy in Russia*, edited by Simon Commander, Qimiao Fan and Mark Schaffer, 52–83. Washington, DC: The World Bank.

Connell, R. 2009. *Gender*. 2nd ed, *Short introductions*. Cambridge: Polity Press.

Dahlberg, Gunilla, and Peter Moss. 2004. *Ethics and politics in early childhood education*. London: Routledge.

Departement Onderwijs en Opvoeding—Stad Gent. 2010. "25 jaar freinetonderwijs in Gent (25 years of Freinet education in Ghent)." Gent. https://biblio.ugent.be/publication/2103707.

Derman-Sparks, Louise. 1989. *Anti-bias curriculum: Tools for empowering young children*. Washington, DC: National Association for the Education of Young Children.

Dewey, John. 1993. "The need of an industrial education in an industrial democracy." In *John Dewey: The political writings*, edited by Debra Morris and Ian Shapiro, 121–4. Indianapolis: Hackett Publishing Company. Original edition, 1916.

Dolanc, Anica, Irena Levičnik, Nuša Kolar, Lea Smasek, and Viktorija Zmaga Glogovec. 1975. *Trideset let socialistične predšolske vzgoje*. Ljubljana: Skupnost vzgojno vrastvenih zavodov Slovenije.

Erzieherin-ausbildung.de. 2023. "Situationsansatz in kita und kindergartent—einfach erklärt." accessed January 8, 2023. https://www.erzieherin-ausbildung.de/praxis/paedagogische-leitfaeden/situationsansatz-kita-und-kindergarten-einfach-erklaert#was-versteht-man-unter-dem-situationsansatz.

Eurofund. 2015. *Working conditions, training of early childhood care workers and quality of services—A systematic review*. Luxembourg: European Union.

European Commission. 2020. *A union of equality: EU Roma strategic framework for equality, inclusion and participation (2020–2030)*. Brussels.

Evans, Peter. 2015. *Creating financing and governance preconditions for inclusive early childhood development and education systems: Latvia, Serbia, Bulgaria, Ukraine and Lithuania*. London: Open Society Foundations.

Galardini, Anna L., Donatella Giovannini, Sonia Iozelli, Antonia Mastio, Maria Laura Contini and Sylvie Rayna. 2022. Pistoia Een cultuur van het jonge kind. Dutch translation edited by Ed Hoekstra, Ine van Liempd and Jan Peeters. Amsterdam: SWP.

Halvorsen, Terje 2014. "Key pedagogic thinkers Anton Makarenko." *Journal of Pedagogic Development, University of Bedfordshire, England* 4 (2):58–71.

Harms, Thelma, Richard M. Clifford, and Debby Cryer. 1998. *Early childhood environment rating scale*. 2nd rev. ed. New York and London: Teachers College Press.

Havlinova, Miluse, E. Hejduk, N. Kozova, E. Sulcova, L. Tomasek, and E. Wienholdova. 2004. "Measuring psychosocial outcomes in the Step by Step Program: A longitudinal study in the Czech Republic." *Educating Children for Democracy* Winter/Spring 2004 (6):20–5.

Hayman, Rachel, and Sarah Lewis. 2018. *Supporting OSF partners to cope with change: Lessons learned from the Step by Step financial and program sustainability review*. Oxford: INTRAC.

Howard, Mimi, Aija Tuna, Cornelia Cincilei, Tahmina Rajabova, Tatjana Vonta, and Dawn Takersley. 2010. *Study on the Implementation of the pedagogical standards and their impact on ECDE policies and practices in the region of ISSA's network and beyond (2001–2008)*. Leiden: International Step by Step Association.

Institute of Educational Development BRAC University. 2010. *Master of science in early childhood development: Selected summaries of student research*. Dhaka.

International Step by Step Association. 2001. *ISSA pedagogical standards for preschool and primary grades*. Budapest.

International Step by Step Association. 2010. *Competent educators of the 21st century: Principles of quality pedagogy*. Amsterdam.

International Step by Step Association. 2019. *Child-centered democratic preschool classrooms*. Leiden.

Ionescu, Mihaela, Dawn Takersley, Zorica Trikić, and Tatjana Vonta. 2018. *A systemic approach to quality in early childhood services for children from 3 to 10 years of age: Documentation study on ISSA's work on quality improvement*. Leiden: International Step by Step Association.

Jensen, Jytte Jull 2018. "Denmark—ECEC workforce profile." In *Workforce profiles in systems of early childhood education and care in Europe*, edited by Pamela Oberhuemer and Inge Schreyer, 262–85. Munich: SEEPRO-R. www.seepro.eu/ISBN-publication.pdf.

Kamara Ferguson, Sia Barbara. 2020. "Open society in Liberia." *Early Childhood Program farewell: Celebrating collaborations and inspiring the future*, online.

Kamerman, Sheila B. 2006. "A global history of early childhood education and care." *Paper commissioned for the EFA Global Monitoring Report 2007, Strong foundations: Early childhood care and education*, edited by UNESCO. Paris: UNESCO.

Kamerman, Sheila B., and Shirley Gatenio-Gabel. 2007. "Early childhood education and care in the United States: An overview of the current policy picture." *International Journal of Child Care and Education Policy* 1 (1):23–34. doi: 10.1007/2288-6729-1-1-23.

Klaus, Sarah. 2004. "Stepping into the future: The history of the Step by Step program." *Educating Children for Democracy* 8 (10th Anniversary Issue):3–13.

Klaus, Sarah. 2013. "In Peru, the fight against poverty starts early." *Open Society Foundations*, accessed July 5, 2022. https://www.opensocietyfoundations.org/voices/peru-fight-against-poverty-starts-early.

Klaus, Sarah. 2020. *Early childhood and open society: Creating equitable and inclusive societies*. London: Open Society Foundations.

Knox, Kathleen. 2004. "Czech Republic, Reform project tackles childhood education 'Step by Step.'" *Educating Children for Democracy*, Summer/Fall 2004 (7):13–14.

Kontić, Boro, and Beka Vučo, eds. 2021. *Thirty years: Open society and its friends*. Sarajevo: Open Society Fund—Bosnia and Herzegovina.

Kreusler, Abraham. 1970. "Soviet preschool education." *The Elementary School journal* 70 (May 1970):429–37.

Lindsay, Gai. 2015. "Reflections in the mirror of Reggio Emilia's soul: John Dewey's foundational influence on pedagogy in the Italian educational project." *Early Childhood Education Journal* 43 (6):447–57. doi: 10.1007/s10643-015-0692-7.

Lombardi, Joan. 2003. *Time to care: Redesigning child care to promote education, support families, and build communities*. Philadelphia: Temple University Press.

MacLeod, Rod. 2017. *Step by Step sustainability strengthening programme: Final evaluation*. United Kingdom: INTRAC.

Magrab, Phyllis. 2004. "Voices of children." *Educating Children for Democracy* 7 (Summer/Fall):8–12.

Malaguzzi, Loris. 1998. "History, Ideas and Basic Philosophy: An Interview with Lella Gandini." In *The hundred languages of children: The Reggio approach advanced reflections*. 2nd ed, edited by Carolyn Edwards, Lella Gandini, and George Forman, 49–98. Westport Connecticut: ABLEX Publishing.

Marti, Maria, Emily Merz, Kelsey Repka, Cassie Landers, Kimberly Noble, and Helena Duch. 2018. "Parent involvement in the getting ready for school intervention is associated with changes in school readiness skills." *Frontiers in Psychology* 9:759. doi: 10.3389/fpsyg.2018.00759.

McCain, Margaret Norrie, J. Fraser Mustard, and Stuart Shanker. 2007. *Early years study 2: Putting science into action*. Toronto: Council for Early Child Development.

McDonald, Christina, and Katy Negrin. 2010. *No data—no progress*. New York: Open Society Institute.

Milotay, Nora. 2016. "From research to policy, the case of early childhood education." In *Pathways to professionalism in early childhood education and care*, edited by Michel Vandenbroeck, Mathias Urban and Jan Peeters, 119–31. London and New York: Routledge.

Misik, Elena, and Zoran Velkovski. 2011. *Scaling up quality in early childhood education in Macedonia: The scaling up of the step by step program (1994–2001)*. Washington, DC: Brookings.

Mooney, Carol Garhart. 2013. *Theories of childhood: An introduction to Dewey, Montessori, Erikson, Piaget, and Vygotsky*. 2nd ed, edited by St. Paul. Minnesota: Redleaf Press.

Moss, Peter. 2007a. "Bringing politics into the nursery: Early childhood education as a democratic practice." *European Early Childhood Education Research Journal* 15 (1):5–20. doi: 10.1080/13502930601046620.

Moss, Peter. 2017b. "Power and resistance in early childhood education: From dominant discourse to democratic experimentalism." *Journal of Pedagogy— Pedagogický časopis* 8:11–32. doi: 10.1515/jped-2017-0001.

Mustard, J. Fraser. 2002. "Early child development and the brain—The base for health, learning, and behavior throughout life." In *From early childhood development to human development*, edited by Mary Eming Young, 23–61. Washington, DC: The World Bank.

Noble, Kimberly G., Helena Duch, Maria Eugenia Darvique, Alexandra Grundleger, Carmen Rodriguez, and Cassie Landers. 2012. "'Getting ready for school:' A preliminary evaluation of a parent-focused school-readiness program." *Child Development Research* 2012:1–14. doi: 10.1155/2012/259598.

Nuhanović, Hasan. 2020. *De tolk van Srebrenica*. Translated by Raoul Nicolaas Schuyt. Amsterdam: Querido Fosfor.

Open Society Foundations. 1995. *Soros preschool project report* Open Society Foundations. Department: Children & Youth Department. New York (unpublished).

Open Society Foundations. 1996. *Summary of expert evaluation reports*. Open Society Foundations. Department: Children & Youth Department. New York (unpublished).

Open Society Foundations. 2018. *Early childhood program portfolio review notes: National systems reform – Liberia*. Open Society Foundations. Department: Early Childhood Program. London (unpublished).

Open Society Foundations. 2020. "The Open Society Foundations and George Soros." Open Society Foundations, Last Modified December 1, 2020, accessed April 6, 2023. https://www.opensocietyfoundations.org/newsroom/open-society-foundations-and-george-soros.

Open Society Initiative for Southern Africa. 2017. *Getting it right: Promoting change through early childhood development and education in southern Africa*. Johannesburg.

Open Society Initiative for Southern Africa. 2020. *Getting it right: Inclusive early childhood development and education rights, vol 2*. Johannesburg.

Open Society Institute. 2000. *Sustainability review of the Step by Step Program*. Open Society Institute. Department: Institute for Education Policy (unpublished).

Open Society Institute. 2008a. *Building open societies through quality early childhood care and education: Case studies of the Step by Step Program*. Open Society Institute. New York.

Open Society Institute. 2008b. *Soros Foundations Network Report 2007*. Open Society Institute. New York.

Peeters, Jan. 2008. *The construction of a new profession: A European perspective on professionalism in ECEC*. Amsterdam: SWP Publishers.

Peeters, Jan. 2016. *UNICEF report: Quality of ECE Services in Albania, Bosnia and Herzegovina, Kosovo and Montenegro*. Geneva: UNICEF.

Peeters, Jan 2018. *Improving the quality of ECEC services in Ukraine*. Ghent: VBJK.
Peeters, Jan 2021. *Report on the Workshop for 9 Georgian Universities: Finalization of BA programmes*. UNICEF Georgia (unpublished).
Peeters, Jan, and Brecht Peleman. 2017. "The competent system or the intersection between research, policy making and practice." In *The SAGE handbook of early childhood policy*, edited by Linda Miller, Claire Cameron, Carmen Dalli and Nancy Barbour, 522–36. London: Sage.
Peeters, Jan, and Lidija Miskeljin. 2018. *Developing and implementing a framework and process to monitor and improve quality of ECEC services in Serbia*. Consulting report for UNICEF SERBIA. Serbia: UNICEF.
Peeters, Jan, and Michel Vandenbroeck. 2011. "Childcare practitioners and the process of professionalization." In *Professionalization, leadership and management in the early years*, edited by Linda Miller and Carrie Cable, 99–112. London: Sage.
Peeters, Jan, Tim Rohrmann, and Kari Emilsen. 2015. "Gender balance in ECEC: Why is there so little progress?" *European Early Childhood Education Research Journal* 23:302–14. doi: 10.1080/1350293X.2015.1043805.
Piattoeva, Nelli, Iveta Silova, and Zsuzsa Millei. 2018. "Remembering childhoods, rewriting (post)socialist lives." In *Childhood and schooling in (post)socialist societies*, edited by Nelli Piattoeva, Iveta Silova, and Zsuzsa Millei 1–18. Cham: Palgrave Macmillan.
Proactive Information Services. 2004. "Transition of students: Roma special schools initiative." Manitova: Proactive Information Services.
Rangelov-Jusović, Radmila. 2007. "Bosnia and Herzegovina—Sarajevo: Radmila Rangelov-Jusovic's Story." In *From conflict to peace building: The power of early childhood initiatives*, edited by Paul Connolly, Jacqueline Hayden and Diane Levin, 33–40. Redmond: World Forum Foundation.
Results for Development. 2019. *Consolidated final report: Evaluation of the program for children and parents: "Strong from the start—Dam Len Phaka"*. Washington, DC: Results for Development.
Riazantsev, Alexander, Sandor Sipos, and Oleg Labetsky. 1992. "Child welfare and the socialist experiment: Special economic trends in the USSR, 1960–90." In *Innocenti Occasional Papers, Economic Policy Series*, Florence: UNICEF. https://www.unicef-irc.org/publications/81-child-welfare-and-the-socialist-experiment-social-and-economic-trends-in-the-ussr.html.
Rinaldi, Carlina. 2005. *In dialogue with Reggio Emilia: Listening, researching and learning*. Edited by Gunilla Dahlberg and Peter Moss, Contesting early childhood. London: Routledge.
Rona, Susan, and Linda Lee. 2001. *School success for Roma children: Step by Step special schools initiative interim report*. New York: Open Society Institute.
Shakira Mukashovna, Mukhtarova. 2013. "Kazakhstan: An overview with special reference to ethnic and linguistic dimensions." In *Education in West Central Asia*, edited by Mah-E-Rukh Ahmed and Colin Brock, 123–38. London: Bloomsbury.

Sharmahd, Nima, and Jan Peeters. 2019. "Critical reflection, identity, interaction: Italian and Belgian experiences in building democracy through pedagogical documentation." In *Understanding pedagogic documentation in early childhood education: Revealing and reflecting on high quality learning and teaching,* edited by João Formosinho and Jan Peeters. London: Routledge.

Sharmahd, Nima, Jan Peeters, Katrien Van Laere, Tajana Vonta, Chris De Kimpe, Sanja Brajković, Laura Contini, and Donatella Giovannini. 2017. "Italy (Pistoia): Colleagiality as basis for PLC." In *Transforming European ECEC services and primary schools into professional learning communities: Drivers, barriers and ways forward,* 49–53. Luxembourg: Publications Office of the European Union. https://nesetweb.eu/wp-content/uploads/2019/06/AR2__2017.pdf.

Shegal, G. 1929. *Down with kitchen slavery!* Moscow: Khudozhestvennoe Izdatelskoe Aktsionernoe Obschestvo AKhR.

Silova, Iveta. 2008. "Championing Open Society." In *How NGOs react: Globalization and education reform in the Caucasus, Central Asia, and Mongolia,* edited by Iveta Silova and Gita Steiner-Khamsi, 43–80. Bloomfield, CT: Kumarian Press, Inc.

Silova, Iveta, and Gita Steiner-Khamsi. 2008. *How NGOs react: Globalization and education reform in the Caucasus, Central Asia and Mongolia.* Bloomfield, CT: Kumarian Press.

Singer, Elly, and Sandie Wong. 2021. "Early childhood theories, ideals and social-political movements, an oral history study of pioneers in the second half of the twentieth century." *Early Child Development and Care* 191 (7–8):1330–45. doi: 10.1080/03004430.2020.1850445.

Snel, Guido. 2022. *Negen Steden: Europa van Wenen naar Istanbul (Nine cities: Europe from Vienna to Istanbul).* Amsterdam: Arbeiderspers.

Sommer, Barbara W., and Mary Kay Quinlan. 2018. *The oral history manual.* 3rd ed, *American Association for State and Local History.* Lanham, MD: Rowan & Littlefield.

Sommer, Barbara W., Mary Kay Quinlan, and American Association for State and Local History. 2009. *The oral history manual.* Lanham, MD: Rowan Altamira.

Soros, George. 2007. *Notes from interview for Rockhopper film.* London.

Soros, George. 2019. *In defense of open societies.* New York: PublicAffairs.

Soros, George, and Alexander Soros. 2021. "The promise of open society." In *Thirty years: Open society and its friends,* edited by Boro Kontić and Beka Vučo, 14–15. Sarajevo: Open Society Fund—Bosnia and Herzegovina.

Stake, Robert. 2006. *Multiple case study analysis.* New York: Guilford Press.

Stasz, Cathleen, Cathy Krop, Afshin Rastegar, and Mirka Vuollo. 2008. *The Step by Step early childhood education program: Assessment of reach and sustainability.* Santa Monica, CA: Rand Corporation.

Stojanovic, Jadranka. 2000. "Impact of Step by Step preschool experience on Roma children's educational success." *Educating Children for Democracy* Summer/Fall 2000 (1):22.

Sudetic, Chuck. 2011. *The philanthropy of George Soros: Building open societies*. 1st ed. New York: Public Affairs.

Sulavek, Chris. 1995. "A head start for preschoolers." *Open Society News* Winter 1995:4–6.

Swarnyk, Mykola. 2002. "What every child with a disability needs." *Educating Children for Democracy* Winter/Spring 2002 (2):7–10.

Trikić, Zorica, Jelena Vranjesevic, Dawn Takersley, and S. Brajković. 2017. *Embracing diversity: Creating equitable society through personal transformation*. Netherlands: International Step by Step Association.

Ulrich, Catalina. 2012. *Scaling-up early childhood development in Romania*, edited by Brookings. Washington, DC: Brookings.

UN General Assembly. 2007. *Convention on the rights of persons with disabilities: Resolution/adopted by the General Assembly*, edited by UN General Assembly. New York.

UNESCO. 2007. "Strong foundations: Early childhood care and education." *EFA global monitoring report*, edited by UNESCO. Paris. https://www.unesco.org/gem-report/en/strong-foundations/ecce.

UNESCO. 2020. *Global education monitoring report summary 2020: Inclusion and education: All means all*. Paris.

UNESCO. 2022a. *Global partnership strategy for early childhood (2021–2030)*. Paris.

UNESCO. 2022b. *Tashkent declaration and commitments to action for transforming early childhood care and education*. Paris.

UNICEF. 2001. "A decade of transition: Regional monitoring report no. 8." In *The MONEE Project CEE/CIS/Baltics*. Florence: Innocenti Research Centre.

UNICEF. 2022. "The situation for children in Liberia." UNICEF, accessed October 15, 2022. https://www.unicef.org/liberia/situation-children-liberia.

UNICEF, and European Social Observatory. 2011. *Preventing social exclusion through the Europe 2020 strategy: Early childhood development and the inclusion of Roma families*. Brussels: Belgian Presidency of the Council of the European Union.

United Nations. 2017. "Legacy website of the International Criminal Tribunal for the former Yugoslavia." International Residual Mechanism for Criminal Tribunals, accessed December 27, 2022. https://www.icty.org/en/about/what-former-yugoslavia/conflicts.

Urban, Mathias, and Carmen Dalli. 2008. "Editorial." *European Early Childhood Education Research Journal* 16 (2):131–3. doi: 10.1080/13502930802141576.

Urban, Mathias, Michel Vandenbroek, Arianna Lazzari, Jan Peeters, and Katrien van Laere. 2011. *Competence requirements in Early Childhood Education and Care (CoRe)*. London and Ghent: University of East London/University of Ghent.

US Agency for International Development. 2012. *2011 CSO sustainability index for Central and Eastern Europe and Eurasia*. Washington, DC: US Agency for International Development.

Vandenbroeck, M., Mathias Urban, and J. Peeters. 2016. *Pathways to professionalism in early childhood education and care*. London and New York: Routledge.

Van der Linde, Irene, and Nicole Segers. 2021. *Bloed en honing: Ontmoetingen op de grenzen van de Balkan (Blood and honey: Balkan encounters on the borders in the Balkan region)* Amsterdam: Boom.

Vonta, Tatjana. 2004. "Teacher evaluation using ISSA standards: A tool for professional development and quality improvement." *Educating Children for Democracy* Summer/Fall 2004 (7):21–5.

Weaver, Kitty D. 1971. *Lenin's grandchildren: Preschool education in the Soviet Union*. New York: Simon and Schuster.

Wittorski, Richard, and Maryvonne Sorel. 2005. *La professionalisation en actes et en questions*. Paris: L'Harmattan.

Zaitsev, Sergey. 2002. "Step by Step: The new role of the teacher." *Educating Children for Democracy* Summer/Fall 2002 (3):11–14.

Index

Abt Associations 75
Academy of Education Development 75
activity centers 10, 67, 86, 166
adult learning 71–2
advocacy 54, 113–14, 120, 173, 180
Africa xiv, 2, 54, 122, 166, 173
Aidzhanova, Dina 118
Albania 74, 83, 95, 194, 241 n.2
Amazon 224
American Psychological Association 4
Amnon, Yukhiko 169
Angola 165
anti-bias education 111, 121, 239
Argentina 74, 160–2, 240
  NGO 83
  Open Society funding 82
Armenia 74, 127, 191
  Getting Ready for School initiative 77, 238
Asia xiv, 2, 54, 156, 166, 173
Asmolov, A. G. 7
asylum seekers 106–8
authoritarianism viii, xi, 8–9, 48–9, 86, 142, 144, 194, 199, 203, 211, 219, 223
autocracy 42
Azerbaijan 35, 61–2, 74, 127

Balkan wars 38, 125
Baltic states, ECE 30
Bangladesh viii, 16, 71, 163, 219, 240
Belarus 37, 70, 147
Belgium xii, 137, 208
Berisha, Driton 114–16, 226
Berlin 207
  Berlin wall, fall of xii, 7–8, 11, 15, 22, 35, 42, 52, 133, 142, 184, 202–3, 222
  Situations Ansatz 208
Bernard van Leer Foundation 184, 190, 207, 209, 239

Bhutan viii, 16, 83, 166–9, 172
Bodrova, Elena, *Tools of the Mind* 25, 27, 30, 38, 105, 226
Bosnia and Herzegovina 31, 36, 74, 125, 131, 194
  Getting Ready for School 77, 110–11, 238
  kindergartens in, rebuilding 128
  lack of teachers 129
  Open Society Fund 127
  rebuilding education system 126
  Step by Step NGO 144, 152–3
  war in 124
BRAC University's Institute of Education Development (BU-IED) 162
Bronfenbrenner, Urie 2–5
  ecology of human development 5, 213
  Two Worlds of Childhood: US and USSR 4
Bubenova, Yelizaveta 87–8
Bulgaria 36, 237
  Roma Special Schools Initiative 111, 239
  Step by Step preschools 68, 109

Central Asia viii, 23, 35–7, 83, 104, 185
  ISSA 152
  national foundations in 75
  NGOs 141–2
  Step by Step expansion 75
Central Europe 40
  early childhood and donor engagement 41–2
change agents x, 15, 51, 86, 162, 171, 175, 204, 216
  teachers as 87–92
change process, ownership of 186–9, 206
Charles Stewart Mott Foundation 143
childcare programs 3, 89, 174, 184, 203
Child-Centered, Democratic Preschool Classrooms: The Step by Step Approach 241 n.1

child-centered pedagogy/approach viii, x, xiv, 9, 13, 15, 59, 63, 67, 88–91, 98–9, 105–6, 111, 116, 131, 142, 164, 172, 182, 184–5, 188, 190–3, 197–9, 203, 205–8, 217, 220, 237–9
   Peru 164
   Step by Step practices 76, 218
   teacher-centered to 85–6, 185, 187, 207, 217
   United States 205
children 213
   agency 6–7, 13, 65, 86, 161, 213, 225
   child development ix, 5, 28, 93, 163
   child rights ix, viii, 2, 42, 103, 212
   choice(s) 10, 86, 161
   impact 34, 77, 98–9, 110, 121, 187
   impact of war on 23, 38, 126–8, 130, 133, 169, 224
   individualization and autonomy 96–8
   longitudinal study 98–9
   mentoring time 90
   social-emotional development 77
Children in Europe xiii
Children's Creative Center 74
children with disabilities viii, 14–15, 37, 45, 54, 105, 145–7, 165, 220–1, 223
   attitudes toward 106–8, 119–22
   inclusion of 116, 146, 209, 218, 238
   rights of people 120
   and their families 104, 116–19
Ciari, Bruno 6
Cincilei, Cornelia 31, 33, 60, 62, 64, 69, 72–3, 76–7, 93, 106, 143–4, 149–50, 152, 154, 157, 192–3, 196, 227
CIP-Center for Interactive Pedagogy (CIP Center) 194–5
citizenship ix, 2–3, 9, 22, 98
civil society x, 2, 9, 16, 58, 92, 165, 173, 180, 182, 199, 203, 210, 213, 217–19, 225
   in challenging political contexts 140–2
   development of 143
   early childhood ecosystem 137–8, 218
   and ECE systems change 191–4

   investments in 220
   reflections on building and strengthening 154–6
classroom community 10, 13, 86, 207
classroom environment viii–ix, 10, 13, 27–8, 32, 76, 81, 96, 103, 105, 111, 145, 168, 192, 217–18
   infant/toddler 69–70
   preschool 63, 66–7, 92, 98, 116, 181
climate change 203
Cole, Michael 30
collectivism 22–3
Comenius Foundation 225
competent system 16, 182–3, 189, 198
Convention on the Rights of the Child 42
CoRe study 182–3, 189, 194
Coughlin, Pam 45, 116, 204
Council for Exceptional Children (CEC) 118
Council of Europe for the Fourth European Roma Platform 112
COVID 79, 113, 220–3
Creating Child-Centred Classrooms (3–5 years old) 241 n.1
Creole, *Tipa Tipa* 160–2
crisis, systems reform 11, 202
critical thinking 9–10, 90
Croatia 48, 109, 124, 128
   NGO 144
   Step by Step kindergarten 96–7
cross-country collaborations 225
"crossing boundaries" 12, 206–11
Cuna Mas 164
Ćurak, Hašima 27–8, 31, 69, 73, 77, 88, 127, 131–2, 153, 214, 227
curriculum 23, 26, 42, 58, 75, 117, 172, 185
   in Bhutan 167
   and new opportunities 40
   preschool 29–33
   reform of 168
Czechoslovakia, dissolution of xii, 15, 37, 202
Czech Republic 36–8, 45, 95, 98–9, 109, 111, 239

Danish early education pedagogy 207
Deák, Éva 74, 105, 107, 112–13, 115, 140–1, 143, 221, 227
defectology 103–4

democracy viii, xiii, 2–3, 15, 50, 68, 79, 83, 94, 157, 161, 175, 203, 208, 214, 223
　and education 6, 76, 212, 214, 218
　forums of 7
　human rights and ix
　interrogating early childhood and 11–13
　learning risks and practicing 97–8
　in northern Italy 6–8
　Open Society Foundations and 8–11
　in preschools 212
　promoting 213
democratically oriented environments 65
democratic approach/pedagogy viii, xiii–xiv, 8, 15–16, 89, 131, 184, 188, 192, 195, 202–3, 207–8, 214–15, 225
　educators, motivation 204–6
　at multiple levels 212–14
　of openness 89–90
　parents, hope and self-confidence 94–5
　teacher-centered to child-centered 85–6
democratic education systems 12, 76
　educational theories/practices/experiences, exchange 206–11
　Europe/Eurasia and beyond 222–5
democratic institutions (*democracia scolastica*) 6
democratic reforms x, 47, 57, 182, 184, 198–9
democratic transitions 202–3
democratic values 164, 185, 198, 202, 205, 213, 220
Denmark 207–8
Derman-Sparks, Louise 209
Dewey, John 2–6, 8, 206, 212–13
D.H. and Others 111–12
disabilities 14–15, 37, 103, 120–1, 221. *See also* children with disabilities
discrimination x, 8, 45, 102, 116, 121, 216, 220–1
diversity 7, 9–10, 14, 26, 92, 102, 108, 133, 162, 209
　of human society 105–6
　and inclusion 77, 101, 212

Diversity in Early Childhood Education and Training (DECET) network xiii, 209
'donor logic' 41–2, 50, 82, 174–5, 196, 211–12, 217

early childhood ix, xiii, 7–8, 13, 82, 142, 148, 153, 156–7, 160, 202, 217
　ecosystem, seed-funding 173
　and societal values 164
early childhood development (ECD) 13, 50, 113, 116, 141, 156, 164, 168, 171, 184, 213, 218, 222
　in SDGs 174
Early Childhood Education and Care (ECEC) 13
early childhood education (ECE)/ECE systems xii–xiii, xv, 4, 13, 21, 30, 57, 59, 78, 85–6, 120–1, 132, 133, 150, 161, 168, 182, 212, 214, 218, 225
　access to and availability of 34–7
　improvements 197
　motivations for 22–6
　policy 16, 23, 37, 112, 146, 170
　political goals of 32
　political transformation of 6–8
　and primary education 24–5
　reform 202–3, 238
Early Childhood Environmental Rating Scale (ECERS) 89
Early Childhood Program viii–ix, xi, xiii–xiv, 3, 6, 54, 83, 122, 156–8, 160, 162–3, 168–72, 207, 223, 238. *See also* Open Society Foundations (OSF)
　decision to launch 42–4
　democratic model 8–11
　designing Step by Step 44–8
　fostering allies and hiring program team 50–2
　national foundations, experiences 48–50
　and OSISA 165
Early Childhood Regional Networks Fund 54, 83
early education systems 2, 11–12, 16, 26, 35, 51, 58, 143, 204, 206, 211, 214–15, 218
　changing national 195–8
　and childcare 184
　democratizing 76, 215, 219, 222–5

Eastern Bloc 21, 24–6, 37, 241 n.1
Eastern Europe viii, xiv, 7–8, 12, 16, 30, 43–8, 57, 103–4, 120, 152, 154, 197, 204, 209–10, 216
East Timor 164
Educating Children for Democracy 240
educational reform viii, xiii, xv, 11–12, 40, 42–3, 48–9, 58, 71, 143–4, 150, 163, 180, 185, 194, 202–3, 211–12, 218
Education and the Culture of Democracy: Early Childhood Practice 241 n.1
education policy 7, 23, 138, 180, 198–9
Education Support Program 122
enrollment rates 37
equity 75–9, 157, 175, 216
  and dignity 216
  human rights and 218
  inclusion and x, 9–10, 16, 76, 103, 121, 171, 174, 185, 220–1
Estonia 94
ethnic minorities 62, 106–8, 220
Eurasia xii, 2, 7–8, 12, 16, 35, 57, 101, 138, 142, 159–62, 173, 189, 202, 204, 209, 238
  democratic early education 222–5
  early childhood and donor engagement 41–2
  early education systems 206–7
  Getting Ready for School 210
  ISSA 154
Europe x, xii, xv, 2, 12, 16, 22, 35, 45, 83, 122, 138, 159–62, 173, 195, 204, 209–10, 238
  democratic early education 222–5
  donors 40
  early education systems 206–7
  ISSA 149, 154
  political transformation of ECE 6–8
European Commission 13, 78, 182, 214, 218
  Childcare Network 207
  Working Group on Early Childhood Education and Care 210
European Union 14, 36, 40, 82, 113, 121, 143, 146, 152
evaluations, reports, and documents xiii, 44, 205, 237–40
  Assessment of Reach and Sustainability (2008) 238
  Getting Ready for School initiative (2012) 238
  National Expert Evaluations (1996) 237
  Program for Children and Families Strong from the Start – Dam Len Phaka (Let's Give Them Wings) 239–40
  Quality Early Childhood Care and Education 238
  Roma Special Schools Initiative (1999–2004) 238–9
  scaling up studies in Macedonia (2011) and Romania (2012) 239
  Step by Step Program (1998) 237
  Step by Step sustainability strengthening program (2018) 239
  survey of national foundations' perspectives (2013) 239
  sustainability review of Step by Step Program (2000) 237–8
exclusion. *See* social exclusion/inclusion

Fidesz 141
Fondation Connaissance et Liberté/ Fondasyon Konesans Ak Libète (FOKAL) 160–1
France, *crèches parentales* 208–9
Freinet 6, 208, 212–13
Fundación Leer 160

Galijašević, Jesenko 125
Gayleg, Karma 167–8, 227
Georgetown University xii, xiv, xvi, 58, 65, 211
  Center for Child and Human Development (GUCCHD) 45
Georgia 33, 74, 193, 197
  bachelor program for preschool teachers 193
Germany 215, 224
Gestione Sociale 208
Getting Ready for School (GRS) initiative 77, 110–11, 210, 238
Ghent, Liana 92, 153, 155, 157–8, 185, 187, 217, 221, 224, 227–8
Greece 224
Grover, Deepa 113, 141, 154, 190, 202, 228
Gvineria, Eteri 39, 72, 86, 144, 228

Haiti 16, 74, 83, 160–2, 173
  community ownership 161
  half-day preparatory program 78

Halimova, Zuhra 24, 39, 49–50, 52–3, 69, 119, 195, 228
Hansen, Kirsten 59, 91, 94, 139, 228
Head Start Program xii, 3, 7, 15, 45–8, 52, 58, 64, 83, 102, 109, 133, 204, 206–9
  evidence-based program 184
  Family Literacy Center 210
  female trainers 215
"H.E.A.R.T" 108
Heimgaertner, Henriette 184, 186, 190, 228
higher education 27, 42, 82, 104, 162, 219
  institutions 171, 181, 193, 197, 214
  model sites and 70–4, 81
  reforms in 163, 197
  Step by Step trainings 199
  and universities as partners 189–91
  "Higher Education Initiative" 71–2, 81, 189, 192
human rights and democracy ix, 9, 102, 218
Human Rights Program 122
Hungary 8, 36, 38, 71, 76, 108, 111, 180, 239. *See also* The Soros Foundation Hungary
  Roma Special Schools Initiative 239
  Step by Step NGO 141
Hyder, Tina 53, 163–5, 168–71, 173–5, 212, 222, 229

inclusion. *See* social exclusion/inclusion
individualized teaching (learning, approach) 2, 68, 98, 205, 239
inequity 35–6, 221
infant/toddler classrooms 69–70
in-service teacher training 71, 75–6, 143, 190, 192, 196, 199
internally displaced people (IDP) 107
International Renaissance Foundation, Ukraine 106
International Step by Step Association (ISSA) ix, xiii–xv, 16–17, 54, 83, 92, 108, 125, 133, 154, 182, 187, 189–90, 199, 209–10, 223–5, 240
  achievement 206–7
  Annual Conference (2017) Ghent, Belgium 137
  growth in membership 152–3
  and NGOs 156–8

and Open Society Foundations 151
  professional learning community within 118
  on quality improvement 93–4, 194–5, 206
  Quality Resource Pack 191, 194, 212
  standards and principles 92–3, 99, 164, 204, 214
  to sustain the movement 147–50
  UNICEF and 153–4
INTRAC 147, 156, 239
Iron Curtain 4, 12
Italy 208–9
  democratic movements 6–8
  professionals 179

Johnson, Lyndon B., "war on poverty" 3, 45

Kamara Ferguson, Sia Barbara 171, 227
Kamerman, Sheila 41
Kaufmann, Roxane 58–9, 63–5, 187, 229
Kazakhstan 35, 37, 66, 74–5, 118, 238
  Getting Ready for School 77
kindergartens 4, 14, 23, 25–7, 33–6, 39–40, 61–4, 67, 70, 72, 74, 77–8, 89, 94, 109–10, 127–8, 205, 208, 241 n.2. *See also* preschools/preschool education
  idea of selecting 62
  Kazakhstan 37
  Kosovo 128, 130
  Latvia 30
  mainstream 99
  pilot and new 66, 194
  rebuilding 128
  in Roma settlements 67, 109–10
  Soviet Union 24, 32, 37
  Yugoslavia 25
Kirandžiska, Suzana 27, 36, 63–4, 67, 72, 78, 110, 124, 130, 132, 144, 147, 156, 196, 229
"kitchen slavery" campaign 23
Klaus, Sarah xiii–xiv, 47, 130, 150, 189
  Early Childhood and Open Society 237
Končoková, Eva 51, 109, 194
Kosovo 74, 124
  rebuilding kindergartens in 128
Kosovo Education Center 144
Kosovo Roma Ashkali Egyptian Early Years Network (KRAEEYN) 114

Krupskaya, Nadezhda 2–5, 22
Kyrgyzstan 68, 74–5, 94, 127, 194, 237
   children with disabilities, mainstream programs 118

Labetsky, Oleg 36
labor force 27
Landers, Cassie 77, 210
Lapham, Kate 104, 142, 151–2, 156, 229
Latin America xiv, 9, 54
Latvia 30, 74, 119, 238
Liberia viii, 16, 163, 174
   Early Childhood Program 169–72
   seed-funding 173
Lică, Carmen 62, 67, 73, 107, 139, 145, 155, 157, 198, 229
Liechtenstein Development Services (LED) 143
Lithuania 78, 96–7
Lombardi, Joan 46, 122, 211, 223, 229–30
long-term investment 12, 16, 203, 211–12, 225
Lorant, Liz 44–8, 51–2, 65, 73, 111, 138, 204, 230
low-resource contexts 165–6
   anchor for regional and global work 173–5
   Bhutan 166–9
   lessons learned from working in 172–3
   Liberia 169–72

Macedonia 69, 78–9, 109–10, 129, 188, 241 n.2
   National Foundation 67
   scaling up studies (2011) 188, 239
Macquarie University 164
Magrab, Phyllis 45, 47–8, 52–3, 116, 139, 148, 150–1, 155, 158, 160, 174, 221, 223, 230
Makarenko, Anton 23
Malaguzzi, Loris 6–7, 206, 212–13
Maltzman, Irving 30
Mečiar, Vladimír 49
Middle East xiv, 9, 54, 122
Mihajlović, Milena 194, 230
Mikayilova, Ulviyya 34, 62, 64, 66, 142, 152, 192, 230
Milinović, Nives 63, 128–9, 193, 230
Millennium Development Goal 42

Ministry of Education (MoE) 4, 30, 61, 67, 82, 137, 140, 172
   collaboration with 170, 194–5, 219–20
   model sites 62, 70–4, 80–1, 192, 205
Moldova 75, 119, 143, 191, 196, 224
   Step by Step NGO 76
Mongolia 74, 83, 119
   inclusion 104
Montenegro 74, 193, 197
Montessori 46–7
Moss, Peter 7, 207
Museum of Mining and Metallurgy, Bor (Serbia) 226
Mustard, Fraser ix, xi, 43–4, 52, 202
Myanmar 71, 83, 163, 219, 240

national early education system
   civil society organizations and institutions 213
   policy reform 211
   politics matter 195–6
   strategic thinking 197–8
   system changes 196–7
National Foundations. *See* Open Society Foundations (OSF)
Neier, Aryeh 49, 52, 63, 80, 102–3, 112, 161, 231
"Neither Black nor White" program 108
the Netherlands. ISSA 54, 92, 149, 152, 210
network x, xiii, 4, 6, 9, 16, 43, 54, 58, 72–5, 83, 92, 113–14, 140, 144–5, 158, 165, 173, 180, 209, 217–18
   investment 211
   NGOs and (*see* non-governmental organizations (NGOs))
   professionals xv, 16, 54, 91, 113, 138, 173, 203, 206, 210
Neuman, Michelle 231
New York, Open Society Foundations 43, 53, 75, 82, 139, 150
Nixon, Richard 5
non-governmental organizations (NGOs) x, xiv, 16, 54, 81–2, 113, 138, 181, 185, 192–3, 204, 210, 218, 220, 239
   civil society (*see* civil society)
   ISSA and 156–8
   managing and expanding 150–4
   spinning off national Step by Step programs 138–40

sustainability
  assessing prospects for 145-7
  challenge of 142-5
  creating ISSA 147-50
  and organizational capacity 155
northern Italy 209
  democratic movements 6-8
  early childhood programs 6
  North-Italian pedagogy of Pistoia 91

October Revolution 22
Ogneviuk, Victor 105
Ogrodińska, Teresa 231
open society x, 8-9, 43, 83, 101, 149, 159, 162, 180, 213-14
Open Society Foundations (OSF) ix-x, xii-xiii, 1, 7, 12, 15, 51, 54, 57-8, 64, 75, 99, 108, 111, 117, 120, 127-8, 142, 148, 162, 172, 179-80, 184, 189, 191, 196-7, 211, 235, 237-8. *See also* Step by Step Program
  child-centered, democratic reforms 198-9
  and democratic ECE 8-11
  Early Childhood Program viii-ix, xi, xiv, 42-4, 52, 54, 122, 156-7, 160, 223
  education reform 49, 180, 235
  funding/funder 82-3, 182, 216-19, 239
  health education program 43, 45, 47, 217
  investments xv, 82, 128, 159, 202, 218
  ISSA and 151
  leadership 120-1
  national foundations 48-50, 61, 64, 68, 75, 79, 140, 204
  new country initiatives 163-5
  new university initiatives 162-3
  pilot projects 170
Open Society Initiative for West Africa (OSIWA) 170, 172
Open Society Institute for Southern Africa (OSISA) 165
Organisation for Economic Co-operation and Development (OECD) 13, 154, 210

Panaite, Olga 88
Panikova, Alena 49, 51, 53, 66, 102, 109, 115, 141, 185, 187-8, 231

parent(s) 2, 5, 11, 46, 51, 63, 66, 130, 203, 207, 213-14
  communication 77, 107
  and community involvement 46, 75, 108, 142, 205, 217
  employment 5, 22
  and families 10, 78, 94, 207, 211
  hope and self-confidence 94-5
  impact of war on 23, 126-8
  involvement and associations 60, 63-4, 67, 161, 185
  parenting 44, 77, 173, 223
  role in preschool 5, 10, 15, 26, 33-4, 60, 69, 94-5
  Roma and 111
  and teachers 24, 38, 68, 86, 90, 98-100, 107, 117, 126-8, 133, 202, 208
  unemployment 39
parent-centered approach 89
Parenting with Confidence 73
Parent Teacher Associations 75
Participation in Education and Knowledge Strengthening (PEAKS) program 75
participative approach 188-9
pedagogic standards/principles 150, 195
Peeters, Jan xiii
Peru 83, 164
Poland 36, 38, 125, 184, 224-5
policymakers 5, 31, 188, 197
political and social transformation/ transition x, xii, xv, 1, 3, 7, 15, 35, 101, 203, 222
Popper, Karl 8
Portugal, Andrea 164
post-socialist education reform 40
poverty 3-4, 6, 15, 45-6, 78, 102, 115, 161, 169
  and building empathy 107
  in Serbia 129
preschools/preschool education viii, 1, 4-5, 13-14, 21, 68, 73, 77, 80-1, 109-10, 211, 213-14, 219-20. *See also* early childhood education (ECE)/ECE systems; kindergartens
  buildings and structural issues 26-8
  children with disabilities 119
  child's day in 28-9
  curriculum and teachers role 29-33

democracy in 79, 212
investments in 25
life in 26
methodologist 32–3
parents, role 5, 10, 15, 26, 33–4, 60, 69, 94–5
and primary methodologies 182
reform of 58
social transformation and patriotism 22
Soviet Union 23, 30, 32
Step by Step Program in 58–69, 92–3, 110, 191, 237
teachers 25, 27–8, 107, 110, 115, 193
training and demonstration classrooms 181
Yugoslavia 36
pre-service training 80, 104, 163, 189–90, 192–4, 197, 199, 219
primary schools xv, 13–14, 26, 42, 58, 73–4, 80–1, 83, 105, 110, 170, 180–1, 211, 214, 219–20
child-centered educational practices 98
children with disabilities 119
demonstration classrooms 181
ECE and 24–5, 197–8
Step by Step expansion 69–70, 75–6, 95, 197
professional development viii, 2, 11, 15, 64, 143–4, 164, 184, 203, 214
building trust through participation 186–7
continuous 100, 150, 192, 206
investment in 186–9
participative approach created committed mentors 187–9
of teachers 15, 76, 80, 92–3, 206, 214, 238
and training 181
professionalism 186, 206
competence and 182
democratic child-centered form 87
professional learning communities 90–1, 118, 189, 205

Quinlan, M. K. xii

RAND Education 81, 238
Rangelov-Jusović (Rada), Radmila 125–7, 129, 131–3
Reading Corner Project 79
reconciliation 126, 132, 206
reform viii, x, 1, 11–12, 34, 40, 42–3, 47–9, 52, 59, 143, 150, 168, 180, 183, 185, 193–8, 218, 235
ECE systems xiii, xv, 57, 143, 196, 198–9, 202–3, 222, 238
of higher education 71, 163
long-term, flexible investments 12, 211–12, 225
of preschool and early primary education 43, 58
pre-service teacher training 189, 197, 199, 219
refugees x, 16, 54, 78–9, 122, 124, 130, 147, 173, 210, 223, 225
attitudes toward 106–8
children affected by war 38, 126, 129, 133, 224
crisis 130, 203
Serbia 109, 128
Reggio Emilia 6–7, 91, 208–9
restoring education 47
Riazantsev, Alexander 36
rights-based pedagogy x
Rinaldi, Carlina 87
Roma Early Childhood Inclusion Reports (RECI) 112
Roma Early Years Networks (REYN) 113–14
Romania 36–8, 61, 68, 70, 109, 237–8
national foundation 139–40
NGO 144–5
scaling up studies (2012) 239
Roma/Roma children 14–15, 37, 72, 82, 103, 146–7, 220
attitudes toward 106–8, 119–22
early childhood workforce 76
equity and inclusion of 103
and families 108–11, 113
investing in 114–16
and refugee families 78, 147, 173, 210
settlements, kindergartens in 67, 109–10
Special Schools Initiative 111–12, 238–9
Royal Education Council 166
Royal University of Bhutan 166
Rudaš, Aljoša 114–15, 231

Russia 7, 22, 35, 117, 127, 163, 219
  language of special education 104
  master teacher trainers, Step by Step 86
  preschools 74-5
  Step by Step expansion 75

Save the Children 75, 224
second language learning 111
seed-funding 173
Serbia 1, 25, 31, 48, 67, 110, 119, 124, 128-9, 193-5, 240
  Fund for an Open Society 108-9
  initial training programs 193
  poverty 129
  refugees 109
  "Years of Ascent" 195
Silova, Iveta 42, 180
Singer, Elly 6
Sipos, Sandor 36
Sklenka, Miroslav 114, 116, 231
Slovakia 36, 38, 48-9, 51, 94, 109, 140-1, 194, 238
  national foundation spun off 141
  REYN 114
  Roma Special Schools Initiative 111, 239
Slovenia xv, 74, 101, 109, 114, 124, 128
  ISSA standards 92-3
  pilot classrooms 66
  professionals 179
  Research Institute 140, 144, 241 n.1
  teacher professional development 76
  teachers in 86, 92
social constructivism, theories 58
social exclusion/inclusion ix, 2, 8, 77, 92, 107-8, 118, 121, 142, 146, 162, 164, 206, 218, 236
  of children with disabilities 76, 103, 116-17, 120, 146, 209, 238
  and civil rights 209
  deep roots of 220-2
  demonstration programs/litigation and monitoring reports 111-13
  and diversity 101, 212
  and equity x, 9-10, 16, 171, 174, 185, 218, 220
  of minorities and refugees 146, 223
  Open Society responds 101-2
  in preschools 119
  rigid systems of education 118
  and segregation of children with special educational needs 102-6
  through networking 113-14
social justice ix, 9, 45, 116, 122, 133, 146, 221
social values 3, 12, 22, 39, 164
Sofiy, Natalia 24, 29, 32, 61, 65, 94, 106-7, 118, 125, 128, 130, 157, 166-8, 197, 232
Sommer, B. W. xii
Sorel, Maryvonne 87
The Soros Foundation Hungary 8, 45, 50, 61, 63, 110, 130, 138, 144, 147, 180, 196
Soros, George viii-ix, xi, 8, 43-5, 47, 50, 52, 80, 82, 159, 197, 202, 212-13, 216
South Africa 74, 83, 160-2, 171, 242 n.4
  Open Society funding 82
Soviet Union 4, 35, 48
  collapse of xii, 15, 39, 86, 104, 127, 133, 202
  ECE systems 3-4, 37
  methodological centers in 33
  preschools/kindergartens 23-5, 27, 29
  social and political underpinnings 2-5
  teachers 32
special educational needs 14, 102-6, 121, 165
Steiner-Khamsi, Gita 42
Step by Step Program viii-xiii, 1-2, 8-9, 11-13, 16, 35, 38, 50-2, 86-9, 101-2, 129, 132, 145-6, 173, 180, 202, 237, 239
  assessing teacher quality 92-4
  child-centered, democratic pedagogy 15
  children's development and well-being ix
  classroom 10
  countries implementing 106, 125, 160-1, 181, 190, 195, 209, 211, 224, 235, 238, 242 n.5 (*see also specific countries*)
  country development model 181
  democratic pedagogy at multiple levels 212-14
  expanding to primary schools and infant/toddler classrooms 69-70

higher education and model sites, replication 70–4
initiatives 79–80, 108, 110, 210
limits of 219–20
longitudinal study 98–9
long-term investment 12
in low-resource contexts (*see* low-resource contexts)
national foundations 50, 54
new pedagogical practices 185–6
partnership initiatives, expansion 74–5
pedagogy xiv, 185
in preschools
  assessing impact 68–9
  expansion to more preschool classrooms 66–7
  First All-Program Meeting 65–6
  methodology and training country teams (US) 58–61
primary program 201
quality, equity, and access 75–9
rebuilding trust 133–4
scope, scale, and impact 79–83
shared goal to change education system 184–5
spin-off programs 54, 75, 79, 91, 138–40, 145, 147, 154, 180, 182, 238
successes and challenges 15
Sula, Gerda 89, 232
sustainability/sustainable change 54, 68, 83, 139, 145, 155, 180, 182, 197, 218, 220, 237–9
  assessing prospects for NGO 145–7
  civil society organizations 58
  competent system 182–3
  ISSA 147–50
  strategies toward 180–2
Sustainable Development Goals (SDGs) 173–4
systems change 11–12, 16–17, 72, 81, 154, 156, 179–80, 182, 196–7

Tajikistan 15, 24, 35, 49, 74–5, 118–19, 127, 140, 142, 241 n.1
  Getting Ready for School 77, 238
  highest fertility rate 36
Tankersley, Dawn 90, 121, 164, 186, 232
Tavedze, Dodo 97

teacher(s) viii–ix, 2–3, 10–11, 39, 63, 68–70, 76, 82, 86, 95, 98–100, 107, 134, 186, 197, 202, 225, 239, 242 n.1
  assessing quality in Step by Step program 92–4
  as change agents 87–92
  impact of war on 38, 126–8
  interactive trainings 91
  lack of 129
  professional development 15, 76, 80, 92–3, 206, 214, 238
  retraining systems 76
  role in preschools 25, 27–33, 107, 110, 115, 193
  Step by Step training 70–3, 81
  and teaching team 213
  training x, 11, 42, 45, 71, 75–6, 94, 108, 111, 117, 146, 161, 170–2, 192, 205, 219
  transformation 86–7
teacher-centered approach 87, 190, 207, 219
  to child-centered 85–6, 185, 187, 207, 217
  professional environment 87
Tipa Tipa 160–2
traditional pedagogy ix
transition/transformation xv, 15, 35, 37, 87, 100–1, 149, 187.
  See also political and social transformation/transition
  collapse and 37–40
  to democracy viii, x, 1, 202–4
  research, policy, and practice 189–91
  teachers 86–7, 187
  women 214–15
Trbić, Dženana 38, 132–3, 179, 232
Trikić, Zorica 25, 31, 108, 110, 115, 129, 153, 166–7, 195, 232
trust 32, 59, 111, 129, 132–4, 186–8, 199, 206, 215, 225
Tuna, Aija 28, 40, 86, 88, 105, 232
Tuscany, early childhood programs 6

Ukraine 16, 24, 36, 41, 64, 109, 117–18, 167, 197, 237–8
  International Renaissance Foundation 106
  ISSA 224–5

preschools 68, 119
war 15, 125, 127, 130, 133, 203, 223, 225, 235
UK, REYN 113
unemployment 36, 39
United Nations Children's Fund (UNICEF) 78, 130, 143–4, 153, 162, 164, 190, 193, 210, 218–19, 225
    Innocenti Research Centre (Italy) 35
    and Roma Education Fund 112
United Nations Educational, Scientific and Cultural Organization (UNESCO) 78
    Global Education Monitoring Report (2006/2020) 35, 102
United States of America 8–9, 12, 45, 116, 121, 124, 204–5, 207, 209
    child-centered approaches 205
    early childhood education systems 4
    Head Start Program xii, 3, 15, 46, 102, 171, 184, 204, 207, 210
    ISSA 149
    methodology and training country teams 58–65
    ReadyNation 145
    social and political underpinnings 2–5
universities 81, 193
    as partners 189–91
    pedagogic 70–2, 104, 214
    and pre-service training institutions 192, 194, 199
US Agency for International Development (USAID) 68, 75, 82–3, 98, 143, 147, 218
    "Improving Educational Quality Project II" 237
Uzbekistan 35, 74–5, 147

Vonta, Tatjana xiii–xv, 26, 33, 60, 86, 89, 119, 124, 126, 134, 140, 144, 148, 152, 188, 194, 198, 232–3
Vučo, Beka 216, 223, 233
Vygotsky, Lev 8, 12, 29–30, 38, 195, 206, 212–13, 226

Walsh, Kate Burke 60, 69–70, 90, 149, 187, 233
war
    after Yugoslav war 132–3
    in Balkans 38, 125
    in Bosnia and Herzegovina 124
    bringing people back together 131–2
    devastating conflict 123–6
    First World War 22–3
    impact of children, parents, and teachers 23, 38, 126–8, 130, 133, 169, 224
    lingering after-effects of 129–30
    rebuilding infrastructure 128–9
    Second World War 3, 6, 23, 124
    secret of Step by Step 133–4
    in Ukraine 15, 125, 127, 130, 133, 203, 223, 225, 235
Wittorski, Richard 87
women ix, 3–4, 6, 78, 115, 126, 188, 203
    employment 3, 22, 27, 39, 214
    equality 23
    in the labor force 3, 23
    transformation 214–15
Wong, Sandie 6
Woodhead, Martin 233, 240
    General Comment 7: Implementing Child Rights in Early Childhood 233
World Bank 42–4, 78, 82, 121, 143–4, 170, 174, 214, 218–19
    Privatization Project 74
    Social Investment Fund 75
World Conference on Education for All 42

Yoshikawa, Hirokazu 155–6, 173–5, 184, 222, 233–4
Youth Cultural Center, Skopje 78
Yudina, Elena 25, 31, 40, 234
Yugoslav Federation 123–4
Yugoslavia xii, 22, 35, 37–8, 48, 127–8, 130, 152, 202
    after Yugoslav war 132–3
    devastating conflict 123–6
    development of ECE system 34
    dissolution of 15, 124, 202
    preschools/kindergartens 25–7, 36
    teachers in 29, 31

Ziegler, Deborah A. 104, 117, 119–21, 143, 148–9, 151, 155, 234
Zimbabwe 165
Zylfiu-Haziri, Hana 74, 108, 128–9, 132, 234

www.ingramcontent.com/pod-product-compliance
Lightning Source LLC
Chambersburg PA
CBHW071812300426
44116CB00009B/1289